The Basic Business Library

The Basic Business Library
Core Resources and Services

Fifth Edition

Eric Forte and Michael R. Oppenheim, Editors

 LIBRARIES UNLIMITED

AN IMPRINT OF ABC-CLIO, LLC
Santa Barbara, California • Denver, Colorado • Oxford, England

Library of Congress Cataloging-in-Publication Data

The basic business library : core resources and services. — 5th ed. / Eric Forte and Michael Oppenheim, editors
   p. cm.
Includes bibliographical references and index.
ISBN 978–1–59884–611–9 — ISBN 978–1–59884–612–6 (ebook) 1. Business libraries—United States. 2. Business—Bibliography. 3. Business—Computer network resources. 4. Business—Reference books—Bibliography. 5. Business information services—United States. I. Forte, Eric J., 1967- II. Oppenheim, Michael R.
Z675.B8B37   2012
016.0276′9—dc23   2011037666

ISBN: 978–1–59884–611–9
EISBN: 978–1–59884–612–6

16 15 14 13 12   1 2 3 4 5

This book is also available on the World Wide Web as an eBook.
Visit www.abc-clio.com for details.

Libraries Unlimited
An Imprint of ABC-CLIO, LLC

ABC-CLIO, LLC
130 Cremona Drive, P.O. Box 1911
Santa Barbara, California 93116-1911

This book is printed on acid-free paper ∞

Manufactured in the United States of America

To Vaughn, Zane, and Jeannee for their patience.
To Christine for her support and encouragement.
To my contributors for their dedication and commitment to excellence.
—Eric Forte

To the memory of my parents, Abe and Frances Oppenheim—the first
librarians I ever knew.
To the memory of Margaret G. Linton, incomparable friend, fellow
librarian, and inspiration of a lifetime.
To Eric Forte, the most infinitely patient, generous, and
supportive co-editor imaginable.
—Michael Oppenheim

Contents

Preface

It has been nearly 30 years since Bernard Schlessinger began *The Basic Business Library: Core Resources*. With its concise treatment of the essential resources necessary to serve business clientele in all kinds of libraries, the book quickly became one of its several publishers' bestsellers, a status that remained through second, third, and fourth editions (the fourth edition seeing Rashelle Karp take over as primary editor as Dr. Schlessinger headed into retirement). Much has changed since that fourth edition, published in 2002. For starters, both Dr. Schlessinger and Ms. Karp fully retired, and with their blessing, Michael Oppenheim and I have moved from contributors to editors for this fully updated and revised fifth edition. What else has changed since 2002? Not much beyond the well-known stampede to electronic sources, with very few of the classic business reference tools remaining as they were 30 years ago, much less even a decade ago.

For this completely revised edition, therefore, Michael and I have been fortunate enough to assemble a stellar cast of contributors, full of recognized leaders in contemporary business librarianship. These contributors have assembled a *Basic Business Library* for a new era, one that has seen a proliferation of amazing new business resources, dramatic updates to existing products, and an ever-widening portfolio of resources, both free and fee, to serve the business patron of today. A slightly revised title, *The Basic Business Library: Core Resources and Services*, reflects the presence of several essays aimed at the practice of business librarianship. Yet at the heart of the book remains an updated assessment of the core resources, followed by expert chapters "drilling down" into the key topics, including startups, marketing research, investment, and the business literature.

The book is designed to be both a single, linear narrative, but also to allow users to jump in at any particular chapter of interest. As each chapter has been written to stand on its own, there will be occasional overlap of sources discussed.

The first chapter serves as both Introduction and a guide to both the most core business resources and concepts, and to the contents of the rest of the book. With its emphasis on the "accidental business librarian," Chapter 1 will introduce both the novice and the returning librarian to the core resources and business concepts most essential for the practice of business librarianship.

Chapter 2, by Lucy Heckman of St. John's University, covers the core databases that are at the heart of so much business research these days. Products from EBSCO and ProQuest/CSA are among those that increasingly aim to serve as one-stop shopping for almost any business information need; the prevalence of these products reflects the extent to which business literature is now delivered and accessed almost exclusively electronically. However, their core function remains indexing and abstracting the periodical literature: the variety of expert reportage and specialty coverage make periodical business literature an ongoing goldmine of business intelligence. These publications may be accessed via many of the databases covered in Chapter 2. Meanwhile, Ruthie Brock and Carol Byrne, of the University of Texas at Arlington, list and describe the key periodicals to know in Chapter 3.

Many key business resources are produced by governments at the federal, state, and local levels. These sources range from economic statistics to the wealth of demographic data in the decennial census to resources produced to support new businesses, from startup to ongoing operations. Chapter 4 covers resources from the government, which have the added advantage of being free.

Chapters 5, 6, and 7 provide in-depth coverage of the most-needed genres of business information: investments in Chapter 5 (Madeleine Cohen, New York Public Library), marketing resources in Chapter 6 (Wendy Diamond, California State University–Chico), and startups in Chapter 7 (Chris LeBeau, University of Missouri–Kansas City). These chapters occasionally overlap with each other in the sources they cover; although, quite frankly, if you see a source coming up again and again, that in itself is a partial testimony to its importance.

With the rest of the chapters, this fifth edition of *The Basic Business Library* may be said to go somewhat beyond the scope in the previous four editions. Gary W. White's (Penn State) Chapter 8 on deep business research highlights many sources that are mainstays of the biggest and best MBA programs. Although smaller academic business programs, and also larger public libraries, may also acquire some of these sources, they are intended for the more advanced academic researcher—and thus are generally far from "core" or even "basic" resources.

Chapters 9 and 10 are aimed at the business library practitioner. Chicago Public Library's Mark E. Andersen discusses collection development in Chapter 9, while Baruch College's Louise Klusek takes on references services in Chapter 10. The book closes with a treat: Howard F. McGinn, who has worked in or headed just about every type of library you can imagine, provides a personal essay on conditions in 2010 and beyond, telling stories about business librarianship in the modern age and looking forward to the key trends and issues that different libraries will need to address in the near future.

Through its many expert contributions, this new edition of *The Basic Business Library* provides both the new or accidental business librarian and the seasoned expert the resources needed to maximize effectiveness in providing support for the business information seeking communities in the cities and towns, colleges and universities, and small and large businesses we serve. We hope you enjoy the latest edition!

—*Eric Forte and Michael Oppenheim*

1

Introduction:
Core Resources for the Accidental Business Librarian

Eric Forte

INTRODUCTION

Welcome to the fifth edition of the *Basic Business Library*! This introduction will briefly review the core resources for locating, finding, and using business information. It will largely serve as a road map to the most core resources covered in the later expert chapters, while also covering a number of key resources that do not fit neatly into later chapters. In addition, you'll find a handful of entertaining and insightful sidebars listing the "Top 5" or "Top 10" business resources from librarians working in diverse settings, describing some of the sources that these working librarians cannot live without.

Business information is among the most frequently sought types of information. With comments such as "The chief business of the American people is business" (Coolidge, 1925) and "It's the economy, stupid" (Carville, 1992) part of the national consciousness, the prevalence of business information—along with the demand for it—is no surprise. Public libraries—especially in troubled economic times—are inundated with entrepreneurs seeking information about starting a business, job seekers researching careers and industries, and individuals managing retirement accounts and other investments. In a 2011 Harris Poll, more than two-thirds of adults "said that the library's assistance in starting a business or finding a job was important to them" (American Library Association, 2011). Academic libraries, meanwhile, serve more students enrolled in business programs than in any other academic subject: in 2008, more than twice as many business undergraduate degrees were awarded as compared with any other discipline (U.S. National Center for Education Statistics, 2011a), and MBA degrees were right behind education degrees among master's degrees earned (U.S. National Center for Education Statistics, 2011b). Students use libraries and information resources heavily in support of research-oriented

1

course work, and faculty conduct in-depth business research in the course of scholarship and publication. Finally, many special and corporate libraries specifically exist to provide research and to serve business and market clientele and customers.

However, finding business information is not always easy. In fact, finding information for most other subjects is relatively straightforward when compared to finding business information. Business intelligence is among the most nuanced and specialized types of information. Sources of business information are infinite in variety. Private publishers, market research and investment firms, governments, scholars, countless trade and industry groups, special interest groups, international organizations—the producers of business information are virtually endless, as are the platforms and models for accessing such information. Several monographs and printed sets remain useful and sometimes even essential, but most business information has rapidly gone online in recent years—and much of it is available online via private, fee-based databases. Wikipedia and the free web may help the patron researching a health condition, a novel, a country, or even a legal subject. The depth and research required to produce high-quality, useful business information, though, is generally such that most of the best business information is rarely free, and thus libraries retain their time-honored role of providing access to resources for the masses, from students to citizens to CEOs.

Most public and academic libraries, no matter how small, serve clientele seeking business information. Sources of business information are countless and could easily fill a budget of millions of dollars. This first chapter covers only briefly the most essential of business sources, and is a survey and guide to the most basic resources covered in the rest of the book. A public library serving a small to medium-size city, or an academic library of almost any size that supports a business program, might reasonably expect to provide access to nearly all of the resources mentioned in this first chapter, and then add to the collection various further materials taken from all of the other chapters, based on need. A very small library might pick and choose selected sources from this first chapter only. Most librarians, meanwhile, will begin here, and then choose many of the rest of the resources covered elsewhere. Special librarians might not use this general chapter at all, and will focus instead on the resources covered in those chapters most relevant to their specific missions.

This introductory chapter is thus aimed at the "accidental business librarian." It covers some basic territory:

- Resources to support discovering business literature, which—
  especially because of the value of the contents of trade and industry

journals and much value-added content beyond the literature—is of critical importance across all business topics

- Resources to provide intelligence on both large, public companies (researched often for investment purposes) and small businesses (researched often for start-ups/competitive purposes); resources to support the small-business owner or entrepreneur, including market research information, legal advice, and management and organizational resources
- In-depth resources to support the investor
- And a sampling of resources for the job seeker and citizen

BUSINESS LITERATURE

The business periodical literature as a whole, consisting of the content of business journals, magazines, newspapers, trade journals, etc., represents perhaps the most core business resource of all, and it is the subject of Chapter 2. The articles and reports contained in that literature cover business topics comprehensively, with the trade journals—specialty magazines often published by trade associations representing a particular industry—being especially useful, providing inside information about specific industries that is generally unavailable from other sources. For the most part, these trade magazines are not the types of journals that will be found for sale at a newsstand or in a bookstore; neither do they offer much of their content free online. (Full access usually requires a membership—or a library subscription.) They serve a critical function, though, to the extent that they report detailed industry and business intelligence, frequently providing key bits of information extracted from business reports and data that in their native formats might well cost thousands of dollars.

The single most core business resource thus will be a database that both indexes—makes discoverable—and provides the full texts for as many of these business periodicals as possible.

Databases and Indexes

Such a business database combines indexing of those key trade journals with coverage of the core business magazines and news sources, regional and local business publications, *and* often some market research and other specialty reports such as country reports, company reports, and commodity reports. The following business databases cover much of the core business intelligence and news that exists, especially for the United States.

There are several primary databases that index this business literature, mentioned briefly here and covered in detail in Chapter 2, on accessing the

Top Five Resources

Patrick Muckleroy
Western State College of Colorado
2,500 FTE, undergraduate business degrees only
Modestly funded, state-supported college

1. Business Source Premier (EBSCO): for marketing articles it is a definite first choice because of trade journal articles related to strategy, new products, market performance, and competitors.
2. Within Business Source Premier, I steer students to the Datamonitor reports because each company is "explained" in nuts-and-bolts language within about 10–12 pages. It is a perfect foundation for a marketing paper.
3. LexisNexis Academic: You cannot beat it for trade newspapers and large-audience U.S. and foreign papers . . . really up-to-date information.
4. Hoover's Handbooks: nice, concise overview of companies. It fits nicely for a background source in marketing papers.
5. *Standard & Poor's Industry Surveys*: the best and seemingly most authoritative reporting on major industries. Each survey includes the major companies, performance of top companies, and most important for marketing research, trends in the industry (where things are going!).

I would be useless without these five!

business literature. Each database included usually both indexes the literature and contains full text itself for the majority of the content covered. These databases do contain a fair amount of overlap; indeed, most libraries—both public and academic—are most likely to choose at least one of these databases. The smallest libraries may be unable to afford any of these specialty business databases, and may rely instead on the business coverage in a general-purpose periodical literature index and multidisciplinary databases. In any case, despite the overlap, each database contains a number of unique items, making the decision about which to purchase more difficult than not.

Arguably the two leading general business literature databases in recent years are ABI/Inform products from Proquest and EBSCO's Business Source products. Other products from Gale Cengage and LexisNexis also compete in this area. An important point to note is that some of these products do actually compete against each other for content, sometimes gaining exclusive access to particular periodicals and sources. For instance, ABI/Inform currently has exclusive access to the full text of the *Wall Street Journal* and the *Sloan Management Review*, among others; EBSCO currently has exclusive access to the full-text *Harvard Business Review*. Although in general these competing databases have great areas of overlap, librarians trying to choose which one on which to spend scarce resources will need to consider what will be left out by any particular database.

Both ABI/Inform and Business Source come in different flavors, with different levels of content depending on which version is purchased—read Chapter 2 for details. For many years, ABI/Inform was relatively secure as the premier, top-end index to the business literature. It indexed all of the important popular business magazines, from *Business Week* to *Fortune* to *Forbes*, key business journals as the *Harvard Business Review*, and important trade journals such as *Nation's Restaurant News*. The past decade has seen an aggressive push by EBSCO to upgrade its business database to take on ABI/Inform (and others). Flavors of the database include, in descending order of size of coverage, Business Source Complete, Premier, and Elite, with the latter offering the smallest amount of coverage and a lesser price. Like ABI/Inform, Business Source covers the basic business periodicals, trade publications, and many scholarly journals; various market, industry, and company reports are also included, as well as monographic content.

H. W. Wilson's Business Periodicals Index Retrospective: 1913–82 (acquired by EBSCO, as part of its June 2011 acquisition of the H.W. Wilson Company) provides unique historical indexing. Gale's Business and Company Resource Center provides a broad complement of business intelligence, including company reportage and data, marketing and investment intelligence products, and indexing and full-text for hundreds of business journals, magazines, and trade publications. For some libraries, Business and Company Resource Center is a complementary database; for others, it is the core resource to support business research. By comparison, LexisNexis Academic has broad, interdisciplinary coverage, almost entirely full-text, and includes thousands of different types of business, general news, legal, and general reference publications. Its robust business module provides coverage of business literature and company and investment intelligence, among other reports; particularly notable is its collection of U.S. and international company directories.

Chapter 2 covers many more database options than can be discussed here. In summary, an academic library supporting a business curriculum and faculty research, or a medium-to-large public library, will likely choose one of the above databases. Bigger libraries will likely choose several or more of the other databases covered in Chapter 2, such as Factiva or LexisNexis Academic. And as noted in Chapter 2, many general-purpose, multisubject periodical databases, such as EBSCO's Academic Search or Proquest's OneFile products, will be sufficient for the business needs for many smaller libraries.

Business Periodicals

As discussed in the preceding section, periodicals, whether in print, digital, or emerging, app-optimized versions, remain a key source for the latest business and industry news. Chapter 3 provides an extensive list of key periodicals in all business disciplines. Generally, these periodicals may be split into four broad categories: newspapers, magazines, research journals, and trade journals.

The smallest library may choose to purchase only some basic titles: a traditional daily, starting with the *Wall Street Journal*, and perhaps also adding in the *Financial Times* or *Investor's Business Daily*. That small library will also want to carry the local newspapers (if they still exist in collectable forms) so as to get coverage of the local business market (EBSCO's Regional Business News, described in Chapter 3, covers regional business publications nationwide). After that, the small library may add one or more of the most basic business magazines, starting perhaps with *Business Week*, *Fortune*, or *Forbes*. And if the small library still has room (and funding!) after making these acquisitions, some of the more specialized yet arguably "basic" trade magazines, such as *Advertising Age* and *Marketing Week*, may be added next.

Most libraries are likely to rely largely on full-text access to many of these sources as purchased through one of the general or business literature databases discussed above and in Chapter 2. Smaller libraries and public libraries especially may actually purchase only a handful of browsing periodicals, relying on full-text access through a database for nearly all of their business periodicals collection.

Chapter 3 also covers the key business journals in which the latest developments in business research are shared. Among the most prominent of these titles are the *Harvard Business Review*, the *Sloan Management Review*, and the *California Management Review*. Beyond those are many additional specialty scholarly journals, covering such topics as advertising, consumer psychology, finance, economics, investing, and more.

Finally, consider the aforementioned category of industry or trade magazines. Usually produced by or affiliated with a trade association, and typically not found in bookstores or at newsstands, these titles are vital sources of industry-specific intelligence. Operating in clothing or fashion? You will want to keep up with *Women's Wear Daily*. Selling bicycles? Read *Bicycle Retailer and Industry News*. Own a restaurant? Try *Nation's Restaurant News*. The list of trade magazines and journals is lengthy, and libraries will generally rely on access via one of the specialty aggregator business databases covered above.

To reiterate, many or most of these titles may be accessed through a subscription to one or more of the databases in the preceding section; refer to Chapter 3 to understand the important titles to watch for in whichever aggregator database seems to be the best choice for your library.

Top Business Resources

Brent Field
Librarian
Santa Barbara (CA) Public Library
Service area approximately 226,000 people

I am the business librarian by default—no other librarian wanted to teach the Business Resources class. We have mainly three groups of patrons who request business resources: the retired, business students, and entrepreneurs.

The retired are mainly interested in managing their investments so we maintain subscriptions to *Value Line Ratings and Reports*, and *Morningstar Mutual Funds*, as well as the publications *Barron's National Business and Financial Weekly*, and *Investor's Business Daily*, all fairly standard reference resources for investors.

For local students taking business classes at institutions without sufficient business resources of their own, we have resources like *Strauss's Handbook of Business Information*, Dun and Bradstreet's *Industry Norms and Key Business Ratios*, Rand McNally's *Commercial Atlas and Marketing Guide*, and a local research publication, *Economic Outlook for Santa Barbara County*.

For entrepreneurs such as the Women's Economic Ventures Self-Employment Training participants, we provide business resources aimed at providing them with information related to writing well-researched business plans: the *Encyclopedia of Associations* and the *National Trade and Professional Associations Directory* (both provide access to trade groups that offer research specific to a particular industry); the Economic Research Institute's *California Economic Growth* and *California County Projections*; the Eureka Group's *California Retail Survey*; and the *SRDS Direct Marketing List Source*.

We also subscribe to the online database *Reference USA*, a business and residential directory, good for market and competitor research. Online sources for demographic information that I find useful are the U.S. Census's http://www.factfinder.census.gov and the California Department of Finance's http://www.dof.ca.gov/Research/Research.php.

For particular patrons interested in inventing and creating devices, or those interested in sourcing materials, my favorite online resource for information on manufacturers, distributors, and service providers is ThomasNet.com.

START-UPS AND MARKET RESEARCH

One of the most important business information services libraries provide is support for the entrepreneur and small-business owner; that service also extends to business students in academic libraries who do frequent business planning exercises. Chapter 7 is devoted exclusively to resources for start-ups, while

Chapter 6, on marketing research, is useful for both start-ups and existing businesses alike. Most of what is covered in those chapters will not be repeated here; instead, we will briefly highlight sources and types of resources of interest to the accidental business librarian.

Support and Legal

Every business has certain legal and accounting requirements. A core business need is basic advice concerning how to start and run a business. An excellent free resource, covered in Chapter 4 on government information, is the U.S. Small Business Administration (SBA) website. The SBA site includes a rich section devoted to starting and nurturing a business, and guidance for such basic tasks as registering and licensing a business, understanding business types (e.g., sole proprietorships, partnerships, corporations), laws and regulations that must be followed, and forms that one must complete. Starting a child care business in Kansas? SBA.gov identifies the resources detailing both federal and state requirements for starting such a business, ranging from business registration to taxes to permits. SBA.gov frequently points to state websites for entrepreneurs: every state in the union features web portals leading to state-specific requirements and advice to foster business creation and start-ups. The state of Virginia, for example, offers a business start-up portal through http://www.virginia.gov/ that includes information on registering, licensing, financing, and researching your potential business. Become familiar with the websites of your state's mechanisms to provide support for business and start-ups. See Chapter 7 ("Start-Ups") and Chapter 4 ("Government Information Sources") for more information.

Many privately published resources also cover the legal basics of starting a business. For instance, the popular self-help legal publisher Nolo Press has a free web page called "Start Your Own Business: 50 Things You'll Need to Do" (http://www.nolo.com/legal-encyclopedia/start-own-business-50-things-30077.html); libraries may also purchase Nolo's basic advice titles such as *The Small Business Start-Up Kit*, *Legal Guide for Starting & Running a Small Business*, *Trademark*, and *Legal Forms for Starting & Running a Small Business*. Numerous other websites and publishers also offer start-up guidance, and these are covered in Chapter 7.

A frequent component of the start-up process is writing a business plan. The websites noted above all have advice on writing the business plan, as do basic monographs about start-ups. The *Business Plans Handbook* is a core resource that reproduces dozens of actual business plans in an ongoing series of relatively affordable volumes. The *Handbook* and other resources discussed in Chapter 7 cover advice and how-tos for this task, and also address the legal requirements for start-ups.

Customers

Aside from the legal requirements for starting up, much research goes into planning and running a successful business. First, consider information about potential customers. Spending habits, income, demographic and socioeconomic statistics: all of these data are useful for entrepreneurs who need to identify and understand their potential customers. This type of people-specific market intelligence generally costs money, and is the fruit of in-depth research by market intelligence companies. However, there is at least one key free resource: the decennial census of population and housing, from the federal government. Federal government information is free from copyright, so is freely available to all. Through the decennial census and the related American Community Survey (ACS), one can get data on race, age, sex, income, occupation, education, etc., about people in every city, town, ZIP code, and smaller entities, right down to a city block. It is extremely useful information. The decennial census and ACS are covered in more detail in Chapter 4 on government information.

As rich a resource as it is, the decennial census does not provide many of the details that are especially valuable to a business owner. For instance, it does not tell who watches television or uses the Internet, or how much or what they watch. It does not tell who buys specific products or types of products, or who uses particular types of services. It does not provide demographics of those who buy any specific product or service. For that kind of information, more detailed and expensive resources are required; those resources are well covered in Chapters 6 and 7.

The smaller library might not be able to afford further customer research products at all. Nevertheless, if possible, a library should try to add in some of the customer market research-based products covered in Chapters 6 and 7, whether those are such relatively inexpensive items as monographs from New Strategist (see sidebar from Melissa Kozel-Gains); the mid-priced Local Market Audience Analyst, from Standard Rate and Data Service (SRDS); or more robust tools for consumer data manipulation, such as SimplyMap, from Geographic Research, Inc.

Local Market Audience Analyst (discussed in greater detail in Chapters 6 and 7) uses survey data to present characteristics of some 100 different lifestyles, such as dining out, travel, art, books, etc. It provides demographic, economic, and geographic statistics for each lifestyle, revealing, for instance, that people who purchase bicycles tend to be male, older than average, and wealthier than average. The resource also presents data on where those who practice the lifestyle are likely to live, among other rich market research data.

Top 10 Resources

Melissa Kozel-Gains
Boise State University
14,000 FTE, many undergraduate and graduate business programs including MBA

1. *Local Market Audience Analyst*—This was fabulous in print when it was the *Lifestyle Market Analyst*, but now it is even better online. The demographic, lifestyle, and geographic information about consumers cannot be beat.
2. *Encyclopedia of Business Information Sources*—This is where I go when I cannot find product information about something anywhere else. From the abrasives to zinc industries, databases, indexes, statistical sources, newsletters, and trade and professional associations' information are suggested here by product or industry. Especially good for those really small niche products.
3. *Business Statistics of the United States*—Robust economic information about the U.S. economy can be difficult to find in government databases, but this great print resource makes it manageable. The latest edition has data that are quite current, including Great Recession information.
4. New Strategist publications contain demographics about, and spending by, selected groups like Baby Boomers, Generation X, Millennials, Older Americans, and others. It simply takes government information that is often difficult to find, and challenging to comprehend, and makes it understandable.
5. *Hoover's* database has public and international companies' information, but, more importantly, it has those harder-to-find private-company data.
6. *Market Share Reporter* has interesting market share data on companies, products, and services. Always worth a look, because one often finds that fascinating factoid or list that just makes a report.
7. *Business Source Premier*—Such a great database, because it is so easy to use, and you have got to love its Datamonitor industry and company reports.
8. *ABI/INFORM*—Arguably, one of the three best general business databases in the world, but I especially appreciate their *Topics* and *Suggested Topics* display right up front on the top of the page after executing a search. Even my students cannot miss those helpful topics and are able to better focus their searching attempts.
9. *Business Rankings Annual*—This is a terrific resource for the same reasons I love *Market Share Reporter*. Love those top 10 lists like "Top Magazines in Advertising," "Top Fortune 500 Companies in Packaging and Containers," and "Best Commercial Health Plans," to name a few.
10. *Reference USA*—My favorite business directory.

SimplyMap, by comparison, features similar demographic and psychographic data built on a robust mapping interface. The Local Market Audience Analyst and SimplyMap are just two of a number of sources to consider to gain access to rich market research data about potential customers. Although many of these resources can be relatively expensive, there remain single-volume print sources that provide much cheaper, if more shallow (and often heavily U.S. Census-reliant) access to richer market research data.

For business librarians and the student or real-world entrepreneurs whom they assist, market research data about potential customers are a key information need. This importance is why both Chapters 6 and 7 cover resources in this area.

Industries and Businesses

Both start-ups and existing businesses need to understand their customers, their industry, and their competition. Chapters 6 ("Marketing Research") and 7 (Start-Ups) both list key sources with which to gain this kind of understanding. Once again, those libraries with limited funds to purchase products do have access to some quality data; and, to reiterate, these free data are available from the government, via the Economic Census and related products. Covered in detail in Chapter 4 on government information, these products contain basic data on the number, size, location, and other basic measures of business activity around the country. These resources reveal how many businesses exist by type within states, counties, and ZIP codes nationwide; and measures of how large or small these businesses are, based on such metrics as the number of employees and the volume of revenues generated. Economic Census data do not provide intelligence on any specific businesses, however, and are presented only in aggregate.

Beyond these free government data, the trade associations noted above are often excellent sources for intelligence on the nature, news, and data about a particular industry. This intelligence may be shared via trade journals, or simply via an association's website—although many data are costly, or access may be restricted to members of the association. For instance, for those who make, sell, or provide services for consumer electronics, the Consumer Electronic Association website provides a wealth of free information about that industry. Other examples illustrating the type and breadth of these organizations are the National Association of Convenience Stores, the Telecommunications Industry Association, the National Athletic Trainers Association, or the Automobile Aftermarket Industry Association. Although association websites can contain some of the most detailed—and sometimes expensive—data about a particular industry, they can also provide a surprisingly rich amount of free data, in the name of advocacy on behalf of the industry. Always explore the websites of appropriate business and trade associations, and always use one of the business databases noted earlier, because business trade journals often feature articles that report key findings of otherwise very expensive market research products (or publish informative announcements from trade associations).

To identify such organizations, it is helpful to have the classic reference tool the *Encyclopedia of Associations* (online either as Associations Unlimited, or as an e-book component of the Gale Directory Library), although a smart web search (using an appropriate industry name or keyword and the exact phrase "trade association") can be quite successful, as is browsing free directories such as http://www.usa.gov/directory/tradeassc/index.shtml.

Commercial products generally provide more consistent and in-depth intelligence about a particular industry than free resources will offer. Dun and Bradstreet's First Research Industry Profiles, for instance, features up-to-date snapshots of some 900 industries in the United States (many Canadian industries are covered as well), providing background and statistics about the industry's size, its nature, its customers, and its trends. A more affordable option (although much less frequently updated) is the monographic *Encyclopedia of American Industries*, featuring several-page snapshots of some 1,000 industries. The classic *Standard and Poor's Industry Surveys*, meanwhile, covers industries in broader strokes (about 50 industries, or sectors; "Telecommunications," for instance) but in much more depth (a typical *Industry Survey* is some 30 pages long). Also useful for industry research are measures of industry ratios, or financial performance benchmarks; because their source is company financial reports, those are covered later in this chapter, under "Accounting."

First Research Industry Profiles, the *Encyclopedia of American Industries*, and *Standard and Poor's Industry Surveys*, among other similar sources, are all covered in depth in Chapters 6 and 7.

Also consult Chapters 6 and 7 for resources to identify potential competitors, using one of several business directories. There are some 14 million businesses in the United States, by at least one count, and the vast majority of those are small (and privately owned) businesses. Detailed intelligence about all of these businesses is hard to come by. The Reference USA database is one of the current premier, nationwide business directories, with information about these 14 million businesses, including name/ownership, address, type of business, and estimates of the number of employees and sales. Dun and Bradstreet's Million Dollar Directory database and the Hoover's Online database also include this type of information. Entrepreneurs and others use these and other databases to identify competitors in their industry, whether locally or nationally, and to create and download lists of business by various relevant criteria. Opening a hair-styling salon in Philadelphia? Each of these resources will provide the names and some measure of the size and sales of all hair salons or barbershops in Philadelphia, along with their addresses and other contact information.

Although these tools tend to be expensive, there is no real low-cost alternative for this type of information; free information from the government reveals nothing specific about small businesses (as noted above, the Economic Census presents only anonymous, aggregate data; similarly, you cannot view a company's tax return), and the free web provides little beyond yellow-page directory-type information. Therefore, although such commercial directory databases may indeed be relatively costly, when they can be managed they will likely be one of the first items purchased with a business library's budget, especially because they also cover the 20,000 or so publicly traded companies in depth, and thereby serve patrons doing investment research as well—the next topic to which we will now turn.

INVESTMENT

The U.S. financial system, whereby anyone can own a share in our largest companies and thereby raise money for the company—and also share in its profits—is one of the pillars of the American economy. Indeed, the markets and exchanges through which such investments in these so-called "public" companies are made, popularly referred to as "Wall Street," represent perhaps the most closely watched measure of business activity, largely because so many Americans own stock or bonds in these companies and are therefore extremely interested in their performance. Although many of us may invest in companies only secondhand, by way of various mutual funds run by those who manage our retirement accounts, many others play the market individually and seek intelligence about the companies and other entities in which they invest. Nor is investment limited to buying stock in companies. Individuals invest in bonds (perhaps issued by a company, but also often by state and local governments, school districts, and other public entities), foreign currencies, and other, more complicated investment vehicles. Such investors seek information about companies' financial health, foreign currencies, bonds, etc., making investment research one of the largest business information needs to be served. A few basics are covered below; investment resources are covered in depth in Chapter 5.

Company Research

For libraries and researchers on a limited budget, there is great news about company research: excellent data are available from the federal government. This is because in the wake of the 1929 stock market crash, laws were enacted requiring public disclosure of financial information from all public companies—meaning those that are traded on the stock markets. For many decades, such intelligence, although technically available to the general public, was controlled by securities and investment firms, and was difficult to access by the independent investor. Luckily, inspired by the possibilities of the web, public information advocate and hero Carl Malamud led the effort to put these reports online, free, for all taxpayers to access (Markoff, 1993).

The mechanism for this access became the EDGAR database ("EDGAR" stands for Electronic Data Gathering and Retrieval). Covered in depth in Chapter 4, EDGAR is managed by the SEC (Securities and Exchange Commission) and features the financial documents filed by thousands of public companies, as required by the law. Available reports for each company include quarterly ("10-Q") and annual ("10-K") financial reports; these documents are key to understanding the health of any company being considered for investment.

Top Business Resources

Daniel Shiffner
Library Coordinator
Free Library of Philadelphia
Service area approximately 1.5 million people

To begin with, know your local municipality's business portal, in my case http://business.phila.gov, and related resources, such as our Greater Philadelphia Sustainable Business Network (http://www.sbnphiladelphia.org/). We would also be remiss if we did not mention the free government resources covered later in the book (Chapter 4), such as the Census Bureau, SBA.gov, and data from the Bureau of Labor Statistics.

Our core paid resources are:

- ReferenceUSA and Dun and Bradstreet's Million Dollar Database: These databases are directory databases that allow users to generate lists of businesses that meet specific criteria. For example: I would like a list of every hair salon in a specific ZIP code.
- SimplyMap and BusinessDecision: Databases that combine Geographic Information System (GIS) data with census data and market research to run demographic and psychographic reports on residents in a defined area.
- *The Business Plans Handbook* (electronically accessed via Gale Virtual Reference Library and published on paper by Gale): Examples of successful business plans. If you have it electronically, you can perform a keyword search.

- Value Line/Morningstar/Standard & Poor's Net Advantage: Stocks, bonds, mutual funds, and industry research.
- Business and Company Resource Center (Gale): Articles, industry research, and company information. EBSCO's Business Source Premier is the best database we used to have but do not anymore: business journal articles, as well as industry and stock research.

Best free resources:

- Mint.com and Google Finance: personal finance resources.
- Yahoo! Finance: current and historical stock quotes (get a quote on a stock from any day in its history).
- Wall Street Journal Online.
- SCORE Philadelphia (http://www.scorephila.org) has been an amazing partner for us, and people can find their local SCORE Chapter at http://www.score.org.
- Two of our local universities have Small Business Development Centers (UPenn and Temple). Many universities have similar centers serving their communities.
- http://www.investopedia.com/: A dictionary of all of those investing terms nobody taught you when you were getting your BA in comparative literature.
- http://us.kompass.com/: Who makes what where, internationally. If you need an iron mine in Turkey, this is the place to go.
- http://Xe.com/: currency conversion.
- http://www.thomasnet.com/: Thomas Register, who manufactures what
- State corporation bureaus (listed here: http://www.llrx.com/columns/round up29.htm): Allow you to see who owns a particular business in a particular state. Not all are searchable and not all are free, but Pennsylvania's is both.

Building on EDGAR, there are several commercially produced databases, which start with data from EDGAR or from a public company's annual report to its shareholders, and add value with additional information, analysis, and other data about public companies. Free sites such as Yahoo! Finance, CNNMoney.com, and the Motley Fool provide surprisingly rich data about public companies and their stock. Multifunctional subscription databases from Mergent, Dun and Bradstreet, and Standard and Poor's are among those also found in this category. All of the latter are relatively expensive, but, because of their sophisticated functionality and depth of coverage in comparison with the freely available websites, they will merit serious consideration by the medium-size public library and by any academic library supporting a business degree. Further, the business databases mentioned above and in Chapter 2, including EBSCO's Business Source, ProQuest's ABI/Inform, and LexisNexis

Academic, frequently contain company information and reports similar (or identical) to those found in the specialty financial information databases. In addition, Chapter 9, on deep business research, although far from a chapter for the "accidental" business librarian, discusses further usually quite expensive products that allow for even more complex data extraction than the more typically available commercial products.

Sources about Markets

Tracking the stock markets themselves is relatively easy to do in the web age. While standard bearers of these data, such as the *Wall Street Journal*, provide relevant basics, including company stock prices, bond information, and mutual fund information, such free sites noted above as Yahoo! Finance, CNNMoney .com, and the Motley Fool all provide near real-time access to stock and market data, as do the online versions of the chief financial news sources noted previously (such as *Barron's*, the *Financial Times*, and *Investor's Business Daily*), as well as "regular" news sources such as the online *New York Times*.

Chapter 5 goes on to cover the classic, in-depth commercial products for tracking markets. Among these sources are Bloomberg, perhaps the most famous of all the sophisticated, real-time investment resources (having even spawned a mayor!), and Morningstar, which has unparalleled coverage of mutual funds, which most of us—knowingly or not—invest in via retirement and pension funds.

Other Investment Resources

Readers of Chapter 5 will want to pay special attention to investment advisory services. Along with company information, these resources also include recommendations and advice for investment. Perhaps the most long-standing and prominent such title used in libraries is *Value Line*, a staple of public and academic libraries of all sizes. Check out the coverage of *Value Line* and similar products, such as Standard and Poor's *The Outlook*, in Chapter 5, which also covers many other resources to support investment research. Further, Chapter 4 (on government information) covers resources used to follow some of the most famous of investment tools, instruments from the U.S. Treasury such as T-Bills and T-Notes.

OTHER BUSINESS AND RELATED RESOURCES

Economic Data

The best-known economic data, such as unemployment, interest rates, foreign trade, prices and inflation, exchange rates, etc., are produced by the federal government, and are relatively easily accessible. Chapter 4 highlights sources of these economic data. The accidental business librarian should know how to find these basic economic data. These measures are also widely reported in the press, and can be found at any news or newspaper site like the *Wall Street Journal, Financial Times, Investor's Business Daily, New York Times,* or Yahoo! Finance.

Employment and Job Seekers

Although it may not be considered a pure business need, information needed by job seekers, inspired by the economic recession that began in 2008, has been dramatically reinforced in the national consciousness as one of public libraries' most in-demand resources. Libraries perform significant patron support for citizens looking for jobs or looking to better their job prospects through resume improvement, etc. The introduction to this chapter referred to the large numbers of citizens using public libraries to find jobs and sharpen employment skills. Part of this demand originates simply because job advertisements are now found mostly online, and people use public libraries' free Internet access to seek opportunities. Several library resources support citizens as they seek employment opportunities.

Once again, freely available titles from governments (at all jurisdictions) are among the basic sources to support the job seeker. Covered in Chapter 4, the *Occupational Outlook Handbook* is a classic, single-volume tool that lists over 400 occupations, describing the nature of the work, educational and training requirements, salary and wages, and the employment outlook for that job in the coming years. The O*NET Online database offers similar information. The Bureau of Labor Statistics, which compiles and publishes a wealth of statistics on employment-related measures, publishes such sources as Wages by Area and Occupation (also covered in Chapter 4), which, as the title implies, lists the typical wages for hundreds of different occupations, for the nation as a whole, for states, and for specific cities.

Accounting and Accountancy

At the core of every business enterprise is its financial record, popularly known as "the books": the records of assets, income, inventories, and profits. By way of recording and analyzing this data, demand for accountancy materials is steady. The bookkeeping basics needed by the many small "mom and pop" businesses are covered in resources treated in Chapter 7, on start-ups. Accountancy will not be covered in particular depth in this book, but the accidental business librarian should be aware of a few basic types of accounting resources.

Top 10 Resources (*A Highly Selective and Idiosyncratic List!*)

Michael Oppenheim
UCLA—Anderson Graduate School of Management
1,600 students enrolled in full-time, part-time, and executive MBA programs and doctoral programs—no undergraduate business program
"Top Twenty, Internationally-Ranked B-School"

- *Best Practice Database*: A truly unique resource—it is not available through any aggregator—for benchmarking data and other strategic research, as originally commissioned by Fortune 500 clients and the like, focusing on real-life best practices in such areas as customer service, sales and marketing, human resources, operations, knowledge management, and the internet and e-business.
- *eMarketer*: Arguably the first-stop resource for virtually anything and everything digital and "e."
- *Faulkner's Advisory on Information Technology Studies (FAITS)*: An extraordinarily practical, beautifully efficient source for superb tutorials and market research reports; no other must-have for IT industry coverage begins to provide more bang for the buck (and the buck is extremely affordable, indeed).
- *First Research* (Hoover's/Dun and Bradstreet): Outstanding coverage of hundreds of difficult-to-research niche industries, conveniently searchable by both SIC (Standard Industrial Classification) and NAICS (North American Industry Classification System) codes (as well as keywords)—also a very handy source for industry ratios.
- *Freedonia Focus Portal*: A wonderfully affordable, easy-yet-powerfully searchable source of real-world market research reports (actually, extremely value-packed, 20-or-so-page "executive summaries") covering often challenging-to-research B2B manufacturing and high-tech industries.
- *IBISWorld*: Full-text, fully searchable (by NAICS, SIC, or keyword) U.S. industry analyses, covering over 790 industries at the five-digit NAICS level—more than 97 percent of the U.S. economy. Reports on global and Chinese industries are also available (depending on the subscription).
- *Kompass*: Time and again this worldwide B2B company directory not only has been the only resource in which MBA teams can precisely identify their client companies' competitors or target customers, no matter the market worldwide, but it is often the only resource in which the client company itself can be found—to student teams' grateful amazement. Kompass's exceptionally helpful and responsive sales support and customer service could not possibly be improved, either.
- *Mergent Horizon*—Not at all just another company financials database, *Mergent Horizon* is simply great for drilling down into the niches, subniches, sub-sub-niches, *and* sub-sub-*sub*-niches of industries (such as software, or biotechnology, to name only two industries that MBA students always seem

to find otherwise "unresearchable" microniches to work on), to identify *publicly traded* competitors, customers, suppliers, market segments, and so much more.

- *SimplyMap* (Geographic Research, Inc.): A key resource for market *and* social research, this web-based mapping application—now easier to use than ever, following its reinvention as "SimplyMap 2.0" in 2011—enables you to create both thematic maps (without having to spend days or weeks to learn GIS!) and purely textual reports, as you slice, dice, and instantly (if desired) rank demographic *and* psychographic, business, and marketing data sourced from both the federal government and commercial data providers (depending on the subscription you create). The unflagging flexibility and incomparable quality of customer service and user support also set an industry standard.
- *Zephyr* (Bureau van Dijk): This premier international mergers and acquisitions database—great for researching and analyzing deals of all kinds—has a remarkably powerful and sophisticated interface, which is also astonishingly easy to use and to teach.

First are the sources specific to the practice of accountancy. So-called "GAAP" and "GAAS" guides cover accounting principles: Generally Accepted Accounting Practices (GAAP) and Generally Accepted Auditing Standards (GAAS) are administered by the Financial Accounting Standards Board (FASB) and the American Institute of Certified Public Accountants, respectively. These principles govern financial reporting and auditing by those who manage the books for companies.

Financial accountants also manage accounting for outward purposes, such as for taxes and required reports to shareholders. Financial accountants, and students training as accountants, follow laws and regulations from governments, in addition to GAAP and/or GAAS. The federal laws on taxation are freely available online as part of the *U.S. Code*, the compilation of all federal law in force. Likewise, tax regulations—more specifically, rules that help to interpret the laws—are freely available in the *Code of Federal Regulations*. However, financial accountants usually seek more powerful, value-added tools to help them interpret tax law. Such publishers as Commerce Clearing House (CCH), RIA (now owned by Thomson/Reuters), and the Bureau of National Affairs (BNA) are all long-standing leaders in practical legal information research, each producing numerous products featuring access to an up-to-date compilation of legal practice materials. For accountants, CCH (via the OmniTax database, and other products, such as CCH IntelliConnect) and RIA (via the Checkpoint database) both produce comprehensive tax accounting solutions that bring together all tax law, tax regulations, tax court rulings, and various rules and memoranda from the Internal Revenue Service all in one place, providing a complete resource for tax-reporting requirements for accountants. Such products are staples of accounting and law firms that specialize in tax law, and at least one or more will also be found in academic libraries that support any undergraduate and above accounting programs. They are usually outside the realm of what public libraries collect, even large public libraries. BNA may be most prominently known in accountancy circles for its Tax Management Portfolios: single-volume, comprehensive guides to special tax topics, such as Divorce and Separation, Corporate Bankruptcy, and Real Estate Mortgages.

Accountancy products also interest non-accountants. For instance, investors may wish to find out who a company's accounting firm is—who audits the company—and thus may need to consult *Who Audits America*. Additional related products of interest to investors and others are the classic financial ratio volumes. These titles, specifically the *Almanac of Financial Ratios*, Dun and Bradstreet's *Industry Norms and Key Business Ratios*, and RMA's *Annual Statement Studies*, provide analysis of the tax returns and SEC-required reports of public companies, by industry, that in turn provide key measures, or financial benchmarks, for the industries covered (which vary by product).

Finally, as in any field, accountants also keep up with the research published in their literature. Accounting journals are covered in the databases mentioned above and in Chapter 3.

International Business

Sprinkled throughout the book are references to resources that cover international and global business topics. The databases treated in Chapter 2 cover international journals, and journals with international perspectives are among those listed in Chapter 3. Chapter 5, on investment resources, includes sources that cover foreign markets, while a few of the market research and start-up resources of Chapters 6 and 7 similarly include some international coverage, especially for exporting information. The "deep business resources" discussed in Chapter 9 likewise cover some international topics.

CONCLUSION: THE CORE LIST FOR THE ACCIDENTAL BUSINESS LIBRARIAN

This chapter has highlighted core resources and concepts recommended for any business librarian and researcher to have, and points to later chapters to gain deeper understanding of those resources. In summary, the accidental business librarian should:

- Understand the business literature and the tools that provide access to it.
- Know the key periodicals and their uses.
- Know the core, free resources available from the government.
- Know how to support research on investments.
- Understand basic resources to identify information about potential customers, competition, industry, and the economy as a whole.
- Know sources to support the entrepreneur and business start-up.

REFERENCES

American Library Association. 2011. "The State of America's Libraries." http://ala.org/ala/newspresscenter/mediapresscenter/americaslibraries2011/publiclibraries.cfm.

Carville, James. (exact origins of phrase unknown; Carville credited for popularizing it during 1992 presidential campaign).

Coolidge, Calvin. "Address to the American Society of Newspaper Editors" (speech), January 17, 1925. http://www.presidency.ucsb.edu/ws/index.php?pid=24180.

Markoff, John. "Plan Opens More Data to Public." *New York Times*, October 22, 1993. http://www.nytimes.com.

U.S. National Center for Education Statistics. "Table no. 298. Bachelor's Degrees by Field: 1980 to 2008." *Statistical Abstract of the United States: 2011*. Ed. U.S. Census Bureau. Washington, DC: U.S. Census Bureau, 2011a.

U.S. National Center for Education Statistics. "Table no. 299. Master's and Doctoral Degress Earned by Field: 1980 to 2008." *Statistical Abstract of the United States: 2011*. Ed. U.S. Census Bureau. Washington, DC: U.S. Census Bureau, 2011b.

2

Accessing the Business Literature

Lucy Heckman

INTRODUCTION

A business researcher requires access to scholarly journals, popular magazines, trade journals, newspaper articles, and equivalent web content. A scholarly journal may report the latest findings on the psychology of product placement; a popular magazine might have the most readable summary of the credit crisis; trade journals—by specializing in an industry or product—provide much of the most inside intelligence about news and trends of an industry or product; and newspaper articles are still the most likely sources for local business information. Overall, research using the business literature may range from keeping up with the latest developments regarding specific companies and industries, to locating scholarly articles on the reasons for the financial crisis of 2008, finding biographical materials about CEOs, and locating quantitative studies about the stock market crash of 1987. The availability of full-text articles related to these and other topics has made locating this material more efficient, but requires librarians and information professionals to teach effective search strategies to end users and business researchers.

In addition, many of the literature databases *now also include other business information*, including company intelligence and market research reports, making traditional business literature databases increasingly one-stop shopping for a variety of business research needs.

It should be noted that in some cases, print indexes/abstracts are still available, but the reality is that they will very, very rarely be used for any current business research. Some libraries may be constrained by lack of space from maintaining print indexes and print copies of journals and newspapers, and increasingly the trend is to "go digital" and purchase online indexes, abstracts, and full-text databases. Indeed, many libraries are not only purchasing electronic materials nearly exclusively, they are also discarding even classic print publications in favor of trusted, digital archival versions. In fact, nearly every periodical covered in Chapter 3 includes online versions.

The focus of the present chapter will emphasize these online databases.

ADVANTAGES OF GOING DIGITAL: SEARCHING ONLINE FOR PERIODICAL, NEWSPAPER, AND JOURNAL ARTICLES

Although some vendors and publishers still offer print indexes and abstracts, digital equivalents are the norm and often the only available format. Additionally, periodical publishers offer these titles digitally to various database vendors, which makes it even more efficient for libraries to go digital in their collections rather than purchasing print and microform copies of journals.

Searching online generally offers the following advantages:

- One-stop access to full-text articles, saving the time required to locate the journal and make copies from either print, microfilm, or microfiche
- Options of downloading, printing, and emailing articles retrieved
- Option of exporting citations to EndNote, EasyBib, Zotero, Refworks, or other bibliographic management software to prepare bibliographies and footnotes or endnotes for research papers
- Ability to receive current awareness services such as "search alerts" or RSS feeds of tables of contents or new articles meeting specified criteria
- Remote access features that allow patrons to access the databases from anywhere after authenticating as a user of the library providing access
- Availability of information that cannot be found in print (e.g., ABI/INFORM is an electronic database that does not have a print equivalent)
- Increased range of retrospective coverage in periodicals (once publishers established web platforms for current journals, they turned their attention to increasing retrospective backfiles)

CURRENT AWARENESS AND EVALUATION

The market for databases offering access to periodicals is ever changing and dynamic—companies can merge, some can acquire another database vendor, and changes in coverage (journals, years included) can take place rapidly. Librarians can keep track of major changes via the literature (e.g., *Journal of Business and Finance Librarianship*, *Choice*, *Library Journal*, *Information Today*, etc.). There are also electronic discussion groups such as BusLib-L, which offer a venue for discussion of new databases and/or changes to existing databases. Also recommended is attendance at meetings of appropriate professional organizations (e.g., the Special Libraries Association and the American Library Association's Business Reference and Services Section) since these venues allow librarians to speak with vendors and colleagues from other libraries. Regional consortia and groups (e.g., METRO, the Metropolitan New York Library Council, and WALDO, the Westchester Academic Library Directors Organization, to name two important New York groups) also allow for information gathering and comparison of databases. Despite these opportunities, some of the databases below are characterized by rather frequent changes in content, often without notice. For instance, as this book was in final editing, the long-running business literature indexing and abstracting tools published by the H.W. Wilson Company quickly ceased, with the June 2011 acquisition of H.W. Wilson by EBSCO. These business information tools are themselves run by businesses, and competitive advantages for these products as pursued through mergers and acquisitions, deals for exclusive content, and other business practices have a direct impact on the information user. Business librarians need to be aware of which databases tend to be more stable than others.

Because there is such a proliferation of databases offering full-text journal access (an interdisciplinary, multi-subject proliferation, and not necessarily a proliferation of business-only databases), librarians need to decide which of those will best serve their patrons' research needs. Librarians can also invite vendors to give presentations and opt for trial subscriptions giving a time of evaluation before a decision is made to begin a subscription. One can also read reviews of databases in the literature, and can run one's own comparison and analysis of title and content lists, bibliographic quality, and interface features. Additionally, librarians still need to decide at times between print and electronic subscriptions of journals; a more difficult decision is deciding to rely on access to a title via one of the aggregated databases that do not guarantee perpetual access.

COVERAGE OF JOURNALS

Other decisions to be made require an examination of coverage of the journals within the databases. Some questions to be considered are these:

- How many titles are covered? How many are scholarly, popular, or trade? How many are uniquely covered in the particular database?
- Is there an "embargo" during which coverage for certain months or years will not be available within a specific database?
- How much full-text coverage is there? How quickly are full-text articles added to the database?

- What is the lag time between appearance of a new journal issue and its indexing and full-text in the database?
- Does the database provide within the articles the tables, graphs, and illustrations that were included in the print publication?
- Is it full coverage or are some articles and "front matter" left out of the database?

ACCESSIBILITY

Beyond such classic metrics as title counts, full-text coverage, exclusive availability of content, and volume of peer-reviewed content, several other factors to consider when evaluating the "fit" of a database include:

- Does the indexing and abstracting provided by a database under review meet the needs of the library's clientele?
- Are the abstracts informative (i.e., do they provide a summary of the document's major content?) or are they merely indicative (do they provide an indication of the document's subject?)
- Is everything in the titles covered by the database indexed and abstracted? Are editorials, advertisements, and cartoons included?
- Does the search interface for the database offer a suggestion of related topics? Is there an online thesaurus of indexing terms used?
- Are subscriptions for unlimited use or are there restrictions on the number of simultaneous users?

ACCESSING PERIODICAL LITERATURE: ONLINE DATABASES

The entries below are listed alphabetically by name of the database. Print equivalents, if available, are noted within each entry.

ABI/INFORM. ProQuest. http://www.proquest.com/en-US/catalogs/databases/ detail/abi_inform_complete.shtml.
ProQuest is a part of Cambridge Information Group (CSA): http://www .cambridgeinformationgroup.com. Pricing varies; contact the publisher.

ABI/INFORM is a long-standing, comprehensive index to popular, scholarly, and trade business periodicals, and is a classic in the genre. Coverage includes journal articles going back as far as 1923. Full text is included for many of the articles added from 1991 to present. At present, approximately 50 percent of the journals are indexed and abstracted cover to cover. It covers articles on global business and on company histories, industries, management, new product development, marketing, accounting, taxation, economics, and finance. ABI/INFORM contains bibliographic citations and 25- to 150-word summaries of articles appearing in professional publications, academic journals, and trade magazines published worldwide. The full text of articles is included for hundreds of journals. It provides related topics for searchers and enables users to select full text only or scholarly only (excluding popular titles).

ABI/INFORM is also a prime example of a business literature database that is more than just literature, as it also includes items such as business cases (very popular for us in classroom settings), working papers, hundreds of company SWOT analyses (Strengths, Weaknesses, Opportunities, and Threats), company annual reports, country reports (summarizing business climate and market conditions for countries), and dissertations. All of this added content must also be considered when looking at the value of a database such as ABI/INFORM.

ABI/INFORM is available in different versions, with varying coverage levels and pricing. Available products include: ABI/INFORM Complete, ABI/INFORM Global, ABI/INFORM Research, ABI/INFORM Trade and Industry, and ABI/INFORM Dateline.

- **ABI/INFORM Complete**: Covers over 5,400 periodicals.
  ABI/INFORM Complete Archive. Covers backfiles of selected journals covered in ABI/INFORM Complete.
- **ABI/INFORM Global**: Covers over 3,300 periodicals.
- **ABI/INFORM Research**: Covers over 1,800 periodicals
- **ABI/INFORM Trade and Industry**: Focus is on trade and industry news reports; concentrates on trade publications. Covers over 1,500 periodicals.
- **ABI/INFORM Dateline**: Focus is on regional and local publications, allowing users to locate material on regional companies, industries, and business news not found elsewhere. Covers 200+ journals.

Always check coverage, as title lists can change. Each of these "flavors" also has different coverage of the extra materials discussed above.

Business Source Complete. EBSCO. http://www.ebscohost.com/academic/business-source-complete. Pricing varies; contact the publisher.

Recent years have seen aggressive development of EBSCO's Business Source product, aligning Business Source alongside ABI/INFORM as complete periodical indexing and full-text solutions for serious business libraries. Business Source Complete is the top-of-the-line offering among the three Business Source products, featuring more coverage than Elite and Premier. Like ABI/INFORM, its coverage goes beyond periodicals, and includes books, faculty seminars (videos), industry reports, scholarly journals, trade journals, market research reports, country reports, and SWOT analysis, among other resources, and features profiles of most cited authors of articles. Other "flavors" of the Business Source line are:

- **Business Source Elite**. EBSCO. http://www.ebscohost.com/ academic/business-source-elite. Pricing varies; contact the publisher.
    Business Source Elite provides full-text coverage of approximately 1,000 scholarly journals in business, economics, and management. Like Complete and Premier, it also features company profiles from Datamonitor.
- **Business Source Premier**. EBSCO. http://www.ebscohost.com/ academic/business-source-premier. Pricing varies; contact the publisher.
    Business Source Premier provides access to business journals, including peer reviewed journals, and covering topics such as business, marketing, management, accounting, taxation, economics, company information, and industries. Full-text coverage is available for more than 2,300 journals. Searches can be limited to full text and/or scholarly journals (peer reviewed) only. All of the Business Source products contain the Business Searching Interface which provides access to articles, industry profiles, company profiles, etc.

Business Periodicals Index Retrospective. H.W. Wilson and EBSCO http:// www.ebscohost.com/academic/business-periodicals-index-retrospective.

As of June 2011, H.W. Wilson and EBSCO announced a merger. **Business Periodicals Index**, a long-standing index to articles in business and economics, is no longer being updated. **Business Periodicals Index Retrospective**, however, is still available from EBSCO.

Dow Jones Factiva. News Corporation. http://factiva.com/.

Dow Jones Factiva is a searchable database of thousands of leading news and business sources among which are over 60 newswires, more than 2,500 newspapers, more than 5,500 business and industry publications, selected television and radio transcripts, and pictures from wire services such as Reuters and McClatchy-Tribune Photo Service. For current business news from around the world, Factiva is unrivaled.

EconLit (American Economic Association). http://www.aeaweb.org/ econlit/index.php (also available through Cambridge Information Group [CSA], http://www.cambridgeinformationgroup.com, and Dialog).

EconLit is the classic index to scholarly research in the field of economics. It indexes and abstracts journal articles, books, dissertations, and working papers. The subject matter covers economic theory and application. Also included is the full text of book reviews published in the *Journal of Economic Literature* since 1993.

Group Gale Group PROMT. http://www.gale.cengage.com/BusinessRC/ Offered as part of **Business and Company Resource Center**. Also available through Dialog.

PROMT contains abstracts and full-text records of articles from trade and business journals, local newspapers, regional business publications, national and international business newspapers, industry newsletters, research studies, investment analysts' reports, corporate news releases, and annual reports. As a whole, Gale's Business and Company Resource Center is a complete solution that may compete with ABI/INFORM and the Business Source products.

Journal Storage (JSTOR). http://www.jstor.org.

JSTOR is a multidisciplinary database that provides an extensive backfile of full-text journal articles. Those researching business can browse related journals divided into categories of business, economics, and finance or search by topic for full-text articles. It enables researchers to locate full-text articles, some going back to the nineteenth century. While JSTOR "embargoes" recent issues and focuses on backfiles, recent enhancements include indexing and linking out to the current coverage of a title when available.

Insurance Periodicals Index (IPI) (EBSCOhost). http://www.ebscohost .com/academic/insurance-periodicals-index.

This database was formerly produced by NILS Publishing Co., Inc., in co-operation with the Insurance and Employee Benefits Division (IEBD) of the Special Libraries Association. It is now managed by EBSCO. It indexes and abstracts approximately 200 journals and magazines representing the insurance industry, with coverage of some going back as far as 1946.

LexisNexis Academic. LexisNexis. http://www.lexisnexis.com/.

Among resources provided by this comprehensive academic product from LexisNexis are several business-related modules: accounting (full-text coverage of accounting journals, among which are *Journal of Accountancy*, *Accounting Today*, and *Accounting Technology*); consumer information (full-text coverage includes *Consumer Reports*); detailed company information pulled from several sources discussed in Chapters 6 and 7; and law reviews and journals (which have contents related to business law).

Beyond the coverage of the literature, however, is extremely robust coverage of company information. While resources may come and go depending on licensing, LexisNexis Academic has long hosted excellent sources of information on both large public companies and larger private companies as well as the millions of small businesses. Additionally, it includes many sources of foreign-company information.

PAIS International and **PAIS Archive Database**. http://www.csa.com/ factsheets/pais-set-c.php.

Available through CSA/ProQuest and through Dialog, this database contains citations to journal articles in addition to books, government documents, statistical directories, gray literature, etc. Newspapers and newsletters are not included in the coverage. The topics covered in business are: banking and finance, business and service sector, economic conditions, energy resources and policy, labor conditions and policy, manufacturing and industry, trade, and transportation.

ProQuest Accounting & Tax Index Full Text. http://www.proquest.com/ en-US/catalogs/databases/detail/pq_accounting_tax.shtml.

ProQuest Accounting & Tax indexes and abstracts more than 2,000 publications with hundreds of these in full text. It includes all journals from the American Accounting Association. It also includes American Institute of CPAs (AICPA) publications, accounting dissertations, and selected conference proceedings.

ProQuest Wall Street Journal and **Wall Street Journal Historical**. http:// www.proquest.com/en-US/catalogs/databases/detail/wall_street_journal.shtml.

Available through separate subscriptions, the combination of these two databases provides full-text coverage from the first issue of the *Wall Street Journal* in 1889 to the present day. It allows searching by limiting to specific time periods or dates, and editorials, editorial cartoons, and letters to the editor from well-known people are indexed. The *Journal* is also available through Factiva, covered above.

RDS Business and Industry. Gale Cengage. http://www.gale.cengage .com/pdf/facts/busind.pdf.

RDS Business and Industry focuses on company, product, and industry information and provides mostly full-text coverage of trade and business journals, industry newsletters, and regional, national, and international newsletters.

RDS Business and Management Practices. Gale Cengage. http://www .gale.cengage.com/pdf/facts/busman.pdf. Also available through Dialog.

RDS Business and Management Practices focuses specifically on the processes, management, and strategies of running a business and includes abstracts and full text of articles. Its search features enable highly specific retrieval of relevant articles. Table of contents records for core source publications contained in the database are also included.

RDS Table Base. Gale Cengage. http://www.gale.cengage.com/pdf/facts/table.pdf.

RDS TableBase, covering more than 90 U.S. and international industries, provides tabular data on companies, industries, products, demographics, and more. In addition to reproducing complete tables, full text of the source article, when it has been published in a professional, trade, or industry publication, is also included. Indexing is extremely fine-grained, enabling users to identify such always-in-demand figures and rankings as "market share" or "market size" quickly and easily.

Regional Business News (EBSCOhost). http://www.ebscohost.com/thisTopic.php?marketID=1&topicID=130.

Regional Business News contains full-text coverage of approximately 80 local business publications from the United States and Canada. Academic library subscribers to **Business Source Premier**, **Business Source Elite**, or **Business Source Complete** receive access to **Regional Business News**.

ScienceDirect. Elsevier. http://www.sciencedirect.com/.

Not for science topics only, this database built around publications of the massive STM (science, technology, and medicine) publisher Elsevier includes full-text articles in economics—econometrics and finance—and business, management, and accounting. It contains scholarly articles, features "search alerts," and allows searching by affiliation of authors (at universities, etc.). It provides PDF formats for article results, allowing users to access tables of contents so they can skip to specific article sections.

OTHER DATABASES FOR BUSINESS RESEARCH

It should be noted that in addition to the business-specific databases listed above, libraries also have the option of purchasing general-purpose article databases to complement those which have already been discussed in this chapter. These databases conceivably fill two main purposes: first, they round out business coverage by including popular and scholarly articles from publications of all kinds, offering a necessarily multidisciplinary view of business topics; and second, for the library unable to afford a dedicated business database, some of the following products include coverage of quite a few business publications among the more general coverage.

EBSCOhost Academic Search Premier. http://www.ebsco.com.

Academic Search is a multidisciplinary journal index, and its coverage includes business and economics. The "Premier" version of *Academic Search* (like its Business Source counterpart, Academic Search is offered in three versions, a Complete, Premier, and Elite; Premier is the middle offering in terms of coverage) covers more than 4,600 journals in full text; of those, more than 3,900 are peer-reviewed titles. It provides access to such popular business titles such as *Fortune* and *Bloomberg Businessweek*, plus journals with specific focus on industries, topics in business and economics, and international management and economics.

Gale Academic OneFile. http://www.gale.cengage.com/AcademicOneFile/.

Gale Academic OneFile covers approximately 14,000 journals, focusing on peer-reviewed, full-text journals, newspapers, and reference sources. It includes full-text coverage of the *Financial Times*, *New York Times*, as well as scholarly business journals, and links with JSTOR as a source of archival coverage of journals.

ProQuest Central. http://www.proquest.com/en-US/catalogs/databases/detail/proquestcentral.shtml.

ProQuest Central is generally similar to EBSCO's Academic Search products, but is also includes newspapers, bringing total access to approximately 13,900 titles, with some 10,900 available in full-text format. It provides full-text access to newspapers including the *Wall Street Journal* and the *Los Angeles Times*. Among its topics are business and economics, and it features access to articles from periodicals and full-text dissertations, plus market reports, with international coverage.

CONCLUSION

Access to the periodical literature is vital. In addition to business magazines and scholarly business journals, the unique and voluminous content available in thousands of individual trade periodicals is necessary to research numerous industries and business topics. Contemporary business periodical databases contain more content than ever before, and are an important basic building block of business information.

3

Core Collection of Business Periodicals

Ruthie Brock and Carol Byrne

INTRODUCTION

Since publication of the fourth edition of *The Basic Business Library* in 2002, the U.S. economy has had to deal with the aftermath of 9/11, wars, a historic recession, a housing bubble, bailouts, a major financial crisis, and a debt rating downgrade. During all of these challenges, technology continued to move forward, bringing new devices for work and play such as smart phones, game-playing consoles, e-readers, tablet devices, and more.

Meanwhile, a communication revolution was taking place. Twitter, Facebook, Skype, and text messaging along with Internet news, blogs, cable television, and talk radio have increasingly changed the way we get our news, analysis, and opinions, shop for goods, and keep up with friends and family. These changes, combined with challenging economic times, have seen some print periodicals cease entirely and others struggle to survive. Should we be worried? Not so fast! Since this transformation is ongoing, it is too soon to know how the publishing world will look in the future, but a bright spot portends for reading in general, and for magazines and newspapers in particular, especially with tablet devices and e-readers. An iPad application that provides access to a magazine with all the color and page-turning ease we love about a print magazine will possibly breathe new life into the genre, reminding some of us why we loved it in the first place and allowing others to discover it for the first time.

The transformations that affect the publishing world inevitably affect libraries. Keeping up with mobile devices and applications for access to library catalogs, research databases, and other resources as well as dealing with rising costs of subscriptions are an ongoing challenge. A growing number of libraries have responded to rising costs by downsizing their print collections. Other libraries are embracing open access and encouraging faculty to consider publishing in open-access journals as an alternative model for scholarly communication.

As our culture, economy, and the world of business change, so must the core list of business periodicals. Titles selected for this chapter will be of interest to managers, business owners, investors, consumers, scholars, educators, and students of business. This periodicals list is intended as a starting point with the understanding that each library has a unique budget situation and patron base. Many titles are included that are affordable for libraries regardless of size; other recommendations are for titles that can be considered as budgets allow. The listing is a mixture of scholarly journals, professional and trade publications, and business-oriented magazines and newspapers. Broad subject areas retained from the previous edition include accounting, economics, finance, insurance, marketing, and management. New subjects added include business communication, case studies research, health care, information systems, supply chain management, sustainability, and taxation. Increased focus on housing and mortgage issues are also new to the fifth edition.

An attempt was made to include publications that are available with full-text articles in at least one major database (as covered primarily in Chapter 2). The ability to identify, locate, and access business articles electronically was a key factor to consider in the selection process. The databases named are simply examples and are not intended to be a comprehensive source for determining where full-text articles from a given journal or magazine can be found. This type of information is not static and therefore is best checked against a library's own databases. Publication and pricing facts were checked in one or more of the standard library reference sources such as *Magazines for Libraries*, and online versions of Cabell's Directories of Publishing Opportunities, Ulrichsweb, WorldCat, and the Directory of Open Access Journals. Websites of the affiliated publisher, society, association, or university and the print copy of the publication were also examined for verification.

There are many subscription pricing variations available from publishers. Most offer either a separate print and electronic model or a combined print and electronic model. Some publishers bundle a group of their publications and offer it as a package. Publishing societies usually offer special prices for their members; universities often offer prices based on enrollment; and subscriptions for public libraries are often based on population. Finally, an individual or institutional rate is a simple, yet common pricing option. The most consistently available option, combined print and electronic, was chosen for this chapter along with one or two additional options when available. Because prices inevitably fluctuate, they are provided for the sole purpose of giving the reader a rough idea of the expense involved. As elsewhere in this book, publication and pricing facts are at the time of the writing; changes are inevitable.

In this chapter, a total of 62 periodicals are included, an increase of 2 titles from the prior edition. New to this edition are four open-access titles, which are free to interested readers worldwide and are also available in full text in major business databases. Twenty-five periodicals from the previous edition, including seven U.S. government titles, were dropped. Some government periodicals have ceased since the fourth edition was published, some no longer issue a print copy, and others are covered in Chapter 4. Twenty-seven periodicals were added to this chapter that were not in the fourth edition.

As librarians are well aware, the publishing world is always in a state of flux, perhaps now more than ever due to the economy and changes in readers' habits. Not surprisingly, some content changes for this chapter were caused by the demise, merger, or absorption of publications. Examples of titles that have ceased include *Across the Board, Far Eastern Economic Review, The Public Interest*, and *Internet World*. *American Demographics*, which was also in previous editions of this book, was absorbed by *Advertising Age*.

Historically, publication prices have risen faster than inflation, which may also explain, in part, the difference in prices from the earlier edition. An attempt was made to compare costs between the previous and current periodical selections, but the effort was complicated by the differences in how the previous author listed print prices whereas the authors of this edition combined electronic and print prices. In addition, the titles selected in the two collections did not lend themselves to price comparisons because of the number of titles dropped and added. Considering only titles that are in both editions, costs for the fourth edition total $4,368.80 and costs for the fifth edition total $8,688.85. From this small sample, it appears that costs have doubled since the last edition, although the lack of a pure comparison renders it somewhat of an apples-and-oranges situation.

In this chapter, the authors chose to substitute lower price alternatives for some of our selections in order to keep the total cost as low as possible and yet maintain the collection's integrity. For example, *Sustainable Development* ($1,350) was chosen instead of the more costly *Business Strategy and the Environment* ($2,700), and *Journal of Business Strategy* ($570) was included instead of *Strategic Management Journal* ($1,600).

Still other price increases may be explained by the trend for associations, societies, and universities to outsource the publishing responsibility to commercial publishers so that the nonprofit organization can concentrate on the content. Publishers such as Wiley and Elsevier have been seeking out and partnering with nonprofits in this way.

In the end, titles selected reflect the preferences of the authors based on awareness of trends and their personal knowledge and experience as business librarians. Since library collections should reflect the needs of their community, this chapter will provide a foundation, rather than a prescription, for making selection decisions.

CORE LIST OF BUSINESS PERIODICALS

Accounting Horizons. American Accounting Association (AAA). 1987–. Quarterly. ISSN: 0888-7993; e-ISSN: 1558-7975. $375, institutions print and e-access. http://aaapubs.org.

Accounting Horizons is a refereed journal that serves as a venue for scholarly accounting research and also provides timely commentaries on issues of importance to practicing accountants, regulators, faculty, and students of accounting. Due to the subject matter and inclusion of both commentaries and research, the target audience of *Accounting Horizons* is broader than the *Accounting Review*, another Association publication. As the premier source for publishing accounting research, *Accounting Review* articles include greater detail in explaining and illustrating research methodologies and design, a feature of interest primarily to the academic community. Larger libraries may want to subscribe to both journals. Subscribers can access full-text *Accounting Horizons* articles back to 1999 on the Association's website. Full-text articles are also available in major databases, such as EBSCO's Business Source Complete and selectively in Dow Jones's Factiva.

Administrative Science Quarterly. Cornell University, Johnson Graduate School of Management. 1956–. Quarterly. ISSN: 0001-8392; e-ISSN: 1930-3815. $237., institutions print and e-access; $227.00, institutions e-access only. http://www.johnson.cornell.edu.

This long-standing and respected academic journal publishes both theoretical and empirical works related to organization studies. Articles encompass a range of disciplines such as economics, public administration, industrial relations, sociology, psychology, strategic management, and organizational behavior. Article approaches vary from micro to macro and from lab experiments in psychology to work on nation-states. Works are published from new authors as well as seasoned scholars. *Administrative Science Quarterly* has been a leader in publishing qualitative research since 1979 when a special issue was devoted to the subject. Full-text articles are available in EBSCO's Business Source Complete database. Full-text back issues are also available in JSTOR. If warranted, another highly respected journal to be considered for academic collections is the *Academy of Management Review*, which publishes related research on organizational theory.

Advertising Age. Crain Communications, Inc. 1930–. Weekly. ISSN: 0001-8899; e-ISSN: 1557-7414. $449, premium package with data center, print, and e-access. Library Site License (IP) also available. http://adage.com.

Advertising Age recently celebrated its 80th birthday. While many publications struggle during economic downturns, this one first emerged during the Great Depression in 1930 when consumer spending had dramatically plunged. Since then, the advertising industry has paralleled the growth in various media from radio to the Internet. Today, this long-standing tabloid provides professionals and students of advertising and media with current trends, advertising-related data, and topical issues facing the advertising world, including the difficulties and challenges of Internet advertising. The periodical *American Demographics* has been absorbed by *Advertising Age*. The adage.com website allows subscribers to access the Data Center, which provides industry awards, rankings and statistics, agency and media profiles, and more. Full-text articles are also available from Factiva, a Dow Jones database, Gale's Business & Company Resource Center, and EBSCO's Academic Search Complete.

American Economic Review. American Economic Association. 1911–.7/yr. ISSN: 0002-8282; e-ISSN: 0065-812X. $910, institutions print and e-access, multiple titles bundled. http://www.aeaweb.org.

One of seven scholarly journals published by the American Economic Association, the *American Economic Review* is considered a core journal for economists. In 2011 it reached a 100 year milestone. This peer-reviewed journal covers a wide range of topics, from comparative economics, health insurance, and international trade to the environmental aspects of pollution. The May issue includes the proceedings and selected papers presented at the annual Association meeting. The journal's website provides search and browse options for current and previous articles that are available full-text to members and subscribers. Full-text articles are also available in EBSCO's Business Source Complete and EconLit with Full Text, and Gale's Business & Company Resource Center. Archival articles are available in JSTOR.

B to B: The Magazine for Marketing Strategists. Crain Communications, Inc. 2000–. Monthly. ISSN: 1530-2369; e-ISSN: 1944-7752. $59, print and e-access. http://www.btobonline.com.

Published under various titles since 1935, this tabloid was given its current name in the year 2000, around the time the dot-com bubble burst. Unlike many of the dot-com companies, *B to B* is still around! "B to B" is jargon for business-to-business, as distinguished from business-to-consumer relationships. The publication celebrated its 10th anniversary under its latest title with a special issue highlighting the top business-to-business trends and changes over the decade. The social media phenomenon is expected to fuel future growth in business-to-business marketing, and this publication is on board to keep its readers informed. The website allows access to the most recent print issue; additional material must be purchased. Full-text articles are available in databases such as ProQuest's ABI/INFORM and Dow Jones's Factiva.

Barron's: The Dow Jones Business and Financial Weekly. Dow Jones, a News Corporation Company. 1994–. Weekly. ISSN: 1077-8039. $199, print and e-access. http://www.barrons.com.

Barron's is part of the Dow Jones group of publications, which was acquired by News Corporation in 2007 following generations of Bancroft family ownership back to 1928. Clarence W. Barron created the publication in 1921. *Barron's* offers a review of the previous week's market activity while also looking ahead, preparing readers for what is likely to happen in the days and weeks to come. A statistical pullout section continues to be available in the print edition, with the market statistics also available at http://barrons .com/data. Analytical writers contribute timely insights to complex financial stories; opinion pieces include sarcasm and humor. Articles are available with full-text coverage in Dow Jones's Factiva database and are also available in ProQuest's ABI/INFORM. The website has free access to some content, and other information is locked for subscribers only.

Best's Review: Monthly Insurance News Magazine. A. M. Best. 2000–. Monthly. ISSN: 1527-5914. $55, print and e-access. http://www.bestreview.com.

Whether the challenge is an oil disaster, terrorism, health care reform, or events on a smaller scale, the insurance industry is impacted along with individuals who are directly affected by the event. This publication, which has existed under various titles since 1900, covers all facets of the global insurance industry. While targeting insurance professionals, it is reader friendly for general audiences interested in insurance as well. The *Best's Review* website serves as an integral part of both the print and digital versions of this magazine, with links to timely articles and resources such as daily insurance news, rating announcements, and audio/video features. Subscribers also have online access to insurance-related directories, lists, archives, and Best's statistical studies in their proprietary database. Full-text articles are available in such major databases as EBSCO's Business Source Complete and ProQuest's ABI/INFORM.

Bloomberg Businessweek. Formerly *BusinessWeek*. Bloomberg Finance L.P. 2010–. Weekly. ISSN: 0007-7135; e-ISSN: 1556-1232. $40, print. http://www .businessweek.com.

In late 2009 *BusinessWeek* was acquired by Bloomberg L. P. With the combined resources of the news organization it purchased plus Bloomberg's own substantial resources, a well-known magazine with a publishing history back to 1929 was given extended life. In its rebirth, the Bloomberg name was added to the title, global business coverage was expanded, and the magazine was redesigned. A simple yet effective system using color and thumb tabs direct the reader from the table of contents to articles within five regular sections. Increased content and improved layout and design keep the reader connected. Interviews with major newsmakers add depth to coverage. Subscribers who access the magazine through their iPad will see the page-turning version of the print magazine. The magazine's website, meanwhile, is updated throughout the day with freely available content. A link is provided to the latest magazine, but not previous issues. The website is loosely affiliated with content in the print magazine. Full-text articles are also available from Gale's Business & Company Resource Center and EBSCO's Business Source Complete.

Business & Society Review. Wiley-Blackwell Publishing, Inc. 1974–. Quarterly. ISSN: 0045-3609; e-ISSN: 1467-8594. $344, institutions print and e-access. http://www.onlinelibrary.wiley.com.

Published by Wiley-Blackwell for the Center for Business Ethics at Bentley University, four to six peer-reviewed research articles are included in *Business & Society Review* each quarter. Articles cover a range of ethical issues from corporate governance, environmental economics, and employee selection to social responsibility. Articles are written by professionals actively working in their respective fields of business, law, and government. The journal publisher's website provides search and browse features for the abstracts of current and archived articles. Full-text articles are available in the Wiley Online Library and EBSCO's Business Source Complete.

Business Economics. Palgrave Macmillan. 1966–. Quarterly. ISSN: 0007-666X; e-ISSN: 1554-432X. $254, institutions print and e-access. http://www .palgrave-journals.com.

This peer-reviewed journal is published by Palgrave Macmillan for the National Association for Business Economists. Each issue routinely includes five or six original research articles along with book reviews. A collection of featured columns related to economics at work, industry and markets information, and statistics is published periodically. Articles are for professional economists and noneconomists alike. Content includes best-practice models, tools, and hands-on techniques as well as analysis and insights aimed at solving business problems and challenges in the workplace. The website provides search and browse features for the abstracts of current and archived articles. Full-text articles are available from EBSCO's Business Source Complete and Gale's Business & Company Resource Center.

Business Horizons. Elsevier, Inc. 1957–. Bimonthly. ISSN: 0007-6813; e-ISSN: 1873-6068. $421, institutions print and e-access. http://www.elsevier.com.

Business Horizons is published by Elsevier on behalf of the Kelley School of Business at Indiana University. This bimonthly scholarly journal publishes original research covering various business disciplines and topics such as executive behavior, corporate costs of social responsibility, and business ethics. Article emphasis is on the identification of business issues and possible solutions. On the journal's web page, readers can browse citation information for the current issue as well as the top 10 most cited and downloaded articles. Full-text articles are available in Elsevier's ScienceDirect database.

California Management Review. University of California–Berkeley, Haas School of Business. 1958–. Quarterly. ISSN: 0008-1256. $190, institutions print and e-access. http://cmr.berkeley.edu.

California Management Review is intended for both the academic and business professional. This quarterly journal publishes timely research articles on such topics as customer relations, product development, strategy and organization, global competitiveness, and technological innovations. Scholars from seven of California's business and management schools make up the editorial board for this prestigious academic journal. The *California Management Review* website provides searching capabilities for current and archive material. EBSCO's Business Source Complete, Gale's Business & Company Resource Center, and ProQuest's ABI/INFORM provide full-text access to this journal.

Consumer Reports. Consumers Union. 1942–. Monthly. ISSN: 0010-7174; e-ISSN: 1058-0832. $48, print and e-access. $26, e-access only. http://www.consumerreports.org.

The United States is blessed with an abundance of consumer choices. With so many difficult and sometimes expensive purchasing decisions to make, consumers are sometimes overwhelmed. As publisher of this magazine, the nonprofit Consumers Union does the kind of extensive research, product ratings, and comparisons an average consumer is not able to do. With new competition from web-based review services, Consumers Union has committed to an even-faster review process in the future, as well as increasing the number of products for review. The organization does not accept free products for testing and excludes advertising, thereby instilling its reputation for independence and objectivity. With a publishing history back to 1936, the name of the magazine changed to its current title in 1942. It has broadened testing over the years to measure health and safety of products and to reflect a growing consumer culture. The print magazine and website rank among the top paid subscription-based sources in both formats. Consumer Reports Mobile is included with a subscription to ConsumerReports.org for subscribers who want to shop and check expert product ratings on the go using their mobile device. Articles from the magazine are available in major databases such as EBSCO's Business Source Complete.

The CPA Journal. New York State Society of Certified Public Accountants. 1976–. Monthly. ISSN: 0732-8435. $42, print. http://www.cpaj.com.

The CPA *Journal* is published by the New York State Society of Certified Public Accountants and is identified by them as a technical-refereed publication. Content is concentrated on current issues facing accounting practitioners and other professionals who are affected by the evolution of standards and practices of accounting. The quality of its coverage and analysis has earned the CPA *Journal* a significant national reputation beyond the level of a state society publication. Each print issue highlights a website of the month pertinent to accounting and finance. In 2009, the online version of this publication began utilizing a digital magazine platform that offers both the advantages of online and visual appeal of a print magazine. Free access to the publication's archives is provided on the website back to 1989. Articles are also available full-text in databases such as Gale's Business & Company Resource Center and EBSCO's Business Source Complete.

The Economist. The Economist Newspaper LTD. 1843–. Weekly. ISSN: 0013-0613; e-ISSN: 1358-274X. $138, print. http://www.economist.com.

The Economist is a weekly news publication that provides reporting, commentary, and analysis on global economics and political affairs. Now in the second half of its second century of existence, *The Economist* has remained true to the principles of its founder, who believed in free trade, internationalism, and minimum interference by government, especially in the affairs of the market. Its plain language writing style has also remained intact. Featured sections include finance and economics, science and technology, and culture. The last two pages of each issue provide selective world economic, financial, and market indicators. A more complete listing of market indicators is available on *The Economist* website. The website offers a vast array of data and information, such as their annual collection of predictions for the year ahead, daily news analysis, country briefings, and special reports. Some content is web-only. A searchable online archive dates back to 1997. Full-text articles are available in ProQuest's ABI/INFORM and Factiva. From politics to culture, whether in print or online, *The Economist* provides a snapshot of world affairs for more than 1 million readers. The United States accounts for at least half of the subscribers.

Euromoney. Euromoney Institutional Investor PLC. 1969–. Monthly. ISSN: 0014-2433. $750, print and e-access. http://www.euromoney.com.

This publication provides a focus on activities of capital markets and banking in the global marketplace. Articles report on monetary and fiscal policies of central banks in both developed and emerging countries, as well as the International Monetary Fund and the World Bank. Articles include in-depth analysis and will often profile a key player who is involved in a controversy. Readers of *Euromoney* are provided a non-U.S.-centric approach to evaluate events with multinational ramifications. Special financial reports and rankings are included periodically. On *Euromoney*'s website, portions of articles are available as teasers with links to subscription information for access to the full articles. Reed-Elsevier's LexisNexis Academic, EBSCO's Business Source Complete, and Dow Jones's Factiva are examples of major databases that provide full-text access to this journal.

Fast Company. Fast Company, Inc. 1995–. Monthly. ISSN: 1085-9241; e-ISSN: 1943-2623. $23.95, print. http://www.fastcompany.com.

Started in the mid-1990s, *Fast Company*'s creators brought a fresh outlook and lively style to business publishing, which had been quite staid up to that point. As its name implies, *Fast Company* offers articles on growing companies, new and innovative products, interesting designs, and next-generation CEOs and entrepreneurs. An underlying theme is concern for the environment, with a frequent focus on environmentally friendly products. The website is organized into these categories: technology, design, leadership, and ethonomics. The magazine defines ethonomics as the coverage of entrepreneurs and companies that are doing good for the world as well as the bottom line. The website features some free content, including the latest print-magazine issue. Articles from the website are also searchable in Factiva, a Dow Jones database. Articles from the *Fast Company* print magazine are available full-text in EBSCO's Business Source Complete.

Financial Analysts Journal. CFA Institute. 1960–. Bimonthly. ISSN: 0015-198X; e-ISSN: 1938-3312. $395, print and e-access. http://www.cfapubs.org.

Articles published in the *Financial Analysts Journal* are of two types: peer-reviewed articles derived from rigorous research, and articles that provide thought-provoking opinions and perspectives. Research topics fall into the following areas: portfolio management, equity investments and alternative investments, financial markets, standards, ethics, and regulation. Articles analyzing various aspects of the financial crisis of 2007–9 are included. Selected full-text articles are available at no cost on the cfapubs.org website. Proquest's ABI/INFORM and EBSCO's Business Source Complete provide full-text coverage.

Financial Times (North American Edition). F.T. Publications, Inc. 1997–. Daily. ISSN: 0884-6782; e-ISSN: 0174-7363. $398, print and e-access. $221, e-access only. http://www.FT.com/home/us.

Printed on its distinctive salmon-pink-colored paper since 1893, the *Financial Times* newspaper is a highly regarded source for international business news and analysis. The UK edition began being printed in New York in 1985, and in 1997 a U.S. edition was launched. Today articles run the gamut of business topics including stories on companies, industries, financial markets, equity markets, and major issues impacting economies of the world. Special reports on important geographic locations or topics are often given comprehensive treatment. The *Financial Times* continues to be primarily focused on business news with content provided by journalists in 50 countries. Understanding the bottom-line need for revenue, the paper charges for online access to most of its content, although registered website users are allowed a selected amount of free content. Access via iPad, BlackBerry, or phone is available to subscribers of the combined or online-only *Financial Times* editions. Dow Jones's Factiva database is an amalgamated source for full-text articles from the print edition as well as the newspaper's web edition, FT.com.

Forbes. Forbes, Inc. 1917–. Biweekly. ISSN: 0015-6914; e-ISSN: 1793-2181. $59.95, print. http://www.forbes.com.

This venerable publication has a history of private ownership by several generations of the Forbes family. The driving principle behind the publication is the unshakable belief in the power of free enterprise. Content often focuses on successful entrepreneurs and innovative companies as well as current trends and topics. Aimed at busy business leaders, articles tend to be concise. A publication known for its lists of the world's rich and famous, as well as rankings of global corporations, *Forbes* seeks to satisfy readers' interests in seeking the best in almost every imaginable category, from best business schools to the fastest-growing Facebook pages. The website provides access to articles at no cost. Recent articles from the website are also available in Factiva, a Dow Jones database. Current and past articles from the *Forbes* print edition are available full-text in EBSCO's Business Source Complete.

Fortune. Time Inc. 1930–. 25/yr. ISSN: 0015-8259. $29.95, print. http://www.timeinc.com.

Fortune is a well-branded business magazine, known for covering news, the economy and global markets, and company, industry, and technology matters. *Fortune* is famous for its annual 500 list of the largest corporations, usually published in the May issue. The *Fortune* website archives the Fortune 500 rankings back to 1955. The free ranking information online is limited to the company name, revenue, and profit information. Complete company and financial information is available for purchase from the *Fortune* website. The World's Most Admired Companies, 100 Best Companies to Work For, and the 100 Fastest-Growing Companies ranking lists are released throughout the year. EBSCO's Business Source Complete, Gale's Business & Company Resource Center, and Dow Jones's Factiva provide access to *Fortune*'s full-text articles. Graduates or business professionals looking to change jobs will find *Fortune*'s company listing a valuable tool to consult when job hunting.

Harvard Business Review (HBR). Harvard Business School Publishing. 1922–. 10/yr. ISSN: 0017-8012. $139, institutions print and e-access. http://hbr.org.

Harvard Business Review is the go-to journal for the latest ideas in leadership, innovation, strategy, and management topics for academic and business professionals. In 2010 *Harvard Business Review* revealed a new layout for both the print version and the website, including two new columnists and several new features to enhance and broaden the scope of the journal. The *Journal*'s website provides several exclusive articles and information in categories for social media, sustainability, blogs, and multimedia. The website integrates social media and includes reader comments. A current case study is posted on the *Journal*'s website allowing readers to comment on the case before it is printed in the journal. *HBR* provides free access to most of the articles on their website. For selective articles indicated by a key icon, access to the first several paragraphs is permitted, but an article purchase or subscription is required to continue. The *HBR* Answer Exchange offers a useful management tool for business professionals. Recent topics concerned delegation of tasks, coaching and mentoring, diversity, and performance review. EBSCO's

Business Source Complete provides full-text access to *Harvard Business Review* articles.

HR Magazine. Society for Human Resource Management. 1990–. Monthly. ISSN: 1047-3149; e-ISSN: 1047-3130. $70, print. http://www.shrm.org.

HR Magazine, an official publication of the Society for Human Resource Management, provides up-to-date information for the HR professional or academics interested in the field. Articles cover a broad range of topics from current news to court rulings, compensation, ethics, and best practices in human resource management. Special reports are available in both the print and online editions. The Society's website provides article access to members. EBSCO's Business Source Complete and Gale's Business & Company Resource Center provide full-text access to *HR Magazine*. Libraries with a larger budget or an international business program should consider adding the *International Journal of Human Resource Management* to their collection for a more global perspective of human resource management.

HRfocus. Institute of Management and Administration. 1991–. Monthly. ISSN: 1059-6038; e-ISSN: 1945-5089. $445, institutions print and e-access. http://www.ioma.com.

This 16-page monthly newsletter is expensive but is recommended for HR professionals or individuals interested in human resource management. The newsletter has been publishing for over 80 years. Recent topics have focused on workplace flexibility, recruitment, the Family and Medical Leave Act, and the legal risks of social media in the workplace. Compensation and benefit news and various work-related legal issues are included in each issue. A subscription permits access to the current and online archives. Subscribers also benefit by receiving an e-mail notification when important new information is added to the website. EBSCO's Business Source Complete and Reed Elsevier's LexisNexis Academic offer full-text access to *HRfocus*.

Inc.: Handbook of the American Entrepreneur. Mansueto Ventures LLC. 1979–. 10/yr. ISSN: 0162-8968; e-ISSN: 0898-1809. $19, print. http://www.inc.com.

Inc. is a popular magazine designed to address the interests of entrepreneurs and small-business owners. Recent articles concern topics such as customer relations, hiring and managing employees, industry trends, and how to advertise on Facebook. A wealth of information is available on *Inc.*'s website, from starting a business to financing and managing a company. The technology and innovation sections cover a broad range of topics from software, computer security, and research and development to intellectual property. *Inc.*'s 500/ 5,000 fastest-growing company lists are available on the magazine's website. The search function provides access to current and archived articles. *Inc.* is available full-text in EBSCO's Business Source Complete, Dow Jones's Factiva, and Gale's Business & Company Resource Center. *Inc.* is a valuable resource for libraries serving both large- and small-business owners and entrepreneurs.

Industrial and Labor Relations Review. Cornell University, School of Industrial and Labor Relations. 1947–. Quarterly. ISSN: 0019-7939. $88, institutions print and e-access. http://www.ilr.cornell.edu.

Industrial and Labor Relations Review is a quarterly journal published by Cornell's School of Industrial and Labor Relations. This interdisciplinary peer-reviewed journal is intended for both the business professional and academics. Recent article topics have included labor relations, education and employment, industry studies, Social Security, wages, and union impact on employment. The in-depth book review section discusses the latest subject-based publications in the field. Full-text articles and book reviews dating from April 2003 are available on the website for subscribers; visitors are allowed access to full-text articles or book reviews that are at least 18 months old. Full-text articles and book reviews are also available from EBSCO's Business Source Complete and Gale's Business & Company Resource Center databases.

IndustryWeek/IW. Penton Media, Inc. 1970–. Monthly. ISSN: 0039-0895; e-ISSN: 1930-8957. $71, print. http://www.industryweek.com.

IndustryWeek/IW is now a monthly, rather than weekly, trade publication targeted at senior-level managers in manufacturing. Articles cover a variety of issues from motivating employees to improving productivity and profits. Regular features are on topics such as facilities and operations, supply chain and logistics, competitive edge, and technology. Each month *IndustryWeek/ IW* spotlights a company from the *IndustryWeek/IW* 50 Best Manufacturing Companies list. Webinars, online conferences, and training session information are also provided in the magazine. *IndustryWeek/IW*'s expansive website offers a wide array of information and data such as the latest industry news, articles, white papers, videos, blogs, forums, and upcoming webinars. The search and browse functions permit searching current and archived issues by topic or date. A majority of the information on the *IndustryWeek/IW* website is free, however, the white papers section requires registration. *IndustryWeek/IW* is available full-text in EBSCO's Academic Search Complete, Gale's Business & Company Resource Center, and Dow Jones's Factiva.

Libraries serving academics and business professionals interested in manufacturing industries will want to include this title in their collection.

Investor's Business Daily (IBD). Investor's Business Daily. 1991–. Daily. ISSN: 1061-2890; e-ISSN: 1553-6580. $389, print and e-access. http://www .investors.com.

Founded by entrepreneur and investment guru William O'Neil in 1984, the *Investor's Business Daily* provides beginners and seasoned investors alike with news and information about stocks, bonds, and markets worldwide. It is the philosophy of *Investor's Business Daily* to arm investors with the tools to be successful. From their database of stocks, lists are generated to reflect investment possibilities that have been screened using the key *IBD* ratings and measures. Investors benefit from the resulting information provided and time saved finding investment ideas. Educational tips, articles, and charts provide investors with practical techniques and explanations in an easy-to-understand format. Features on innovative firms and companies on the move help the reader discover the next big investment idea. Regular biographical articles on leaders from all walks of life are included as well as regular features on *IBD*'s 10 traits of successful people. Print subscribers have access to the investors.com website content. Selected content on the website is available at no cost for nonsubscribers. A digital subscription known as *eIBD* is available that provides a facsimile of the print newspaper. Reed Elsevier's LexisNexis Academic and Gale's Business & Company Resource Center databases provide full-text articles.

Journal of Academic and Business Ethics. Academic and Business Research Institute (AABRI). 2009–. Routinely updated. ISSN: 1941-336X. Open access. http://www.aabri.com.

The *Journal of Academic and Business Ethics* is published by the Academic and Business Research Institute. This peer-reviewed, open-access journal publishes original articles on ethics-related topics of interest to both academic and business professionals. Issues of academic integrity, cheating, and plagiarism may be of greater interest to the education audience while articles on corporate social responsibility, corporate crimes, medical record ethics, and employee attitudes will be of interest to those studying and dealing with ethics-related problems in the business environment and the general culture. The articles from this journal are available at the Institute's website listed above at no cost and are also available from EBSCO's Business Source Complete and the Directory of Open Access Journals at http://www.doaj.org. As an open-access publication, it is free to interested readers worldwide. AABRI journal volumes are printed when an online volume has 12 manuscripts accepted. Libraries with a larger budget or with a need for more journals in the business ethics field should consider adding the *Journal of Business Ethics* to their collection. It is more expensive, but is an outstanding journal in the field.

Journal of Accountancy. American Institute of Certified Public Account-ants. 1905–. Monthly. ISSN: 0021-8448; e-ISSN: 1945-0729. $75, print. http://www.journalofaccountancy.com.

When the first issue of the *Journal of Accountancy* was published more than a century ago, the accounting profession itself was in its infancy and accounting education was practically nonexistent at the university level. It could be said that the *Journal* and the accounting profession have had a symbiotic relation-ship since 1905. The publication continues to be a mainstay for practicing accountants today with a broad array of accounting, auditing, and financial issues presented and analyzed. Each issue includes a section for keeping up with drafts of new accounting rules, and provides full text of new official releases of standard setting bodies. The *Journal's* user-friendly website provides free access to articles back to 1997, with various browsing and searching options. Full-text articles are also available in databases such as Reed Elsevier's LexisNexis Aca-demic and EBSCO's Business Source Complete.

Journal of Accounting Research. Wiley-Blackwell Publishing, Inc. 1963–. 5/yr. ISSN: 0021-8456; e-ISSN: 1475-679X. $984, institutions print and e-access; $855, institutions print or e-access only. http://onlinelibrary.wiley .com.

Published by Wiley-Blackwell in partnership with the Accounting Research Center at the University of Chicago Booth School of Business, the *Journal of Accounting Research* includes four regular issues and one conference issue. Original research is published across a broad area of accounting using analytical, empirical, experimental, and field study meth-ods. All articles are available in the Wiley Online Library. EBSCO's data-base, EconLit with Full Text, has a 12-month embargo, delaying access to the latest year's articles.

Journal of Business Communication. The Association of Business Com-munication. 1973–. Quarterly. ISSN: 0021-9436; e-ISSN: 1552-4582. $453, institutions print and e-access; $408, institutions e-access only. http://www .sagepub.com/home.nav.

Published for the Association of Business Communication by Sage Publi-cations, this journal aims to contribute to the knowledge and theory of busi-ness communication as a distinct, multifaceted field. Included are articles about English as the business lingua franca between native and non-native speakers in multinational corporations, CEOs' letters in annual reports, employer e-mail monitoring, and workplace discourse. Articles are peer reviewed, and may focus on written, verbal, nonverbal, or electronic communication in profit-oriented businesses or not-for-profit organizations. Full-text articles are available in EBSCO's Business Source Complete and Communication & Mass Media Complete. The Association publishes another journal, *Business Communication Quarterly* (BCQ), which focuses on the teaching of business communication. BCQ is included free with a subscription to their primary publication, the *Journal of Business Communication*. Both are refereed journals.

Journal of Business Strategy. Emerald Group Publishing Ltd. 1980–. Bimonthly. ISSN: 0275-6668. $569, institutions print and e-access. http://www.emeraldinsight.com.

The *Journal of Business Strategy* is one of the few journals dedicated to business strategy and is somewhat unique in that its editors seek articles geared toward middle and senior-level managers of companies rather than CEOs. Articles cover the strategic aspect of diverse topics applicable to organizations and industries of all types. Whether mergers and acquisitions, marketing, technological developments, or other issues faced in the real world, the *Journal* addresses situations that affect profitability and performance. Each issue includes a mix of authors who are academics, business executives, and policy makers. Case studies and best practices are also included. The publisher's website provides nonsubscribers with a search option and article abstracts. Full-text articles are available in the Emerald Management Xtra database and in ProQuest's ABI/INFORM Global (with a one-year embargo). EBSCO's Business Source Complete provides indexing and abstracts of the *Journal*'s articles. Libraries with a larger budget or with a need for more journals in the strategy area should consider adding *Strategic Management Journal* to their collection. It is more expensive, but is also a high-quality journal.

Journal of Case Research in Business and Economics. Academic and Business Research Institute (AABRI). 2008–. Routinely updated. ISSN: 1941-3378. Open access. http://www.aabri.com.

This peer-reviewed, open-access journal is published by the Academic and Business Research Institute. The *Journal of Case Research in Business and Economics* publishes original case studies written by academic professionals. Case study topics include managerial economics, legal and ethical issues related to the Americans with Disabilities Act, strategic planning, corporate reorganization, bank acquisition, and financial performance. AABRI journal volumes are printed when an online volume has 12 manuscripts accepted. Full-text articles are available from the Institute's website, from the Directory of Open Access Journals at http://www.doaj.org, and in EBSCO's Business Source Complete database.

Journal of Economic Literature (JEL). American Economic Association. 1969–. Quarterly. ISSN: 0022-0515. $910, institutions print and e-access, multiple titles bundled. http://www.aeaweb.org.

One of seven journals published by the American Economic Association, the *Journal of Economic Literature* contains four or five research articles written by distinguished economists in each issue. Books that represent original research are reviewed and new journals are listed and described. The entire *JEL* Classification System is provided in each issue, reflecting a broad outline and breakdown of all fields of economics. New books with brief annotations are listed within subject categories according to the *JEL* Classification System. Each December the journal includes a list of doctoral dissertations in economics conferred during the previous academic year for U.S. and Canadian universities. The Association's website for the *Journal* provides information about forthcoming articles, webcasts, and conference information. The search function on the website provides subject access to current and archived articles; however, to retrieve the full-text articles a membership is required. Full-text articles are also available in EBSCO's EconLit with Full Text and Gale's Business & Company Resource Center databases.

Journal of Finance. Wiley-Blackwell Publishing, Inc. 1946–. Bimonthly. ISSN: 0022-1082; e-ISSN: 1540-6261. $502, institutions print and e-access. $456, institutions e-access only. http://www.afajof.org.

As the official publication of the American Finance Association, the *Journal of Finance* includes original research articles in all major areas of finance and is especially dedicated to the study and promotion of financial economics. The *Journal of Finance* is cited widely in the fields of both finance and economics. Published topics include research related to stock and bond markets, corporate finance and governance, banking, venture capital, bankruptcies, foreign exchange markets, and other international finance and analysis, including various theoretical and financial models. The Association's website provides article access to members. All articles are available full-text in the Wiley Online Library. EBSCO's EconLit with Full Text has a 12-month embargo, delaying access to the latest year's articles.

Journal of Government Financial Management. Association of Government Accountants. 1976–. Quarterly. ISSN: 1533-1385. $95, print. http://agacgfm .org.

Content in this peer-reviewed journal addresses topics that are relevant at the federal, state, and local levels of government. Articles are often submitted by accountants, auditors, budget analysts, or attorneys who are members of the Association of Government Accountants and provide insights and expertise for specific challenges that other government practitioners may face, without being excessively technical. With passage of major legislation affecting large segments of the economy, such as stimulus spending, bailouts of banks and automobile industries, as well as health care and financial reform, demand for transparency and accountability in government accounting is high. Financial managers, taxpayers, and students of governmental accounting will find timely articles of interest. Full-text articles are available to members on the Association's website and also in EBSCO's Business Source Complete database.

Journal of Housing Research. American Real Estate Society. 1990–. Semiannually. ISSN: 1052-7001. $240, institutions print and e-access. http://www.aresnet.org.

Timely topics covered in the *Journal of Housing Research* include economics of the housing markets, residential brokerage, home mortgage finance and mortgage markets, and international housing issues. Full-text articles are available online for members only. The journal is also available full-text in EBSCO's Academic Search Complete. Issues published prior to 2006 were published by the Fannie Mae Foundation.

Journal of Interactive Advertising. American Academy of Advertising. 2000–. Semiannually. ISSN: 1525-2019. Open access. http://jiad.org.

This open-access, online refereed journal was founded in 2000 and was an official publication of the Departments of Advertising at Michigan State University and The University of Texas at Austin until 2008, when the American Academy of Advertising became the publisher. Articles focus on interactive advertising, marketing, and communication in a networked world. Examples of topics include in-game advertising, effectiveness of advertising promotions within social networking sites, advertising in Second Life, and Internet marketing communication in China. The concept of interactivity is having a major impact in the fields of advertising and marketing, and this journal provides the opportunity to address the challenges. Full-text articles are available and searchable on the *Journal*'s website listed above and in EBSCO's Business Source Complete. Libraries with larger budgets may also want to consider the *Journal of Interactive Marketing*, published by Elsevier, Inc., since 2009, on behalf of the Direct Marketing Education Foundation.

Journal of International Accounting Research. American Accounting Association. 2002–. Semiannually. ISSN: 1542-6297; e-ISSN: 1558-8025. $175, print and e-access; $160, e-access only. http://www.aaapubs.org.

Articles published in the *Journal of International Accounting Research* may focus on a single country and the international implications of its accounting practices, or may feature differences of practices among several countries. Published by the American Accounting Association, this journal is peer reviewed and covers a broad array of topics including auditing, financial or managerial accounting, tax, and systems. Full-text articles are available in EBSCO's Business Source Complete, ProQuest's Accounting and Tax database, and for members and subscribers via the Digital Library on the Association's website.

Journal of International Business Studies (JIBS). Palgrave Macmillan Ltd. 1970–. 9/yr. ISSN: 0047-2506; e-ISSN: 1478-6990. Subscription based on enrollment. http://www.palgrave-journals.com.

Published by Palgrave Macmillan for The Academy of International Business, the *Journal of International Business Studies* is a scholarly journal with papers on such topics as foreign investments, technology licensing, global accounting, management strategies, and cultural diversity in an international environment. The publisher's website for *JIBS* provides search and browse functions for reviewing the abstracts of current and archived issues. Editorials and the top 25 most cited articles are available to all for download. Full-text articles are available from the publisher and EBSCO's Business Source Complete and JSTOR. Academics and business and government professionals engaged or interested in the international business arena should include *Journal of International Business Studies* on their reading list.

Journal of Marketing. American Marketing Association. 1936–. Bimonthly. ISSN: 0022-2429; e-ISSN: 1547-7185. $450, institutions print and e-access; $375, institutions e-access only. http://www.marketingpower.com/jm.

A publication of the American Marketing Association, the *Journal of Marketing* is the leading scholarly journal in marketing. Articles undergo a blind review process. The *Journal*'s prestige allows a highly selective acceptance rate, providing articles of top research quality. Articles are intended to address the interests of scholars as well as advance the practice of marketing. *Journal of Marketing* has expanded from quarterly to bimonthly issues, and the full-text articles are available within EBSCO's databases Business Source Complete and Communication & Mass Media Complete. Members may access the Association's website for online access to the *Journal of Marketing*. Large academic libraries may also want to include the related *Journal of*

Marketing Research in their collections. It is also highly regarded and frequently publishes original research that is theoretical and quantitatively based.

Journal of Personal Selling & Sales Management (JPSSM). M.E. Sharpe. 1980–. Quarterly. ISSN: 0885-3134; e-ISSN: 1557-7813. $395, institutions print and e-access. $345, institutions e-access only. http://www.jpssm.org.

Published for Pi Sigma Epsilon National Educational Foundation by M.E. Sharpe, this unique peer-reviewed journal is dedicated exclusively to publishing articles related to selling and sales management. Within that focus, article topics cover a wide range, from the virtual marketplace and avatar salespersons in Second Life to work-family conflict and job satisfaction. Targeting sales executives, professors, researchers, trainers, and students, articles include both theory and practice. A biannual special feature is an abstracts section that tracks and reviews personal selling and sales management literature from more than 60 academic and trade publications. The *JPSSM's* website provides table of contents and abstracts of articles. Full-text articles are available in EBSCO's Business Source Complete.

Journal of Retailing. Elsevier, Inc. 1925–. Quarterly. ISSN: 0022-4359; e-ISSN: 1873-3271. $476, institutions e-access only; $520, institutions print only. http://www.elsevier.com.

Published by Elsevier for the Leonard N. Stern School of Business at New York University, the *Journal of Retailing* concentrates on research related to the economics and behavior of the consumer, supply chains and distribution channels that serve retailers, and services marketing. Lengthy nontechnical summaries of the articles in each issue are provided for general readers. Founded in 1925, the *Journal of Retailing* is the oldest marketing journal, preceding *Journal of Marketing*, which began in 1936. Using the ISI Web of Science Impact Factor, *Journal of Retailing* ranks as one of the top research-oriented journals in the field of marketing. Full-text articles are available from major databases such as Elsevier's ScienceDirect and ProQuest's ABI/INFORM Global.

Journal of Supply Chain Management. Wiley-Blackwell Publishing, Inc. 1999–. Quarterly. ISSN: 1523-2409; e-ISSN: 1745-493X. $321, institutions print and e-access. http://onlinelibrary.wiley.com.

This quarterly peer-reviewed journal is published by Wiley-Blackwell on behalf of the Institute for Supply Management. *Journal of Supply Chain Management* includes empirical and theoretical papers written by leading scholars in supply chain management and other related disciplines. Recent article topics include: outsourcing to low-cost countries, corporate social responsibility, and supply chain taxonomy. The *Journal* publisher's website offers a search feature, content alerts, RSS feed options, and access to the abstracts for both the current and archived issues. The Wiley Online Library and Gale's Business & Company Resource Center provide full-text access to the articles and papers. International business programs or companies engaged in international business should consider including *Journal of Supply Chain Management* in their reading collection.

Journal of Sustainability and Green Business. Academic and Business Research Institute (AABRI). 2010–. Routinely updated. ISSN: 2156-5325; e-ISSN: 2156-5317. Open access. http://www.aabri.com.

The Academic and Business Research Institute recently added the *Journal of Sustainability and Green Business* to its collection of free, open-access journals. The *Journal* strives to publish both qualitative and quantitative original research papers that discuss the issues of green accounting, sustainably initiatives, social media, organizational culture, and international business enterprises. The full-text papers are published on the Institute's website, and a print version of the journal is available once 12 manuscripts have been accepted online. Public and academic communities that consider sustainability and green business to be of the utmost importance will appreciate the business focus of this new open-access journal. As it matures, it intends to publish articles that discuss the issues involved in incorporating sustainability and/or environmental considerations into organizational strategies. Its full-text articles are also in EBSCO's databases and the Directory of Open Access Journals at http://www.doaj.org.

Journal of World Business. Elsevier, Inc. 1997–. Quarterly. ISSN:1090-9516; e-ISSN:1878-5573. $492, institutions print and e-access. http://www.elsevier.com.

International in scope, this peer-reviewed journal publishes relevant articles of interest to academicians and professional managers. The *Journal* focuses on leadership, strategic management, marketing, and human resource management in the global environment. Examples of topics covered include international entrepreneurship, national corruption, cross-cultural training, innovative environmental management, and international mergers and acquisitions. Readers can browse citation information for the current issue as well as the top 10 most cited and downloaded articles. Full-text articles of this journal are available in Elsevier's ScienceDirect database and EBSCO's Business Source Complete.

Kiplinger's Personal Finance. Kiplinger Washington Editors, Inc. 2000–. Monthly. ISSN: 1528-9729. $23.95, print. http://www.kiplinger.com.

Kiplinger's Personal Finance provides readers with basic financial information for day-to-day living such as buying insurance, investing, record keeping, saving money on taxes, and retirement planning. Its publishing history dates back to 1947. Articles are written for consumers, with technical jargon avoided. As a long-standing publication with some variant titles along the way, *Kiplinger's Personal Finance* has provided sound practical advice for achieving financial security and has done so in a reader-friendly style. Many articles are available at the Kiplinger website at no cost. Subscribers log on for additional material. Articles from this magazine are available in EBSCO's Academic Search Complete and Business Source Complete.

Management Science. Institute for Operations Research and the Management Sciences (INFORMS). 1954–. Monthly. ISSN: 0025-1909; e-ISSN: 1526-5501. $855, institutions print and e-access. http://www.informs.org.

A refereed journal published by the Institute for Operations Research and Management Sciences, *Management Science* is aimed at academics from a cross section of disciplines including economics, mathematics, psychology, and statistics. The *Journal's* papers emphasize the theory and applications of management science and operations research. Each issue publishes 10 to 15 mathematical research papers. The Management Insights section briefly explains each paper's importance to the practice of management. This information is available in print and online. The journal is accessible from the INFORMS website. Search and browse features are available for the abstracts of both the current and archived papers. Electronic companions, known as e-companions, are the appendices for the *Journal's* papers and are available only online. A subscription to the *Journal* provides online access to current and archived papers. A two-year embargo delays access to the full-text papers in EBSCO's Business Source Complete database.

MIS Quarterly. Management Information Systems Research Center (MISRC) of the University of Minnesota. 1977–. Quarterly. ISSN: 0276-7783. $1,225, institutions print and e-access. http://www.misq.org.

MIS Quarterly is a well-known, peer-reviewed journal in the information systems discipline. The journal strives to publish quality research articles regarding the development, management, and economics of information technology services and resources. Articles are arranged in four sections: issues and opinions, research, theory and review, and research notes. Previous topics have covered mobile computing, digital technology, strategic information systems, electronic commerce, and search engine marketing. Current and archived abstracts can be viewed on the *Journal*'s website. MIS *Quarterly* is available full-text in EBSCO's Business Source Complete, Gale's Business & Company Resource Center, and ProQuest's ABI/INFORM.

MIT Sloan Management Review. Massachusetts Institute of Technology. 2001–. Quarterly. ISSN: 1532-9194; e-ISSN: 1532-8937. $187, institutions print and e-access. http://sloanreview.mit.edu.

This well-known scholarly journal bridges the gap between management research and practice by alerting its readers to new research and providing analysis and interpretation to benefit practicing managers. Under different titles, it has existed for over 50 years. Articles focus on strategy, leadership, global business, ethics, technology, and innovation. This quarterly journal contains two distinct sections: the Features section provides 8 to 10 in-depth research articles, and the Intelligence section contains shorter, timely articles focusing on the latest management ideas and trends. The *Journal*'s website provides access to the latest print articles, new research issues, and links to the *Journal*'s online-only articles. Other features on the website include an improvisations blog, special reports, and a category for sustainability and innovation. Current and archived articles can be searched on the website, and subscribers have online access to three years of full-text articles. Articles are available full-text in EBSCO's Business Source Complete, Gale's Business & Company Resource Center, and ProQuest's ABI/INFORM Global.

Modern Healthcare. Crain Communications, Inc. 1976–. Weekly. ISSN: 0160-7480; e-ISSN: 1944-7647. $280, institutions print and e-access. http://www.modernhealthcare.com.

This weekly publication is geared toward managers and executives of health care facilities, providing them with late-breaking health care news and events occurring around the United States. *Modern Healthcare*'s website features current health care news, survey data, special reports, videos, podcasts, webinars, and job listings. Special reports, such as the top 100 hospitals of the year, are also available. This trade publication is recommended for academics, practitioners, and individuals working in the health care industry. *Modern Healthcare* is available full-text in Dow Jones's Factiva as well as CINAHL and Academic Search Complete, two of EBSCO's databases.

Mortgage Banking: The Magazine of Real Estate Finance. Mortgage Bankers Association. 1981–. Monthly. ISSN: 0730-0212; e-ISSN: 1930-5087. $75, print; $65, members. http://www.mortgagebankingmagazine.com.

Published under various titles since 1939, *Mortgage Banking* covers the real estate finance industry. Interviews with industry executives and key Washington politicians provide readers with insights and an inside-the-beltway look at Congress and regulatory agencies, including how their legislation and regulations impact mortgage lenders and consumers. While intended for industry professionals, articles will be of interest to individuals seeking to understand the complexities of home financing and its role in the U.S. economy. For industry professionals this magazine will also keep them apprised of relevant technology, software, demographic data, and industry-related statistics. *Mortgage Banking* is available full-text in major databases such as EBSCO's Business Source Complete and Dow Jones's Factiva. The table of contents of the current issue is featured on the magazine's website along with indexes of past issues. Articles are for sale for nonsubscribers.

National Real Estate Investor. Penton Media, Inc. 1958–. Monthly. ISSN: 0027-9994. $129, print or e-access only. http://nreionline.com.

Focusing on commercial real estate, this trade magazine's coverage includes news and in-depth articles related to the multifamily, office, industrial, retail, and hotel markets. A feature called City Review spotlights commercial real estate issues of one U.S. metro area per month, including data on vacancies, occupancies, and square footage. Datapoints, a Monthly Meter of Various Industry Trends, uses charts to display the data graphically. Full-text articles are available from major databases such as EBSCO's Business Source Complete and Dow Jones's Factiva.

Operations Research. Institute for Operations Research and the Management Sciences (INFORMS). 1956–. Bimonthly. ISSN: 0030-364X; e-ISSN: 1526-5463. $525, institutions print and e-access. http://www.informs.org.

Operations Research, the flagship journal for the Institute for Operations Research and the Management Sciences, is a bimonthly scholarly journal that serves academics and practitioners in the operations research profession. Articles typically include decision analysis, supply chain operations and telecommunications, manufacturing, and networking topics. Each issue contains 15 to 20 research articles. The *Journal* begins with an overview of each paper and its importance to operations research. This section is freely available on the *Operations Research* website. Electronic companions, known as e-companions, are the appendices for the *Journal*'s papers and are available only online. The INFORMS website is the home for *Operations Research*, featuring abstracts of both the current and previous articles. A subscription provides access to current and archived papers. A two-year embargo delays access to the full- text papers in EBSCO's Business Source Complete database.

Real Estate Issues. Counselors of Real Estate. 1976–. 3/yr. ISSN: 0146-0595. $48, print. http://www.cre.org/publications/rei.cfm.

Real Estate Issues has been published since 1976 by the members of The Counselors of Real Estate, a not-for-profit organization of the National Association of Realtors. Articles are timely and provide insights into real estate issues that have evolved in recent years, such as the real estate bubble, housing glut, Islamic financing, and foreclosures, as well as analysis of legislation affecting real estate transactions. The website provides articles at no cost back to 1976. Full-text articles can also be accessed from major databases such as ProQuest's ABI/INFORM and EBSCO's Business Source Complete.

Sustainable Development. John Wiley & Sons, Inc. 1993–. Bimonthly. ISSN: 0968-0802; e-ISSN: 1099-1719. $1,500, institutions print and e-access. http://onlinelibrary.wiley.com.

Sustainable Development is an international peer-reviewed journal published by Wiley. The journal seeks articles that contribute to the discussion and debate on how sustainable development can be achieved. Recent articles include topics such as corporate sustainability strategy, environmental policy, sustainable development, and environmental responsibility. The *Journal* publisher's website offers a search feature, content alerts, RSS feed options, and access to the abstracts for both the current and archived issues. The journal also includes book reviews. Sustainability is growing in importance and as such this journal should be of interest to academics, practitioners, and business professionals. Full-text articles are available from Wiley Online Library. EBSCO's database, Business Source Complete, has a 12-month embargo, delaying access to the latest year's articles. Libraries with a larger budget or with a need for more journals in the sustainability area should consider also adding the more expensive *Business Strategy and the Environment* to their collection.

T+D (Training + Development Magazine). American Society for Training & Development. 2001–. Monthly. ISSN: 1535-7740; e-ISSN: 1943-782X. $300, print. http://www.astd.org.

A monthly magazine published by the American Society for Training and Development, *T+D* magazine is a leader in the field of training and development and workplace learning. Articles provide a wealth of information: from training trends, skill shortages, recruitment, e-learning, and job performance to leadership competency. *T+D*'s website is just a "click away" from international and virtual conferences to webcasts. Podcasts are available for featured articles back to 2007. The Archives section permits search and browse functions for current and archived articles to 2007. EBSCO's Business Source Complete and ProQuest's ABI/INFORM provide access to the full-text articles. Membership is required to access the *T+W* webinars. Libraries serving academic and business professionals engaged or interested in workplace learning, training, and development should include *T+D* on their list of core journals.

Tax Adviser. American Institute of Certified Public Accountants (AICPA). 1970–. Monthly. ISSN: 0039-9957. $106.25, print; $85, members. http://www.aicpa.org.

The *Tax Adviser* is a monthly AICPA publication aimed at tax practitioners. Articles provide tax planning techniques and strategies as well as interpretation of recent tax law changes and trends. Readers are kept abreast of IRS rulings, decisions, and legislation. The magazine also provides educational opportunities for the reader using case studies. The latest issue and articles published since 2007 are available at no cost online. *Tax Adviser* is also available full-text from major databases such as Gale's Business & Company Resource Center and EBSCO's Business Source Complete.

Thunderbird International Business Review. John Wiley & Sons, Inc. 1998–. Bimonthly. ISSN: 1096-4762; e-ISSN: 1520-6874. $840, institutions print and e-access. http://www.onlinelibrary.wiley.com.

Thunderbird International Business Review is a bimonthly journal published by Wiley and edited by the Thunderbird School of Global Business Management. This scholarly journal is aimed at business professionals and academicians interested or engaged in international business. Articles cover a wide spectrum, from globalization strategies, mergers and acquisitions, and cross-cultural management to sustainability and ethics. Cultural, economic, legal, and political issues affecting the global business environment are also addressed. The Wiley Online Library provides journal search and browse features, a content alert option, and citation export capabilities as well as the full-text articles. EBSCO's Business Source Complete provides full-text but delays full-text access to current issues with a one-year embargo.

Wall Street Journal (WSJ). News Corporation. 2007–. Daily (except Sunday). ISSN: 0099-9660; e-ISSN: 0163-089X. $441, print and e-access; $155, e-access only. http://www.WSJ.com.

The world's leading business publication with a publishing history back to 1889 was purchased by Rupert Murdoch's News Corporation in 2007. Since then, the *Wall Street Journal* has become one of the largest U.S. newspapers by paid circulation with more than 2 million print and online subscribers. The online paid-subscription model has proven successful, unique in the newspaper industry. The new ownership has increased coverage of U.S. and world political and general news while retaining its strong coverage of business. The *Journal*'s website, WSJ.com, is replete with business and financial news and analysis. The publisher has embraced new technology and methods for delivering content for mobile devices. The *Journal* has been the recipient of 33 Pulitzer Prizes for outstanding journalism, and in 2010 was ranked #1 for the 11th consecutive year in *B to B*'s annual Media Power 50. In addition to WSJ.com, access to the *Wall Street Journal* full-text is available in Dow Jones's *Factiva* database from 1979 to current. ProQuest offers the *Wall Street Journal* as a stand-alone article database and also as a full-image archive that includes the entire historical run of the newspaper from 1889 to 1993, with an additional year of content added annually.

Workforce Management. Crain Communications, Inc. 2003–. Monthly. ISSN: 1547-5565. $79, print. http://www.workforce.com.

This monthly magazine provides the latest trends, resources, tools, and problem-solving strategies to assist HR personnel in all aspects of human resource management. The *Magazine*'s website provides Research, Commerce, and Community centers that provide access to archived articles, vendor directories, and a venue for human resource professionals to communicate with other. Each center is organized by a topic area such as benefits and compensation or training and organizational development. Blogs, webinar information, and white papers are also available. An online subscription is required to access each center's information. Full-text articles are available from EBSCO's Academic Search Complete and Dow Jones's Factiva.

4

. . . .

Government Information Sources

Eric Forte

INTRODUCTION

Governments, none more so than the U.S. federal government, compile and publish a wealth of information and data related to the nation's economy, business and industry, workers, and consumers. More specifically, government research measures the state of business and economic activity; government surveys collect rich demographic and socioeconomic data that are the cornerstone of market intelligence about the nation's citizens; other government surveys classify and quantify U.S. business activity by sector, industry, and location; government regulatory and administrative initiatives provide information about public companies, foreign trade, and intellectual property; governments support the infrastructure and success of American business, whether large or small, domestic or foreign, through various advocacy efforts; and government agencies strive to regulate a fair labor market, and to support and protect workers and consumers alike.

All of this government-produced information, with very few exceptions, is published (nearly all on the web) and is free—paid for by taxpayers, and intended for citizens. Nearly every source described in this chapter is freely available online. A much diminished number of printed federal government documents, meanwhile, continues to be distributed free of charge to a nationwide network of some 1,300 federal depository libraries, an acquisitions and distribution system that has been in place for well over 100 years. Most citizens live fairly close to a depository library (typically, a public or academic library that has received Congressional designation to be "a depository library"), and thus may see and borrow government publications just as they would borrow a new bestseller. Especially popular government documents are available for sale from the government, just like any other book—except that usually a free web version of the item is also available.

Note that government information does not reproduce any data about individuals or, for the most part, about specific businesses. The Privacy Act of 1974 (P.L. 93-579, current version at 5 USC 552a) prohibits sharing of identifiable information in government records, including those used for statistical reporting, although there are a few government programs and services (such as patents and trademarks, and the EDGAR database of company financial information, both discussed below) that do explicitly name names, and thereby provide key primary intelligence about individual companies.

STATISTICS AND DATA

In a business environment that is increasingly data-driven, the need for statistics about markets, industries, and consumers is truly insatiable. The U.S. federal government, through various legislatively-mandated programs, produces a huge array of statistical data about the nation. From the decennial census and its detailed socioeconomic and demographic data for the nation and its places, to economic censuses providing data on the number, size, and type of the country's businesses, to all kinds of macroeconomic data, to reports and data sets on such specific topics as telecommunications, health, education, transportation, and the labor market—there are thousands of government statistical reports and databases.

Many sources discussed in this chapter feature statistics. Although a complete understanding of government sources for statistics requires superior knowledge of government publishing and civics, a key source, the *Statistical Abstract of the United States*, compiles and indexes government-produced statistics across the spectrum of topics.

Top Source

Statistical Abstract of the United States. U.S. Census Bureau. Annual, 1878–. http://www.census.gov/compendia/Statistical Abstract/. Free online; $39 in print.

One particular federal government publication is by far the single most wide-ranging and useful government resource: the annual *Statistical Abstract of the United States*. Every user of statistics needs to be aware of the *Statistical Abstract*. The *Statistical Abstract*, published annually since 1878, is a compilation of statistical data about the United States, covering nearly every conceivable topic. Specifically, the Census Bureau collects popular statistics, whether published by government agencies, research and nonprofit organizations, or private market research companies, and reprints excerpts ("abstracts") thereof in the *Statistical Abstract*. Each one of these statistical tables cites the original source as well, leading the user to much more detailed and robust data on the topic. And this point is key: the *Statistical Abstract* serves not only as a source, but also as an incredibly useful *index* to statistical data published elsewhere, in governmental and nongovernmental sources alike. It is the place to begin almost any search for statistics, and more often than not, it leads to the most important statistical sources on any given topic, either in the volume itself, or in the sources it cites.

The *Statistical Abstract* covers virtually all topics, and data useful for business and economics are especially plentiful throughout the volume. Look at the broad contents of the 2011 edition of the *Statistical Abstract*: nearly half of the content addresses topics of concern and value to business. Need information on income by age in a particular city? The *Statistical Abstract* provides some broad information, and cites an original source—the decennial census, accessed on the web via American FactFinder and covered next—that leads to much more data. Need to know how many hairdressers are in a Manhattan neighborhood? The *Statistical Abstract* provides data on the number nationwide, and cites a source (the Economic Census, also covered below) leading to the exact needed data. Demographics on broadband users? The federal interest rate over the years? Unemployment rates for California? Wages for doctors? The costs of concrete? All of these questions may be answered, if not in the *Statistical Abstract* tables themselves, then in sources cited in the *Statistical Abstract*.

The free online version of the *Statistical Abstract* features an excellent table of contents, and also allows for searching the entire volume by keyword. This keyword search, however, is no match for the excellent, detailed index, which is available as part of the print and online PDF version (look for the link to the PDF version, then scroll down to the index). This detailed index leads to every table that might be relevant to a given query, and consistently performs more effectively than the keyword search does. Power users of the *Statistical Abstract* use this index.

A final feature of this most useful of sources is its appendices. These list key statistical resources and agencies, including their statistical programs and products, and encompasses sources covering the entire nation, each state, and foreign countries and international sources.

Note an **important** addendum to the discussion of this singular resource: as of this writing, the Statistical Compendium office of the Census Bureau, which produces the *Statistical Abstract*, is under serious threat to be eliminated in FY2012, perhaps bringing the publication of this most popular of sources to an end.

Fedstats. Office of Management and Budget. http://www.fedstats.gov. Free. And **Data.gov**. Office of Management and Budget. http://www.data.gov. Free.

With the potential demise of the *Statistical Abstract*, these two sites warrant mention, although neither approaches the general usefulness of the Abstract. Fedstats.gov launched back in 1997, and attempts to link to statistical publications and tables from across the federal government. It provides a subject index, keyword searching of the statistics sites indexed, and lists of key agencies and key datasets and publications, among other tools.

Data.gov, meanwhile, is an initiative of President Obama's open government efforts. It provides access to hundreds of raw datasets from the government, and is of special usefulness to researchers. Unlike the *Statistical Abstract* or even fedstats.gov, data.gov does not provide easy access to the statistics themselves. However, it does facilitate creation and re-use of the data by researchers, businesses, and publishers alike. Note that it is also under threat by FY2012 budget negotiations.

Market Research: Consumers

The federal government plays a key role in market research, as many market research products use U.S. government data, and specifically data from the Census Bureau, as the basis for their products (see Chapter 6 for detailed coverage of market research resources of all types). Market research products aiming to provide a portrait of people, whether by some demographic group (for instance, 45–64 years old, or Hispanic Origin), a geographic area (Portland, Maine, the state of Florida, a ZIP code, or a smaller geography such as a census tract, block group, or block), or some combination of the above (i.e., people of Hispanic origin aged 45–64 who make over $100,000 per year and live in Houston, Texas), all are based on data from the U.S. decennial census, or its companion American Community Survey. Such market research firms as Mediamark, Nielsen Claritas, and Experian Simmons all have popular products that use such data as their basis, to which are added other features, such as proprietary data, sophisticated search interfaces, enhanced output mechanisms, and other value-added elements.

American FactFinder (United States Decennial Census and American Community Survey). U.S. Census Bureau. http://www.factfinder.census.gov. Free.

The decennial census, a constitutionally mandated count of the population of the United States, serves primarily to provide the data for the state-by-state apportionment of representatives to the House of Representatives. Recent data from the U.S. decennial census is made freely available online via the Census Bureau's American FactFinder system. The decennial census—by essentially surveying every single household and person in the United States—is the government's single most important statistical effort for intelligence-gathering about the nation's citizens (and consumers); as such, it is prominently covered in Chapter 6 on market research.

The decennial census provides social, demographic, and economic information about the entire population; measured levels of detail are such that data is available for even very small geographies, such as ZIP codes and for smaller Census-defined places, such as Census tracts and blocks. These smaller geographies are key for business research at the local level—for business owners and operators who most need to understand local areas. Using American FactFinder, one may search for data using a specific address, or search by many variables such as race, age, sex, income, and family status: decennial census data are rife with opportunities for extracting socioeconomic and demographic segments, not to mention the capacity to parse those by precise geographies. Special reports exist for many topics of potential interest to the business and marketing community.

Although the decennial census is taken only once each 10 years (in years ending in zero), and thus can become somewhat dated in the interval between the changing of decades, its companion American Community Survey (ACS, http://www.census.gov/acs/www) asks similar questions of citizens during this intervening period, and provides similar data. Specifically *not* a "census," nor a match for the comprehensive decennial census, the ACS is itself a massive survey in terms of number of people questioned. Certain data elements are not updated by the ACS between censuses—especially data for smaller geographies, which requires many more survey instances to yield usable data.

Herman (2008) offers an excellent overview of the issues surrounding the ACS in general and moving averages in particular. Statistics from other census demographic and population programs may be accessed from the Census Bureau's Population website at http://www.census.gov/population/www/.

Consumer Expenditure Survey. U.S. Bureau of Labor Statistics. Annual. http://www.bls.gov/cex. Free.

As important and wide-ranging as the decennial census and the ACS are, neither program answers perhaps the most basic of market research questions: how do people spend their money? The government does measure consumer spending, although not in enough detail to inform most specific products nor in enough volume to provide data for specific, smaller geographies such as cities and ZIP codes. The survey that does exist is the Bureau of Labor Statistic's Consumer Expenditure Survey (CES). As the name implies, the CES addresses how people spend their money. It covers some 20 categories of spending: housing and housing specifics such as mortgages, home repairs, and utilities; transportation expenses such as automobile purchases, gasoline, and mass-transit spending; personal expenditures such as those for apparel, health care, and personal products; and entertainment and recreation expenditures. Like the decennial census, the CES can form the basis of more in-depth, private market research products, but its lack of coverage for smaller geographies limits its application somewhat. Although it does not have data for specific states, it is able to break down data by some market segments for the nation as a whole, such as by age, race, region, broad occupation, and family type (single, dual earner, married with children, etc.).

Industry and Company Research

Just as it gathers data about citizens via the decennial census, the federal government also surveys businesses, through which activity it produces quite a bit of information about the state of U.S. industries and business enterprises. The primary government sources for industry/sector data are statistical programs from the Census Bureau. Whereas government data efforts generally only aggregate data, and typically provide no specific company intelligence, several government services do produce intelligence about specific companies. This section addresses industry and specific company information available from the government.

Economic Census. U.S. Census Bureau. Information on 2007 edition at http://www.census.gov/econ/census07/; data at http://americanfactfinder.gov. Free.

The economic census is similar to the decennial census of population and housing covered above: with some exceptions, nearly every business in the country that has employees receives an economic census questionnaire every five years (in years ending in "2" and "7") and is required by law to complete it. The economic census asks every business to report its type of business, its size (measured by number of employees or size of payroll, and by sales, shipments, or output of the business), and its location. Thus every business, from Google to a corner barbershop in Philadelphia, provides information to the economic census. This means that business researchers can find the number of establishments by size and location for nearly any type of business (as classified by the SIC [Standard Industrial Classification] or, as of 1997, by NAICS [North American Industry Classification System] codes). So the barbershop owner can find out how many other barbershops may be operating in the same area (such as its ZIP code or county), and Google can get data on other Internet services companies around the country.

Economic census data are available via the American FactFinder system. As with the decennial census and ACS, data may be found by searching for a specific geography, including by focusing on a specific address. Also available are "Economic Fact Sheets" for industries, which provide detailed information about a given industry as a whole in the United States.

Census Bureau Business & Industry. U.S. Census Bureau. http://www .census.gov/econ. Free.

Just as the *American Community Survey* updates decennial census data, other economic surveys provide some timely updates to economic census data, although not in as much detail as the economic census itself does. These may be accessed from the Census Bureau's Business and Industry site. For instance, a popular data set is the *County Business Patterns* (CBP)/*ZIP Code Business Patterns* (ZBP)/*Metro Business Patterns* (MBP) series. These series are similar to the economic census in that they provide counts of the number of establishments by NAICS code and by location, but they lack the important data about output. *Current Industrial Reports* is another long-standing Census Bureau product, reporting quarterly on manufacturing activity by product. Other annual surveys available here include the *American Survey of Manufacturers*, the *Service Annual Survey*, and more.

EDGAR. U.S. Securities and Exchange Commission. http://www.sec.gov/ edgar.shtml. Free.

Although the federal government is not generally engaged in gathering intelligence about specific businesses for publication, a notable exception is the Securities and Exchange Commission's (SEC) EDGAR system, which exists for the explicit purpose of making basic company financial information public for companies traded on a stock exchange. (EDGAR stands for Electronic Data Gathering. Analysis, and Retrieval.) This effort traces its origins to laws passed after the 1929 stock market crash, enacted to ensure that investors have access to accurate financial information about companies in which they own or may be considering the purchase of stock shares.

The law requires a wide range of financial reports to be published in the SEC's free EDGAR database, based on company actions affecting current or potential shareholders. For instance, each company has an annual 10-K report in EDGAR, which features much of the same data that companies provide to shareholders via glossy, typically highly illustrated annual reports. EDGAR reports are also used as part of the available intelligence in various commercially-produced company research products, which often add features such as downloadable spreadsheet versions of the data, and various more robust query and retrieval options.

United States Patent and Trademark Office. Patents and Trademarks databases. http://www.uspto.gov. Free.

Another source of government information about individual companies is patents, documents that are frequently scoured by competitors and the media for clues to new products and services. Both patent applications and actual granted patents are public, and may be searched and retrieved via the U.S. Patent and Trademark Office website. That said, the business of effective patent searching is often undertaken by trained law librarians and intellectual property lawyers. Patents feature their own classification system. Understanding this system, as well as interpreting the content of patent applications themselves, is important for effective patent searching. Industries watch the patent space for new inventions, hoping to find clues as to future product development of competitors. Patents and patent applications can also be a key source of any intelligence at all about otherwise "invisible" private companies.

GOVERNMENT FINANCE AND PROCUREMENT

Finances of governments themselves are of frequent interest. Information about government budgeting and spending, government contracts and bids, and government finance and investment is widely used by the business and investment community. This section covers sources of government spending information, including procurement, government contracts, and doing business with the government; government finance, including government borrowing and bonds, is also considered here.

Budget of the United States Government. Office of Management and Budget. http://www.gpoaccess.gov/usbudget/index.html and http://www.gpo.gov/fdsys/browse/collectionGPO.action?collectionCode=BUDGET. Free.

Federal government finance begins with the federal budget. The president's office and the Office of Management and Budget transmit a proposed budget to Congress each February. These volumes are only proposals for the current year (to find actual current-year budgets requires finding the appropriate spending laws passed by Congress, available via THOMAS, http://thomas.loc.gov), but this multivolume set includes detailed data on actual spending for past years. Data are detailed, and include spending on such specific programs as AIDS research and the Peace Corps, to name only two. The *Historical Perspectives* volumes contain even more historical budget data, in most cases dating back to 1940, although the earlier dates are presented in less programmatic detail than is used in the most current edition of the Budget.

Combined Statement of Receipts, Outlays, and Balances of the United States Government, http://www.fms.treas.gov/annualreport/index.html, *Daily Treasury Statement*, http://www.fms.treas.gov/dts/index.html, and *Monthly Treasury Statement*, http://www.fms.treas.gov/mts/index.html. U.S. Department of the Treasury. Free.

The Department of the Treasury ultimately manages actual federal finance. The *Combined Statement* is the annual financial report of the U.S. government, and it details all receipts and outlays of the federal government for the fiscal year by source. It is one of a triad of publications that also includes the *Monthly Treasury Statement* and the *Daily Treasury Statement*, which detail how much money came in and out of the federal government each "business" day, by function. For instance, one can find out exactly how much money came in as tax revenue, or from bond sales, each day or month. One can likewise track exactly how much went out, such as spending on specific government programs (say, for Social Security, or for school lunches), or on debt interest.

TreasuryDirect. U.S. Department of the Treasury. http://www.treasury direct.gov. Free.

The TreasuryDirect website is the government portal for buying federal bonds and securities. Investors purchase treasury bonds, loaning the government money in order to do its business, similar to the way in which corporations, schools, or other entities might issue interest-bearing bonds to raise money for operations or projects. There are several different types of bonds and securities, from U.S. savings bonds to Treasury notes and bills. All have different returns and durations. Widely considered to be among the safest investments, Treasury bonds may be purchased and tracked right from Treasury Direct.

FedBizOpps.gov. General Services Administration. https://www.fbo.gov/. **USASPENDING.gov**. Office of Management and Budget. http://usaspending .gov/. Free.

FedBizOpps, the web-only successor of a venerable print and electronic government publication called *Commerce Business Daily* (which lasted until 2002) is the official portal listing opportunities for business to contract with the federal government to provide goods and services. It lists all government needs costing over $25,000. It is searchable by award recipients and by many other criteria, including the agency for which the work is to be done, the industry (the nature of the work), and the location. Another website, USASPENDING.gov, was specifically created to provide transparency on recipients of government contracts (it was created by the Federal Funding Accountability and Transparency Act of 2006, P.L. 109-282, 120 Stat. 1186, cosponsored by Senators Obama and McCain). It also allows searching by various criteria. For instance, one can see government contracts awarded by agency, company, type of award, or product. Listed are awards to companies such as Halliburton, or Lockheed Martin and its $23.2 billion in federal contracts awarded in FY2010.

START-UPS AND BUSINESS SUPPORT

Governments at all levels in the United States offer support for businesses. The federal government and each state government have offices providing advice and information on starting and operating a business, covering everything from the legal basics, such as how to register a business, to practical tips on how to manage, grow, research, and document business activities, and how to access market research and other business intelligence sources.

SBA.gov. U.S. Small Business Administration. Free.

The U.S. Small Business Administration (SBA) is an independent agency that exists solely to nurture and guide small businesses in the United States. SBA.gov is a portal to most business information from the government that supports new and existing businesses. It is extremely useful and the closest thing to an official, cross-agency U.S. government business portal for any business or prospective business—an entrepreneur or small-business owner's best friend. Much of the information provided here is specific to each state, and links lead to legal instructions on how to start and register a business in each state, write a business plan, determine the appropriate legal form of business (sole proprietorship, partnership, or some type of corporation), find local zoning and real estate information, find financing, and get expert help. A must-use portal for anyone starting a business, SBA.gov pulls together information from across all appropriate levels of government—everyone from the Internal Revenue Service (IRS), to the Environmental Protection Agency (EPA), to state licensing agencies.

State and Local Resources. Free.

Among the most important resources provided by state and local governments is information intended to help local businesses. State and local portals abound; these sites generally include state- or local-specific information on registering a business, securing proper licenses, and complying with state and local regulations. All states have portals to such information. Idaho's business portal (http://www.idaho.gov/business), for instance, features the

Idaho Business Wizard (http://www.idahobizhelp.org/bizwiz.htm), which allows an entrepreneur to enter a type of business and see the applicable regulatory and licensing requirements. Texas has a similar service called MyTexasBiz (https://business.texas.gov/oog/bizq), found as part of the rich information on starting and maintaining a Texas business at http://texas.gov. Government information librarian Lynn Williamson's sidebar includes mention of both state and local portals appropriate to her location. Business owners—both existing and potential—should definitely become familiar with the available state-provided business support information and services.

SBA Small Business Planner. U.S. Small Business Administration. http://www.sba.gov/smallbusinessplanner/index.html. **SCORE**. U.S. Small Business Administration. http://www.score.org.

SBA's Small Business Planner Portal guides both prospective and current small businesses to useful information. Also notable from SBA are its expert help services, such as SCORE. SCORE (Service Corps of Retired Executives)

Beginner's Guide to .gov sites for Entrepreneurs

Lynn Williamson
Government Publications Department
Free Library of Philadelphia

1. http://www.sba.gov: Small Business Administration
2. http://www.newpa.com: Pennsylvania Department of Community and Economic Development
3. http://www.dos.state.pa.us/portal/server.pt/community/corporation_bureau/ 12457: A Guide to Business Registration in Pennsylvania, Corporation Bureau of the Pennsylvania Department of State
4. http://www.dli.state.pa.us: Pennsylvania Department of Labor and Industry
5. http://www.phila.gov/commerce: Philadelphia Department of Commerce
6. http://fedbizopps.gov: Federal Business Opportunities
7. http://factfinder.census.gov: The Decennial Census, the American Community Survey, the Economic Census of the US, and Annual Economic Surveys
8. http://www.census.gov: Economic Census, Economic Indicators, and Survey of Business Owners
9. http://stats.bls.gov: Consumer Price Index Detailed Report, Wages by Area and Occupation, Occupational Outlook Handbook, and more
10. http://www.census.gov/compendia/statab: Statistical Abstract of the United States

is an SBA program that has provided expert advisory services to small-business owners for decades. There are hundreds of SCORE offices around the nation, covering most cities.

LAW, CONSUMERS, AND CITIZENS

Another key component of government involvement in business is to support individual consumers. For instance, Congress has passed hundreds of laws over the years protecting citizens from dangerous and harmful business products and practices. Many of these laws then triggered the executive agency rule-making processes that spell out in detail how laws will be enforced, resulting in regulations, also referred to as administrative law. A recent example is the Credit Card Accountability, Responsibility, and Disclosure (CARD) Act of 2009 (P.L. 111-24, 123 Stat. 1734), which included numerous provisions to protect consumers with credit cards from certain card-issuer practices. Laws and regulations are the key source for information about consumer and citizen protections, whether financial, environmental, labor-related, etc. Laws and legislation may be discovered and tracked via Thomas.loc.gov, while regulations and the rule-making process may be found at regulations.gov. Researching both laws and regulations can be difficult, and experience or expert help is frequently necessary.

Business Laws and Regulations. Small Business Administration. http:// www.sba.gov. **EPA's Laws and Regulations**. Environmental Protection Agency. http://www.epa.gov/lawsregs. **Department of Labor Compliance Portal**. U.S. Department of Labor. http://www.dol.gov/compliance. Free.

Several key executive agencies offer plain-language summaries and compilations of laws and regulations under their purview. For instance, the Environmental Protection Agency (EPA) and the Occupational Safety and Health Administration (OSHA, under the Department of Labor) both summarize, respectively, appropriate environmental and occupational laws and regulations with which businesses must comply. The SBA.gov portal conveniently links to these compliance websites as well as to others across the range of laws and jurisdictions.

Federal Trade Commission. http://www.ftc.gov/. Free.

The Federal Trade Commission (FTC) also offers materials that synthesize and educate about laws and regulations related to consumers and businesses. For instance, instead of finding and reading through all of the appropriate laws and regulations related to credit cards, one can navigate to the consumer protection portion of the FTC website and find the concise document *Credit and*

Your Consumer Rights (http://www.ftc.gov/bcp/edu/pubs/consumer/credit/cre01.shtm). This is one of dozens of documents available online from the FTC aimed at protecting consumers, covering such topics as credit, identity theft, health and the environment, buying a car or a house, getting an education and/or a job, and shopping online and avoiding online scams.

The FTC also regulates antitrust activity. Famous antitrust activity related to technology companies has included action against IBM in the 1970s and 1980s, Microsoft in the 1990s, and Google in the 2000s.

Consumer Product Safety Commission. http://www.cpsc.gov/. Free.

Another prominent agency supporting consumers is the Consumer Product Safety Commission (CPSC). The CPSC is charged with preventing injury caused by consumer products. The CPSC website lists recalls and safety warnings, and also provides publications to promote consumer safety, such as those on creating a safe baby nursery, keeping pools and playgrounds safe, preventing fire, electrical, and carbon monoxide hazards, and being aware of dangerous toys.

MyEnvironment. U.S. Environmental Protection Agency. http://www.epa.gov/myenvironment. Free.

As noted above, there are very few government initiatives that provide information about specific, named companies. The SEC's EDGAR and the U.S. Patent and Trademark Office's databases, discussed earlier, do name names, however. There are also names associated with environmental- and pollution-monitoring efforts led by the EPA. The agency's My Environment database provides information about potentially harmful output arising from the production of certain goods. Companies that produce over a certain threshold of air pollution or who may have material runoff into water sources are monitored and required to report to EPA certain data which are then made public via My Environment. Enter a location at the site (an address, or ZIP code, city, county, waterbody, park name, etc.) to retrieve a location-specific list of companies or facilities that produce emissions required to be reported to the government.

IRS Tax Statistics. Internal Revenue Service. http://www.irs.gov/taxstats. Free.

In addition to providing access to federal tax forms and instructions for individuals and businesses, the Internal Revenue Service (IRS) collects and publishes a remarkable wealth of data related to income taxes. For instance, data from all individual, business, or corporate income tax returns are compiled and published. For example, one can find the number of returns that use various deductions, such as an individual retirement account (IRA); breakdowns of adjusted income by age, marital status, and income; and, for corporate and business returns, tax data by industry or sector. Traditionally, this statistical information was made available via the Statistics of Income (SOI) series. Although SOI still exists, the IRS tax statistics site is the place to begin to find data related to tax collection.

ECONOMIC INDICATORS

Perhaps the most newsworthy business information disseminated by the federal government are the reports of economic indicators for various economic and business activities throughout the country. Economic indicators are those statistics about the economy taken as indicative of economic health; when released (often monthly, sometimes quarterly) they are usually the leading stories, in both the business and general press. Depending on how one defines an "economic indicator," there could be hundreds of them. There are, however, several key resources that compile most of the important economic indicators. Note that the book *Major U.S. Statistical Series: Definitions, Publications, Limitations*, by librarians Juri Stratford and Jean Slemmons Stratford, describes the nature of most current economic indicators, and is an excellent place to go to learn about the nature of economic indicators and other government statistical measures.

Economic Indicators. Council of Economic Advisers. Monthly. http://www.gpoaccess.gov/indicators/index.html and http://www.gpo.gov/fdsys/browse/collection.action?collectionCode=ECONI. Free.

Many of the nation's key economic indicators are compiled into the monthly *Economic Indicators*, transmitted to Congress from the president's Council of Economic Advisers, which has been published since the 1940s. Among the 46 currently compiled statistics in *Economic Indicators* are popularly reported data such as gross domestic product, unemployment, inflation and prices, interest rates, and foreign trade. All tables in each monthly issue generally include annual data for the last 10 years and quarterly data for the last 2 years. The Federal Reserve also archives the data from *Economic Indicators* via its FRASER (Federal Reserve Archival System for Economic Research) system (http://fraser.stlouisfed.org/publications/ei/).

Economicindicators.gov. U.S. Economics and Statistics Administration. Free.

Economicindicators.gov (not to be confused with *Economic Indicators* above) compiles most key data releases from the two Department of

Commerce subagencies, the Census Bureau and the Bureau of Economic Analysis (BEA), each of which compile economic data. Data available here include retail sales (often reported on in the media as consumer spending), popular data about the housing market such as sales and construction of new and existing homes, GDP (gross domestic product—the most basic, complete indicator of the output of the nation's economy), and foreign-trade statistics.

Economy at a Glance. U.S. Bureau of Labor Statistics. http://www.bls.gov/eag/eag.us.htm. Free.

The Bureau of Labor Statistics compiles and publishes a number of prominent economic indicators, available from its Economy at a Glance website. Data on unemployment and consumer prices (usually called inflation) highlight BLS's data. Another popular indicator available from Economy at a Glance is productivity, a measure of the productive output of the nation's workers. Unlike many economic indicators, many of those available from the BLS, including unemployment and prices, include data at the state and metro level (also available from Economy at a Glance).

Federal Reserve Statistics & Historical Data. Board of Governors of the Federal Reserve System. http://www.federalreserve.gov/econresdata/releases/statisticsdata.htm. Free.

Another preeminent producer of popular economic indicators is the Federal Reserve ("the Fed"), whose mission is largely to manage the nation's money supply. The Fed and its highly visible chairman have become more prominent in recent decades as their role in managing the economy has become perceived as more influential than may have been the case earlier. Key indicators from the Fed measure consumer credit and money stocks. Arguably the Fed's best-known activity is its control of the interest rate (popularly known as the prime rate or the federal funds rate), which may change after a meeting of the Fed's Open Market Committee. Announcements of changes to the prime rate are very closely watched by business, economic, financial, and even general interests. FRASER—the Federal Reserve Archival System for Economic Research (http://fraser.stlouisfed.org/)—also contains data from the Fed, as well as other U.S. economic data.

Economic Report of the President. Council of Economic Advisers. Annual. http://www.gpoaccess.gov/eop and http://www.gpo.gov/fdsys/browse/collection.action?collectionCode=ERP. Free.

The long-standing *Economic Report of the President* (ERP), published annually by the Council of Economic Advisers (an agency within the president's office established by Congress in 1946), is the best place to find historical time series of economic data about the nation. Nearly all of the categories mentioned above—prices, employment and unemployment, GDP and output by sector or industry, foreign trade, government spending, interest rates, and over 100 more items—are included in the ERP. The ERP begins with a narrative analysis of key issues in the U.S. economy, and then includes its statistical tables. The ERP is available via the FDsys/GPO Access platform, and is also archived on FRASER (http://fraser.stlouisfed.org/).

Regional Economic Conditions (RECON). Federal Deposit Insurance Commission. http://www2.fdic.gov/recon/index.asp. Free.

Regional economic indicators are perhaps not as prominent as national ones, although measures such as unemployment are available for many geographies, as noted above. An excellent compilation of economic indicators for states is the Regional Economic Conditions database (RECON) from the Federal Deposit Insurance Corporation (FDIC). FDIC created RECON in order to assess financial risk of banks, the better to measure the economic health of the areas in which those banks operate. Data include housing and real estate, employment, wages, and spending. All of the data compiled here come from original sources noted above.

EMPLOYMENT AND LABOR

Basic economic indicators such as employment and productivity are discussed above, but there is much more government information that is related to labor and employment, such as data on occupations and wages, productivity, and earnings. Nearly all of the key sources for employment and labor are provided by the Department of Labor and its subagency, the Bureau of Labor Statistics.

Occupational Outlook Handbook. U.S. Bureau of Labor Statistics. Annual. http://www.bls.gov/oco/home.htm. Free. Print, $23.

This is one of the most popular government information sources. A biennial survey of occupations, the *Occupational Outlook Handbook* (OOH) describes hundreds of occupations, including each occupation's qualifications, schooling, training, necessary professional certificates, salaries and wages, and the outlook for the occupation. The OOH is perhaps the classic source for people researching careers.

Wages by Area and Occupation. U.S. Bureau of Labor Statistics. http://www.bls.gov/bls/blswage.htm. Free.

BLS's Wages by Occupation provides median and average salaries and wages for more than 800 occupations, and includes breakdowns for states and metropolitan areas. It counts the number of people employed in each occupation in each metro area, state, and the nation as a whole.

INTERNATIONAL INFORMATION

Our much-discussed global economy requires its own suite of information resources to measure business and economic activity, and to support businesses operating internationally.

Export.gov. U.S. International Trade Administration. http://export.gov. Free to U.S. citizens.

Export.gov compiles information to help U.S. businesses export goods or services and to succeed in foreign markets. Its most valuable data are in its Market Research Library (from the U.S. Commercial Service). Key sources here are highlighted by Country Commercial Guides (CCG). Prepared by U.S. embassies, these annual guides for most of the world's countries describe the business climate of each country, as well as political and economic factors that affect American businesses' operations. The CCGs include details about the local labor force, physical and telecommunications infrastructure, the legal and judicial system, and government involvement in the business climate. There are also discussions of key markets, as well as details on exporting such as tariffs. CCGs also discuss strategies for entering the market, including franchising, finding a local distributor for your product, and how to make sales in the local climate. Finally, CCGs describe business customs and etiquette, such as the prevalence of long lunches in one country, or the appropriateness of electronic communication in another.

The Market Research Library also includes a collection of Market Research Reports, in-depth reports containing intelligence about a particular product or business type, and often in a specific location. Although these reports vary greatly in detail and usefulness, they are notable simply because they offer for free data and analysis that is usually fairly expensive when sold as commercially produced content, because the U.S. government, in order to support U.S. business abroad, provides access to these reports at no cost.

UNdata. United Nations Statistics Division. http://data.un.org/Explorer .aspx. Free.

UNdata is the premier portal to data collected by the United Nations and affiliated international agencies. Data here are country by country. UNdata includes the Energy Statistics Database, FAO Data from the Food and Agriculture Organization (FAO), INDSTAT from the United Nations Industrial Development Organization (UNIDO; data for countries resembling U.S.

Economic Census data), International Financial Statistics, from the International Monetary Fund (IMF, a very popular compilation of country-by-country financials), National Accounts databases, and LABORSTA from the International Labor Organization (ILO, with prices and employment data).

While UNdata itself is free, several of its constituent databases, such as International Financial Statistics, have independent versions with many more features, often at a subscription cost.

World Development Indicators. World Bank. http://data.worldbank.org/. Some data free; full database pricing varies; contact the publisher.

The World Bank also publishes a comprehensive, easy to use international statistics database, *World Development Indicators*. Only a subset of recent years is available for free; access to the entire database requires a subscription.

USA Trade. U.S. Census Bureau. http://www.usatradeonline.gov/. Single user: $300/year. Institutional price varies; contact the publisher. **TradeStats Express**. U.S. International Trade Administration. http://tse.export.gov/. Free. **U.S. Census Bureau Foreign Trade**. http://www.census.gov/foreign-trade. Free.

There are several sources for foreign trade statistics. U.S. export and import data are gathered at ports of entry by Customs and Border Protection (CBP), a subagency of the Department of Homeland Security (known, until 2003, as the U.S. Customs Service). These data are then compiled and published by the Census Bureau in the fee-based usatrade.gov. Usatrade.gov has statistics by type of good, the country of destination or origin, the amount of goods, and the port.

Some of these data are available for free from the International Trade Administration (ITA). ITA's primary trade statistics product is TradeStats Express, which provides total volume of U.S. imports and exports by foreign nation, and by product both for the United States as a whole and for each state.

Some U.S. foreign trade data are also available via databases at the Census Bureau (see http://www.census.gov/foreign-trade) and the International Trade Commission (http://dataweb.usitc.gov) websites. Note that trade data uses its own systems for product classification, different from the industry classifications in NAICS or the SIC Manuals. The classification used for imports is the *Harmonized Tariff Schedule of the United States*. For exports, it is *Schedule B: Statistical Classification of Domestic and Foreign Commodities Exported from the United States*.

International Trade Statistics. World Trade Organization. http://www.wto.org/english/res_e/statis_e/statis_e.htm. Free online; print yearbook

50 CHF/Euros. *Direction of Trade Statistics.* International Monetary Fund. http://www2.imfstatistics.org/DOT. Single user: $300/year. Institutional price varies; contact the publisher. Print, $240.

These two sources provide trade data for trade between two foreign countries (not just the United States). The *Direction of Trade Statistics*, from the IMF, in print and as an online subscription database, compiles data on the value of trade between any two countries (but not data about the product or commodities involved). The World Trade Organization (WTO), meanwhile, compiles and publishes data about exports and imports of a country by commodity and product, but does not have these data specifically between any two countries. And the *UN comtrade* database (http://comtrade.un.org) further compiles trade data from several UN sources.

CONCLUSION

While somewhat out of context here, the Clinton-era catchphrase "It's the economy, stupid" nicely summarizes much of government information. The United States is largely about business, and its federal, state, and local governments produce a vast body of information about the business climate and the economy. Some of these sources are unique, and the information may be found nowhere but from the government. Other sources discussed in this chapter might be used mainly, or only, because they are free, with more demanding business information users choosing pricier, superior commercial products such as those covered elsewhere in this book. In any case, knowledge of civics is an excellent supplement to understanding business resources, and that knowledge opens up hundreds of useful government-produced business resources.

REFERENCES

Hernon, Edward. 2008. "The American Community Survey: An Introduction to the Basics." *Government Information Quarterly* 25, no.3: 504–19.

Stratford, Jean Slemmons, and Juri Stratford. 1992. *Major U.S. Statistical Series: Definitions, Publications, Limitations.* Chicago: American Library Association.

5

Investment Sources

Madeleine Cohen

INTRODUCTION

In the past few years we have lived through a subprime mortgage crisis, a stock market crash, failure of major banks, a recession, and unemployment at historic levels. In such an uncertain economy, we may wonder who is investing, and what should a business library collect? While there may be hesitancy on the part of individual investors due to recent swings in the market, people have not stopped investing, and many look to financial advisors for guidance. Students of finance have an ongoing need for financial information, as do individual investors, brokers, and financial analysts. The financial crisis has led to increased demand for financial information, as investors seek to better understand and track their investments. Business libraries can meet the needs of their users by staying up to date with online financial databases and websites and by acquiring some of the sources for investment research noted in this chapter.

Sources listed in this chapter are organized in the following sections:

- Online Databases
- Advisory Services
- Reference Serials
- Periodicals
- Free Websites
- Books for Circulating or Reference Collections

DATABASES FOR INVESTORS

Bloomberg Professional. Inc. http://www.bloomberg.com/apps/feedback?site=sales (for services and pricing) or by phone, offices worldwide (212-318-2000). Price varies; contact the publisher.

Bloomberg provides access to news, analytics, charts, and screening through a proprietary online system offering access to sophisticated tools for investment research. It is very costly, but pricing may be lower for academic libraries able to limit to program-enrolled students.

Business Source Premier (EBSCO). http://www.ebscohost.com/academic/business-source-premier. For pricing, see http://www.ebscohost.com/pages/contact-ebsco-publishing.

Available in many public and academic libraries, Business Source Premier provides excellent coverage of publications for investor research. Investment journals combined with trade publications for financial professionals comprise nearly 100 of the titles in the database. (Regional Business News, which includes many trade publications for investors, is provided to subscribers of BSP at no additional cost.). This is covered in more detail in Chapter 2.

Business Source Complete (EBSCO), a "premium" version of the Business Source EBSCO database, available in some academic business libraries, incorporates additional content for investment research, and includes financial data and investment research reports in addition to trade publications.

Factiva (Dow Jones). http://factiva.com/. Pricing varies; contact the publisher.

Factiva, a searchable full-text database with rich content, provides access to thousands of sources in 23 languages from over 150 countries. It provides search features for search by company, stock quotes, and charting. Financial and news publications are full text and often available on Factiva on or before the date of publication. It is recommended for business libraries of all types, including smaller libraries.

Investext (Thomson Reuters). http://thomsonreuters.com/products_services/financial/contactus/. Pricing varies; contact the publisher.

Investext is a database of research reports by brokerage firms and analysts. Thomson categorizes Investext as an "embargoed analyst research collection." As such, it offers libraries the ability to offer individual investors and academic users online access to quality research used by financial professionals. The information is delayed by a week or two weeks. Investext's global coverage includes research reports from over 1,600 firms. Investext analyst reports are also available through the One Source database. Note: As of 2011, the Investext database direct from Thomson has been integrated into Thomson's Banker One, without a separate interface, which may be a drawback for libraries subscribing to the Investext product without the full Banker One subscription.

Mergent Online. http://www.mergent.com/productsServices-desktop Applications-online.html. Pricing varies; contact the publisher.

Mergent Online is a "modular product" platform, whose basic subscription includes U.S. Company Data and/or International Company Data. Libraries can choose to add many other modules, which can be integrated into the main Mergent Online service. Modules available include: U.S Annual Reports, U.S. Company Archives, Institutional Holdings Data, Insider Trading Data, Expanded Long-Term Debt, a Private Company database (with data from Dun and Bradstreet's) and Equity Portraits. Mergent Online provides sophisticated advanced search functions to conduct comparisons and financial analysis of companies and securities. Pricing varies based on size of the library and the modules included. (A small library can license Mergent Online at a price starting under $3,000 per year, which would offer basic U.S. company data, including company history and business descriptions, along with financials for three years.)

Morningstar Investment Research Center. http://corporate.morningstar .com/us/asp/detail.aspx?xmlfile=115.xml. Pricing varies; contact the publisher.
Morningstar Research Center provides easy access to financial data on mutual funds, company stocks, stock quotes, ETFs, analysts' (Morningstar analysts) reports, and more. It provides a variety of screening tools for research by company, industry sector, performance, mutual funds, and recently added coverage of ETFs (exchange-traded funds). A Portfolio X-ray enables investors to view a hypothetical portfolio and see how its securities work together. The Research Center includes portfolio-planning tools and an excellent set of online investment courses within the database. It is highly recommended for business libraries.

Standard & Poor's NetAdvantage. http://www.netadvantage.standardand poors.com/ Pricing varies; contact the publisher.
S&P NetAdvantage is a comprehensive online source of investment information providing access to Standard and Poor's publications. Content in the database depends on which publications a library has licensed. Publications that can be searched in NetAdvantage include the Bond Report, Company Profiles, the Register of Corporations, Directors & Executives, Stock Reports, Industry Surveys, the Outlook, and S&P's Security Dealers of North America Directory; these individual titles are covered below under "Periodicals." Screening tools and advanced search functions allow users to build searches and print or save data to an Excel format.

Thomson One Banker and Thomson One Banker-Analytics. http:// thomsonreuters.com/products_services/financial/contactus/. Pricing varies; contact the publisher.

Thomson One Banker provides access to company overviews and financials, stock quotes, earnings estimates, corporate filings, ownership information, M&A deals, private equity information, and equity analyst reports on companies and industries. It is for academic business libraries.

Thomson One Banker-Analytics, meanwhile, offers company financials, earnings estimates, real-time market data, and stock quotes from multiple sources, including Thomson Financial, Datastream, Extel, First Call, Worldscope, and Disclosure, along with advanced filtering and screening capabilities. Users can download and analyze data with an Excel add-on. It is for academic business libraries.

Value Line Investment Research Center. http://www.valueline.com/ Institutional/ProductsD2/The_Value_Line_Research_Center_Library_Edition .aspx. Pricing varies; contact the publisher.

The Value Line Investment Research Center, a premium suite of investment publications and screening tools, provides online access to these classic publications: Value Line Investment Survey Library Edition, Value Line Expanded Library Edition, The Value Line Mutual Fund Survey, Value Line Daily Options Survey, Value Line Special Situations, and Value Line Convertible Survey. The Research Center allows investors to customize screens, compare companies and funds, customize graphs, and track their own portfolios. Larger libraries will clearly prefer the Investment Research Center subscription, while smaller collections will be well served by subscribing to the Standard or Expanded Edition. Although some investors may prefer a print version of the Value Line Investment Survey, the online database is quite easy to use and provides PDFs of the print issues. The online version also provides screening tools and company search functions, which eliminate the need to consult a printed index issue, as is often required when investors consult the print issues.

Value Line online databases. http://www.valueline.com/Institutional/ Libraries/. Pricing varies; contact the publisher.

Value Line offers institutional pricing to libraries for its electronic database, allowing them to provide investors with easy access to a variety of Value Line publications. Online editions, which can be licensed at varying levels, currently include:

The "Library Edition"—the Value Line Investment Survey online version.

The "Expanded Library Edition"—includes the main Investment Survey online, and adds research for 1,800 small- and mid-cap companies.

Zephyr. Bureau van Dijk. http://www.bvdinfo.com/Products/Economic -and-M-A/M-A/Zephyr.aspx. Pricing varies; contact the publisher.

Zephyr is an excellent database to research and track mergers and acquisitions, containing information on over 700,000 companies, with 10 years of global deals, and providing information related to IPOs, private equity and venture capital deals, rumored deals, announced deals, leveraged buyouts, completed deals, and more. Coverage is global, and searching may be done on multiple criteria including private equity, joint ventures, IPOs, etc. Libraries can customize the screens for their users, and users can save searches and download details of M&A deals. Zephyr is recommended for libraries who serve a community of serious investors and financial professionals.

REFERENCE SERIALS

While nearly all of the sources listed in this section are classic print publications (and generally still available in print format), it's likely that the print versions will cease in the coming years as publishers abandon that increasingly unsustainable format, especially as investment professionals demand the more robust functionality that often accompanies the online versions. These titles are now usually either available via one of the broader databases listed above, or in stand-alone online versions.

Many of these core sources for business libraries are now published by two main publishers, Standard & Poor's and Mergent (formerly Moody's), and each has long-standing credentials in the financial information world. Larger libraries serving financial professionals may have the luxury and the acquisitions budget to offer access to publications from both of them (and perhaps in both print and online formats); smaller libraries with more limited budgets may instead choose between similar publications issued by either S&P or Mergent. For example, both produce reports on stocks, bonds, and industry surveys, with similar coverage. In some cases electronic access to company information is updated daily or weekly, so for currency of information, electronic is clearly preferable. Note: prices below are for print versions only, unless otherwise indicated. Electronic access options vary, and one should contact the publisher.

Annual Guide to Stocks: Directory of Active Stocks. South Plainfield, NJ: Financial Information Inc. (2010 edition; 98th year). http://www.fiinet.com.

This is a directory of information on outstanding domestic and foreign stocks, including both listed and unlisted stocks. For each listing, it provides corporate title (place of incorporation), company address, telephone number and website, stock descriptions, lead underwriter, par value, CUSIP number, initial issue description, transfer agent, transfer charge, dividend disbursing agent, changes in capital structure, and stock dividend information. Note: it is available as a set of three main sections, which includes a separate directory for inactive securities. For securities of corporations that are no longer in existence see the **Directory of Obsolete Securities: Annual Guide to Stocks**, second section, from the same publisher, Financial Information, Inc., South Plainfield, New Jersey.

Listings contain inactive securities due to changes in name, merger, bankruptcy, acquisition, liquidation, reorganization, redemption, charter cancellation, or other capital changes since 1926. The third section, **Legal Requirements**, is an outline of necessary requirements to complete legal transfer of stocks.

Bond Guide, Standard and Poor's. New York: Standard & Poor's Publishers. Monthly. $473 per year.

S&P's Bond Guide provides comparative financial and statistical information on over 7,300 issues. Standard & Poor's ratings are included for most corporate bonds. Available in print and online through S&P Net Advantage.

Mergent Bond Record (and Annual Bond Record) (Formerly Moody's Bond Record). New York: Mergent Inc. Monthly. $840 per year; includes year-end annual.

A monthly, the Mergent Bond Record contains summaries and details on over 68,000 issues. It lists name of corporation with coupon dates or dates of maturity. It covers corporate bonds, convertibles, government, municipals, and includes Moody's ratings. Available in print and in Mergent Online.

Mergent Dividend Record and Annual Dividend Record. New York: Mergent, Inc.

The Mergent Dividend Record is published twice weekly, with a semiannual cumulative issue published in June of each year and three tax supplements published annually. It provides updated information for common and preferred dividend-paying stocks and mutual funds. It includes cash and stock dividends. The Annual Dividend Record provides full-year dividend summaries for more than 12,000 dividend-paying stocks and 18,000 mutual funds.

Note regarding Mergent Library Packages:

Mergent offers their most popular publications in print to libraries in various packages, based on the type of library and size. Some details and pricing from the Mergent website, checked October, 2010, for various print packages are listed here:

> **Reference Library Service Package**—$1,445 (http://www.mergent.com/findSolution-libraries-referenceLibrary.html): Annual Dividend Record, Handbook of Common Stocks, Handbook of NASDAQ Stocks, Industry Review, Unit Investment Trust Payment Record
>
> **Investment Guide Package**—$1,420: Bond Record, Handbook of Dividend Achievers, Dividend Record, Handbook of Common Stocks, Handbook of NASDAQ Stocks, Industry Review
>
> **Custom Library Service Package**—$2,366 (http://www.mergent.com/findSolution-libraries-customLibrary.html): Industrial Manual with News Reports, Over the Counter Industrial Manual with News Reports, Annual Dividend Record, Bond Record, Handbook of Dividend Achievers, Handbook of Common Stocks, Handbook of NASDAQ Stocks, Unit Investment Trust Payment Record

Mergent Manuals. New York: Mergent, Inc.

Mergent Manuals are primary reference sources for business and financial research. Manuals issued in print include: The Mergent Industrial Manual, OTC Industrial Manual, OTC Unlisted, Transportation Manual, Public Utility Manual, Bank and Finance Manual, International Manual, Municipal Manual, U.S. Company Archives Manual, and the International Company Archives Manual.

The manuals are updated by monthly News Reports (for online subscribers, updates are weekly). Larger business libraries may have the funds to subscribe to all of the manuals, while smaller libraries may need to focus on just a few, such as the Industrial Manual and the Municipal, Bank and Finance Manual; possibly Transportation and others depending on the type of library.

CRB Commodity Yearbook. Chicago: Commodity Research Bureau. 1939–. Annual. $150.

The CRB Commodity Yearbook is a comprehensive source for 100+ commodities, U.S. and international. It includes current and historical pricing data and statistical information. It is also available on CD-ROM.

Capital Changes Reporter. New York: CCH. Wolters Kluwer Law & Business. Available as a loose-leaf service or online in several versions based on timeliness of updates.

This classic service for investors covers stock transactions that have taxable income losses or gains due to capital changes. It covers federal tax consequences of capital changes for more than 58,000 corporations and organizations resulting from stock dividends, stock splits, reorganizations, exchanges, rights, and other changes in capital structure. It is available in print as a weekly, and online every two weeks. It is also available as Capital Changes Daily, on the web and as a direct data feed. It also includes lists of worthless securities.

Handbook of Common Stocks. New York: Mergent, Inc. (formerly Moody's). Quarterly. Cost of single copy, fall 2010: $105.

The Handbook provides one-page profiles of 900 NYSE securities including business summary, stock price, ratios, 10 years of income statements, dividends, and institutional holdings. It is available as a single title and is also part of Mergent's various library services packages, e.g., Investment Guide Package.

Handbook of NASDAQ Stocks. New York: Mergent, Inc. Quarterly. Cost of latest edition, summer 2010: $95.

Like the preceding title but covering stocks traded on NASDAQ, this handbook also provides one-page profiles containing market data, performance ratios, stock prices, dividends, and future prospects. It also lists officers, address, phone and fax numbers, websites, transfer agents, auditor, and investor contacts. It is available as a single issue and as part of Mergent's Library Services Packages.

Ibbotson SBBI Classic Yearbook. Chicago: Morningstar. 1983–. Annual. (Former title: "Stocks, Bonds, Bills and Inflation Yearbook").

Contains data on U.S. capital markets including total returns and index values dating back to 1926 for large- and small-company stocks, long-term corporate bonds, Treasury bills, and inflation. It is a useful reference work for financial advisors, financial planners, and brokers to analyze asset class performance.

Mergent Book of Dividend Achievers. New York: Mergent, Inc. Quarterly. $53 single issue.

Similar in format to other related Mergent titles, this provides one-page profiles of companies that have increased their regular cash dividends annually for the past 10 or more consecutive years. Each profile provides the company's stock performance chart, dividend record, business description, analysis, and seven years of financial results and ratios. It is available as a single issue and as part of Mergent's Library Services Packages.

Mergent Industry Review. New York: Mergent, Inc. Semiannual $675 per year.

The Mergent Industry Review is a statistical reference tool with comparative figures and rankings on 6,000 leading companies in 137 industry groups. It is available as part of Mergent's Special Library Service Package.

SRC Book of 12 Year Charts. Auburn, MA: Securities Research Company. Quarterly. $195 per year, combined print and online subscription.

This provides investment information on over 1,500 of the most actively traded stocks on the NYSE and AMEX stock exchanges. Each 12-year stock chart traces the monthly price ranges, relative-to-market performance, 48-month moving average, trading volumes, plus earnings and dividends. Data are adjusted for stock splits and dividends, and notable events in the company's history are included. Subscription to the print version also includes online access to the charts, which are updated daily. Screening filters available in the online version allow investors to filter and create multiple portfolios.

SRC Green Book. Auburn, MA: Securities Research Company. $397 per year, print and online.

Provides 50 years of information for 900 of the NYSE and NASDAQ's most active stocks. View how a stock has performed during and after each economic downturn from 1960 to the present. The print subscription includes online access to charts, updated daily. Screening tools are provided in the online version.

Standard & Poor's Analyst's Handbook. New York: Standard & Poor's. Annual.

The Handbook provides statistics and selected income and balance sheet items and ratios for the Standard & Poor's 500 index applying industry codes in GICS (global industry classification standard). Using the data supplied, investors can analyze performance and price of companies against others in their sector.

Standard & Poor's Corporation Records. New York: Standard & Poor's. Monthly. $3,012.

This is a financial service with a news edition and daily news section. It is available online in S&P NetAdvantage database. It contains descriptions of public companies including those listed on the NYSE, the AMEX, and larger unlisted and regional exchanges. Daily edition ceased in print, and continues online.

Standard & Poor's CreditWeek. New York: Standard & Poor's. Weekly. Cost for print subscription: $4,200 per year. CreditWeek is also available in PDF format.

Standard & Poor's CreditWeek provides news and highlights of developments in global credit markets and adds industry analyses, market commentaries, and ratings trends. Articles are written by Standard & Poor's credit analysts. It provides in-depth information on credit markets for financial professionals, and is appropriate for large business libraries serving financial professionals.

Standard & Poor's Dividend Record. New York: Standard & Poor's. 1925–. Quarterly. $725 per year.

Available in print, as a data feed, and online, this product allows investors to track cash, stock, and other distributions, including tax consequences and dates. It covers more than 26,000 equity securities.

Standard & Poor's Global Ratings Handbook. New York: Standard & Poor's. Monthly. $1,500 per year.

This print directory provides S&P ratings information including short- and long-term issuer and issue credit ratings, CreditWatch and ratings, and outlooks for taxable issues. It includes Standard & Poor's ratings for global issuers, structured finance, and industrial revenue bonds.

Standard & Poor's Stock Reports. New York: Standard & Poor's.

The Stock Reports are classic reports with data and description for stocks on the New York Stock Exchange, the American Exchange, and the OTC. There are quarterly or weekly updates, and the reports are available online through Standard & Poor's Net Advantage.

S&P Trendline Current Market Perspectives. Monthly. $750 per year.

This reference title contains charts of 15,000 stocks in the S&P indexes: S&P 500, MidCap 400, and SmallCap 600.

ADVISORY SERVICES

Two popular advisory services for individual investors offered in many academic and public libraries are **Morningstar** and **Value Line**. For many libraries, these may be the most heavily used investment publications. Each service uses a proprietary system for ranking securities and mutual funds, and each provides its publications to subscribers in print or electronic format. Both publishers maintain websites (http://www.morningstar.com and http://www.valueline.com), which provide valuable financial information at no cost to nonsubscribers, although the services available by subscription offer more robust sets of screening tools and PDFs of many of their print publications.

Morningstar Mutual Funds. Chicago: Morningstar. Print edition. Biweekly. $795 per year, institutions.

Subscribers receive a binder containing reports on 1,500 mutual fund reports and regular updates. Reports are updated throughout the year; issues are published every three weeks. The *Summary* and *Analysis* sections are published 20 times per year. Summary issues include commentary, benchmark data, and performance data on all 1,500 funds. Analysis issues provide updates on approximately 150 specific funds. Subscribers to the print version receive access to the reports online, and can download the latest issue as a PDF file, review entire groups of funds, or search for specific funds. Morningstar rates mutual funds from one to five stars based on the fund's performance in comparison with similar funds. Morningstar Mutual Funds is a popular advisory service, and is appropriate for public as well as academic business libraries. (See the Databases for Investors section of this chapter for information about Morningstar Investment Research Center.)

Value Line Investment Survey. New York: Value Line, Inc. 1936–. Weekly in three sections. Pricing varies for libraries.

The Survey, Value Line's leading "original" publication, focuses on stocks, issued weekly in three sections:

1. Ratings and Reports: Provides full-page reviews and analyst commentaries on approximately 1,700 of the most actively traded stocks, in over 90 industries, with price and earnings projections, charts, "Timeliness Safety," and "Technical Rankings," all based on Value Line's propriety ranking system.
2. Summary & Index: Covers performance, ranking changes, and price/ earnings projections.
3. Selection & Opinion: News and commentary on markets and the economy from Value Line's analysts.

Value Line, along with Morningstar, is an obvious choice for many public and business libraries. (See the Databases for Investors section of this chapter for online Value Line products.)

OTHER ADVISORY NEWSLETTERS

Investment advisory publications may focus on general investment advice, offer market forecasts, and offer recommendations to buy, hold, or sell securities, depending on market conditions and the rating or ranking system observed by the publication. Providing access to such publications can be costly, and as such, most will not be appropriate for small libraries with limited budgets. What follows is a very selective list for libraries which may want to provide a few advisory newsletters to their users:

Dick Davis Digest. Salem, MA: Dick Davis Digest. Semimonthly. $129 per year.

Every issue presents investors with excerpted ideas and investment opportunities as identified by authors of a broad range of investment newsletters.

Dow Theory Letters. La Jolla, CA. $300 per year.

This long-standing advisory newsletter, in publication since 1958 with Richard Russell, editor and publisher, provides technical analysis of financial markets. It covers the U.S. stock market, foreign markets, bonds, precious metals, and commodities. It includes a daily "Primary Trend Index" (PTI). Issues are mailed every three weeks, and online access is provided to print subscribers.

Drip Investor. Hammond, IN: Horizon Publishing Co. Monthly. $109 per year.

Edited by Charles Carlson, the Drip Investor provides tips and news for investors in DRIPs (dividend reinvestment plans). Dividend reinvestment plans allow owners of securities to purchase additional shares directly from the company.

Grant's Interest Rate Observer. New York. Published 24 times per year. $950 per year.

"An independent, value-oriented and contrary-minded journal of the financial markets." It is available in print and online. (Subscribers to the print edition receive online access at no extra charge. Note: online access requires a security plug-in, which may complicate providing online access in some libraries.) Subscribers receive access to archived issues back to 1983, which are searchable online.

The Hulbert Financial Digest. Springfield, VA: Hulbert Financial Digest, Inc. Monthly. Available in e-mail or print version. Price varies.

Mark Hulbert is the editor of this highly regarded digest of investment advisory newsletters. Hulbert tracks approximately 180 stock recommendation letters each month. The newsletter has been published since 1980.

The Digest's aim is to "provide objective performance data on various investment strategies."

Moneyletter. Ashland, MA: PRI Financial Publishing. Biweekly. $180 per year.

This advisory newsletter for mutual fund investors has been published since 1980. It is available in a print or online subscription. The online version is currently a PDF version. Walter Frank, editor, provides recommendations of mutual funds.

No-Load Fund Investor. Brentwood, TN: The No-Load Investor, LLC. P.O. Box 3029, Brentwood, TN. Monthly. $199 per year.

Another popular newsletter, this one provides information on stock funds and bond funds, fund comparisons, and best buys.

NoLoad FundX. San Francisco: DAL Investment Company. Monthly. $179 per year.

The NoLoad FundX newsletter uses a technical ranking system that compares funds in a FundX score. The score is made up of averages of past total returns plus ratings.

S&P Outlook. New York, NY: Standard and Poor's. Print and online. Pricing varies; contact the publisher.

The S&P Outlook provides recommendations, S&P Stars Stock Reports, screening tools, and more. It is available through S&P NetAdvantage online or as a separate online publication.

The Street.com Ratings Guide to Common Stocks. New York: The Street.com, Inc. Quarterly. (Formerly Weiss Ratings). Contact for pricing.

This popular investment ratings service provides investors with an evaluation and opinion on each stock's risk-adjusted performance. The Street.com also publishes guides covering mutual funds, banks and thrifts, and bond and money market mutual funds. It is available in print and online.

Zacks Earnings Forecaster. Chicago: Zacks Investment Research, Inc. Biweekly, monthly, or quarterly editions. Biweekly: $495 per year; Monthly: $375 per year; Quarterly: $225 per year.

Zacks summarizes earnings and related data and provides consensus earnings estimates based on Wall Street brokerage analysts' earnings forecasts. It includes recent earnings results, earnings growth, stock recommendation ratings, and Zacks ratings. Zacks is a good choice for public libraries as it is easy to use, and provides earnings estimates based on Wall Street brokers' analysis.

INVESTMENT PERIODICALS

Many of these titles are listed as core resources in other chapters of this book, so only brief mentions are made here. Note that many of these titles are available within the databases discussed earlier as well.

AAII Journal. Published monthly by the American Association of Individual Investors. Chicago. $49 per year.

This journal is for a general audience. It does not promote specific-investing techniques, but provides information about stock strategies, financial planning, stock screening, portfolio management, and model portfolios. It is recommended for public and business library investment collections.

Barron's. Dow Jones & Company. $199 per year.

Familiar to even many casual readers, this leading investment publication has been published since 1921. It provides news on companies, market analysis, company insights, reports, articles, and interviews. It is available online at http://online.barrons.com, and also through the Factiva database, and, depending on publishing agreements, may be included in other databases, as well.

Financial Times. Financial Times Ltd. http://www.ft.com. $348 per year, individual subscribers. Contact publisher for library pricing.

This essential daily newspaper, published in London, competes with the *Wall Street Journal* to be **the** leading business daily. It is recommended for business libraries.

Forbes. New York: Forbes, Inc. Biweekly. 1917–. $59.95 per year.

This top business magazine is geared toward executives, managers, and investors. The online version is available at http://www.forbes.com. *Forbes* provides a great deal of information on their website free, including articles and lists.

Fortune. New York: Time, Inc. Biweekly. 1930–. $20 per year.

Another of the leading business magazines, *Fortune* covers financial topics and business trends, and is known for its rankings, the most popular being the Fortune 500 list, published annually. The online version is available at http://money.cnn.com/magazines/fortune/.

Futures. Erlanger, KY: National Underwriter Co., DBA Summit Business Media. Monthly. $78 per year.

Futures provides news and information for the commodity-, futures-, options-, forex-, and stock-trading communities. Paid subscribers to *Futures* receive full access to all content on the Futuresmag.com website.

Institutional Investor. New York: Institutional Investor. Monthly. U.S. edition, 1967–. $445 per year. (Also available through LexisNexis).

This publication is recommended for large business libraries and libraries serving financial professionals. It is available online at http://www.institutional investor.com. (Current issues are available through EBSCO's Business Source Premier with a one-month embargo.)

Investor's Business Daily. Los Angeles: Investor's Business Daily, Inc. 1991–. $329 per year.

Although perhaps a notch below the *Wall Street Journal* and the *Financial Times* in renown, this daily business newspaper also offers news, business and investing tips, charts, and rankings. The online version offer tools for investors. It is available at http://www.investors.com/.

Journal of Portfolio Management. New York: Institutional Investor Journals. Quarterly. $851 per year. Print subscription provides access to online version.

This is a journal of research and theory for financial professionals. For business libraries, Institutional Investor publishes 10 additional journals for financial managers and professionals. A list of titles is available online at http://www.iijournals.com. (It is not appropriate for a general public library.)

Kiplinger's Personal Finance. Washington, DC: Kiplinger Washington Editors, Inc. Monthly. 1947–. $23.95 per year.

Kiplinger's provides advice and tips on investing and personal finance for a general audience. It is recommended for public library business collections.

Money. New York: Time, Inc. Monthly. $15 per year.

This popular magazine for a general audience includes articles on personal finance, investing, credit, banking, retirement, etc.

Pensions & Investments. New York: Crain Communications. Biweekly. 1973–. $259 per year.

This news publication is for managers of institutional assets. It is appropriate for business collections used by financial professionals.

Smart Money. New York: Dow Jones & Company. Monthly. 1992–. $26 per year. Print and online at http://www.smartmoney.com.

Smart Money is a popular magazine for investors.

Wall Street Journal. New York: Dow Jones & Company. Daily. Published since 1889. $363.48 per year in print. *Wall Street Journal* print subscribers can add the WSJ online for an additional $49 per year.

The leading financial newspaper, the *Wall Street Journal* is essential for all business and public libraries. It contains articles, tables, charts, news, world events, markets, financials, personal finance and more. It is available online at http://online.wsj.com/. There is a fee for online access. The *Wall Street Journal* is also available online through Factiva and ProQuest (recent issues and historical archive).

Wall Street Transcript. New York: Weekly. $1,890 per year.

Weekly print issues focus on transcripts of interviews with CEOs and analysts, and profile one area within an industry sector. Online access to TWST includes PDF files of articles. It is available online at http://www.twst.com/, and via Business Source Complete. TWST is appropriate for business libraries serving financial professionals and serious investors.

RECOMMENDED FREE WEBSITES FOR INVESTMENT INFORMATION

As librarians know, the Internet is a never-ending fount of information, much of it good, some very bad. For investors, the challenge is to seek out the most reliable sites among the thousands they will come across, and ignore those that push hot tips or offers to make millions. Sites that are provided by government agencies or organizations are clearly more impartial and trustworthy than commercial sites, and many industry organization websites provide valuable data for investors. Commercial websites will generally include advertising, but the information provided on the sites may be exactly what an investor needs. A brief selection of some reputable free websites is provided here:

- http://www.bankrate.com
- http://bigcharts.marketwatch.com/
- http://www.emma.msrb.org (EMMA for municipal bonds)
- http://www.federalreserve.gov/econresdata/releases/ surveysreports.htm
- http://finance.yahoo.com/

- http://www.finra.org (Financial Industry Regulatory Authority)
- http://www.investinginbonds.com
- http://www.investopedia.com (Articles, dictionary of financial terms, tutorials)
- http://www.investoreducation.org (Alliance for Investor Education)
- http://www.nasdaq.com/
- http://www.nypl.org/help/getting-oriented/financial-literacy/resources
- http://www.nyse.com
- http://www.sec.gov/edgar.shtml (SEC)
- http://www.sec.gov/investor.shtml
- http://www.smartmoney.com/
- http://www.treasurydirect.gov

SELECTED BOOKS FOR AN INVESTMENT COLLECTION

Sources listed here would be appropriate in either a reference or circulating collection, depending on the needs of the library and its users. Some recent titles are included, as are some that are considered "classics" by financial professionals. All are available in print, and some are available as e-books direct from publishers.

Barron's Finance & Investment Handbook. 7th ed. Hauppauge, NY: Barron's Educational Series, 2007.
>   This handy source for checking facts and quick reference is useful for both investors and students.

Bernstein, William. *The Four Pillars of Investing: Lessons for Building a Winning Portfolio.* New York: McGraw-Hill, 2010.
>   In this classic work for the independent investor, Bernstein explains his theory of investing and building wealth.

Bogle, John. *Common Sense on Mutual Funds: New Imperatives for the Intelligent Investor.* 10th ed., rev. New York: Wiley, 2009.
>   Bogle provides investment advice from the founder of the Vanguard family of mutual funds.

Bookstaber, Richard. *A Demon of Our Own Design: Markets, Hedge Funds, and the Perils of Financial Innovation.* Hoboken, NJ: Wiley, 2007.
>   Bookstaber gives an insider's view of the complex financial instruments that have made the markets more dangerous for investors.

Buffett, Warren. *The Essays of Warren Buffett: Lessons for Investors and Managers.* Durham, NC: Carolina Academic Press, 2008.
>   This is a collection of Buffett's letters to shareholders of Berkshire Hathaway over several decades.

Chen, James. *Essentials of Technical Analysis for Financial Markets*. Hoboken, NJ: Wiley, 2010.
This clearly written guide explains the fundamentals of technical analysis and trading.
Dictionary of Finance and Banking. 3rd ed. New York: Oxford University Press, 2005.
This updated edition covers the terms and vocabulary of global finance and investing.
Edwards, Robert D., John Magee, and W. H. C. Bassetti. *Technical Analysis of Stock Trends*. 9th ed. Boca Raton, FL: CRC Press; New York: AMACOM, American Management Association, 2007.
This is a classic work on chart analysis and technical investing.
Fabozzi, Frank J. *Bond Markets, Analysis, and Strategies*. 7th ed. Upper Saddle River, NJ: Prentice Hall, 2009.
The first edition of this work was published in 1989. This edition covers products and analytical techniques and strategies for investors and students of finance.
Ferguson, Niall. *The Ascent of Money: A Financial History of the World*. New York: Penguin Press, 2008.
This is a popular history of how financial institutions and events have influenced and transformed the world.
Fisher, Philip. *Common Stocks and Uncommon Profits*. New York: Wiley, 2003.
Originally published in 1958 and considered a classic by professional investors, this book presents fundamentals of stock and business analysis. Fisher emphasized investing in companies with the best long-term growth prospects.
Graham, Benjamin. *The Intelligent Investor: The Definitive Book on Value Investing*. Rev. ed. New York: HarperCollins, 2003.
With the preface written by Warren Buffett, this book includes commentaries by Jason Zweig. Originally written in 1949, this work on value investing has been revised and continues to appear regularly on lists of best investment books.
Graham, Benjamin, and David Dodd. *Security Analysis*. 6th edition, New York: McGraw-Hill, 2009.
Benjamin Graham, considered the father of value investing, wrote the original edition of this work in 1934. The original "classic 1934 edition" is still in print, and also available in electronic form, as is this print edition.
Homer, Sidney, and Martin Leibowitz. *Inside the Yield Book: The Classic That Created the Science of Bond Analysis*. Princeton: Bloomberg Press, 2004.
This classic work on bond analysis has been updated with revisions by Martin Leibowitz.
Isaacman, Max. *Investing with Intelligent ETFs: Strategies for Profiting from the New Breed of Securities*. New York: McGraw-Hill, 2008.
Exchange-traded funds are the new kids on the block and very popular with investors. Isaacman provides explanations and investment strategies using ETFs.

Lewis, Michael, ed. *Panic: The Story of Modern Financial Insanity*. New York: Norton, 2009.

This is a collection of articles by a variety of authors about recent market crashes, from the 1987 stock market crash up to the 2008 subprime mortgage crisis.

Lynch, Peter, and John Rothchild. *One Up on Wall Street: How to Use What You Already Know to Make Money in the Market*. New York: Simon & Schuster, 2000.

This book gives investing advice from the former manager of Fidelity's Magellan Fund.

Malkiel, Burton. *A Random Walk Down Wall Street*. 10th ed. New York: Norton, 2011.

Originally published in 1973, this book is often mentioned as a "must read" for new investors. Malkiel recommends that investors diversify and invest in index funds.

O'Neil, William J. *How to Make Money in Stocks: A Winning System in Good Times or Bad*. 4th edition. New York: McGraw-Hill, 2009.

This is a best-selling guide to investing by the founder of *Investor's Business Daily*.

Orman, Suze. *The Road to Wealth: A Comprehensive Guide to Your Money: Everything You Need to Know in Good and Bad Times*. Revised and updated. New York: Riverhead Books, 2010.

This book gives investment advice from best-selling media personality Suze Orman, a leading personal finance author. (Investment resources in a business library could include a range of books in the category of personal finance. Orman is just one example.)

Rothchild, John. *The Bear Book: Survive and Profit in Ferocious Markets*. New York: Wiley, 1998.

Rothchild focuses on protecting assets and minimizing losses during a bear market.

Siegel, Jeremy. *Stocks for the Long Run*. New York: McGraw-Hill, 2008.

Siegel provides investors and financial professionals with a long-term perspective on investing in stocks, including how stocks have performed in bad and good times.

Teweles, Richard J., and Edward S. Bradley. *The Stock Market*. 7th edition. New York: Wiley, 1998.

This popular guide has clear explanations "intended to teach students, investors, brokerage house employees and others how the stock market works and operates" (authors' intent from the preface).

Thomsett, Michael C. *The Options Trading Body of Knowledge: The Definitive Source For Information about the Options Industry*. Upper Saddle River, NJ: FT Press, 2010.

This reference work provides definitions of options terms and explains basic and complex options trading strategies.

Thomsett, Michael C. *Options Trading for the Conservative Investor: Increasing Profits Without Increasing Your Risk.* Upper Saddle River, NJ: Prentice Hall/Financial Times, 2005. (The 2010 second edition is also available.)

This book gives strategies and advice from a well-known options expert on minimizing risk and improving return with options.

CONCLUSION

The financial crisis in 2007–9 that led to the failure of large companies and financial institutions was a shock to investors and the public, with implications beyond the financial markets. The U.S. government stepped in to take over companies under the controversial Troubled Asset Relief Program, federal legislation was enacted to reform financial markets, and regulatory changes are still being debated.

In spite of high unemployment, the weak economy, and other instabilities, the economy rolls on. At times such as these, with interest rates in banks still near record lows, people continue to seek higher returns on their money by investing in stocks, bonds, mutual funds, ETFs, or alternative investments. Business librarians need to become fluent in a variety of investment resources and tools, and know what is important to acquire and what is important to watch, so they can anticipate the changing needs of their users.

6

Marketing Research

Wendy Diamond

INTRODUCTION

Due to globalization, the financial crisis, the replacement of smokestack industries with entrepreneurial start-ups, and other radical changes in the world's economy, *marketing* has a new prominence on Main Street, on Wall Street, and even on "University Quad Street." Previous editions of this book did not have a distinct chapter on marketing. However, marketing is so ubiquitous in our daily lives and so essential to commerce that it is unthinkable now to imagine a business library guidebook without a chapter devoted to marketing research sources.

As defined by the American Marketing Association's online dictionary, "Marketing is an organizational function and a set of processes for creating, communicating, and delivering value to customers and for managing customer relationships in ways that benefit the organization and its stakeholders" (American Marketing Association 2010). Marketing has always been an essential component of for-profit enterprises, but its tools are also used by nonprofit organizations, government agencies, academic institutions, and anyone else who needs to promote visibility and improve customer response rate. Marketing's breadth is expressed by "The Four P's": Promotion (communication with customers), Product (fulfilling needs and wants of customers), Pricing (exchanging with customers), and Place (distributing to customers). By understanding these four functions, librarians can better serve the information needs of their patrons.

This chapter discusses reference tools, subscription databases, and free websites for information about advertising history and planning, finding and describing customers, researching market conditions for products and services, and exporting to the global market. These are the core sources for typical reference questions encountered in an academic setting with a business curriculum, and for public libraries serving small-business people in their local communities.

READY REFERENCE

Marketing Power.com. American Marketing Association. http://www
.marketingpower.com. Free, with some restricted content.

The American Marketing Association (AMA) is the national professional
organization for academics and practitioners in the field of marketing. The
organization's web page has a catchy title, *MarketingPower.com*, and offers
career management and professional development tools and opportunities, such
as virtual workshops, conferences, podcasts, and blogs. Although some content
is restricted to members, there are useful areas accessible to the general public.

The "Resource Library" offers several core resources. The AMA Dictionary is based on Peter D. Bennett's *Dictionary of Marketing Terms*, published
in 1995 as the second edition of the AMA dictionary. The online version is
continually updated with new definitions related to e-marketing, social networking, online media, and even "obscure phrases" (American Marketing
Association 2010).

The Association regularly publishes substantive reports and papers that
may be accessible without a member's password. There is access to a varying
assortment of full-text content from AMA scholarly journals, magazines,
white papers, best practice reports, and newsletters. Some materials are spot-
lighted; all are available via a "quick search" box and a topical listing including such subjects as Advertising, Brand Management, Nonprofit Marketing,
Packaging, and Services Marketing.

The Marketing Resource Directory lists professional products and services,
such as advertising agencies, data management, market research, new product development, sales and training, and so on. However, AMA does not
post information about how the firms and consultants are selected, and thus
the listings should be regarded as paid advertisements.

In summary, *MarketingPower.com* is an authoritative resource for articles,
major reports, and general information about the marketing profession.
In libraries, its most useful feature will be the Dictionary of Terms in the
Resource Library Section.

KnowThis.com. http://www.knowthis.com/. Free.

KnowThis.com: Knowledge Source for Marketing since 1998 is a marketing
portal that is both educational and practical. It offers a free set of tutorials
on the principles of marketing. These provide fundamental information on
marketing concepts, key functions, and resources. The site highlights its
news blog, and also includes a dictionary of marketing terms, a textbook, an
article archive, a directory of associations and publications, and a searchable
listing of web resources.

KnowThis.com has good credentials as a quality resource with educational scope. The site was conceived by a professor of marketing and a business librarian, and is still edited by the former. The site has been cited in marketing textbooks and has been listed as a reference resource by many university, college, and public libraries.

KnowThis.com is well organized and easy to navigate. Although supported by advertisements, these are relatively restrained and do not interfere with the content or usability of the site.

ADVERTISING AND MEDIA PLANNING

Advertising Age Encyclopedia of Advertising. McDonough, John, and Karen Egof. New York: Fitzroy Dearborn, 2003. $595.

The *Advertising Age Encyclopedia of Advertising* addresses several areas of marketing information in a library's business reference collection. First, it is unique in its depth of historical coverage of advertising agencies, and includes company histories, notable biographies, and mergers and acquisitions. Second, it is an outstanding source for the general history of advertising: there are detailed entries on historic advertising campaigns (e.g., Burma Shave); brand development (e.g., Doritos); marketing strategy (e.g., military advertising); music and jingles; and logos. The entries cross-reference creative campaigns and effective techniques with the advertising agencies that created them. The academic study of advertising and its role in social history is well covered, with sections on children, minorities, and representations of advertising in literature, motion pictures, and television. The scope is also international, covering the nature and development of advertising in specific countries.

This excellent two-volume work was compiled from the resources of several premier advertising research collections, such as Duke University's Hartman Center (see *Ad*Access*), the Museum of Broadcast Communications, *Advertising Age* magazine, and many corporate archives. Each entry is enhanced with a bibliography of "Further Reading," which may include trade journals and scholarly articles, monographs, research papers, and websites. Although primarily textual, the set is well illustrated with numerous full-page and four-color photographs.

Ad*Access. Duke University Libraries. John W. Hartman Center for Sales, Advertising, and Marketing History. http://library.duke.edu/digital collections/adaccess/. Free.

Ad*Access is a digital collection of several thousand images of American and Canadian advertisements from the years 1911 through 1955. Its content is limited to five product categories—Beauty and Hygiene, Radio, Television, Transportation, and World War II propaganda—because these are subjects of typical research interest. The images are a resource for social historians, graphic designers, advertising professionals, and students. Comprised of the "Competitive Advertisements Collection" from the archives of J. Walter Thompson, this "clipping collection" was used by their staff to research the work of competing agencies. The website contains only a small portion of the entire Hartman repository.

Encyclopedia of Major Marketing Campaigns. Volume 2. Gale Cengage Learning, 2007. http://www.cengage.com/us/. $429; for e-book pricing information, contact the publisher.

This work describes nearly 500 memorable, creative, and socially significant advertising campaigns from the period 1999 to 2005. It examines ads that appeared in print, radio, and television, and on billboards and the Internet. Designated as Volume 2, this publication updates the previous edition of the same title and complements other advertising history sources.

Advertising Red Books. Biannual with supplements. New Providence, NJ: LexisNexis Group. http://www.redbooks.com. Print $2,499/year; online $1,499/year and up.

The *Advertising Red Books* have been published for over 100 years as a directory of advertising agencies and the companies that use their services. The two distinct files, the Agency database (*Agency Red Book*) and the Advertiser database (*Advertiser Red Book*), can be purchased separately in either print or online format. However, they are most useful when purchased together in order to take advantage of the cross-referencing and indexes that link companies and their ad agencies.

In the *Agency Red Book*, the data elements include annual billings with a breakdown by media, new accounts, industry specialization, and names of key personnel on both the creative and business side. In professional settings, the agency information is used for sales prospecting, networking, and competitor analysis. In libraries, that information is valuable for students and other job seekers looking for positions in advertising, public relations, media, and sales promotion. The company listings in the *Advertiser Red Book* are useful for research projects related to the advertising activities of competitors. The listings include a succinct description of the company, their agency and account executive names, ownership structure, major industry including Standard Industrial Classification (SIC) and North American Industry Classification System (NAICS) codes classifications, company size, headquarters location, sales totals, brand ownership, and current news. Of particular interest to media buyers, entries include the month the company sets its advertising budget.

The combined *Advertising Red Books* database consists of 15,000 U.S. and international agency profiles, more than 20,000 global companies, and 125,000 brand names. The print edition is issued twice a year with quarterly updates, with indexes by geography, special markets, personnel, and agency responsibilities. The online version is updated twice a week and offers more features and information than the print version. For example, agency and advertiser profiles contain recent news from LexisNexis. The publisher ensures the accuracy, completeness, and currency of the data with a rigorous strategy including numerous routines for "data mining" of public company documents, the Internet, trade publications, and news sources.

SRDS Media Solutions. Des Plaines, IL. http://srds.com. For pricing information, contact the publisher.

As the authoritative provider of media-planning information, *SRDS Media Solutions* describes and categorizes over 100,000 advertising sources. The suite of SRDS databases covers magazines, trade journals, newspapers, television, radio, websites, outdoor advertising, and direct-marketing lists. Each source is classified into SRDS's proprietary system, enabling media planners and ad agencies to create campaigns targeted to the desired audience.

With the growth of web advertising, SRDS has integrated print sources with their companion online versions. In *Consumer Media Source*, magazines and their related websites are classified into 80 lifestyle categories; *Business Media Source* offers 190 industry categories. The listings for print sources provide the essential information needed by media buyers, including advertising rates, specifications, special issues, publication schedules, and circulation figures. Because pricing for broadcast and interactive media is negotiable and variable, SRDS does not publish rates for television, radio, and websites. However, audited audience metrics are included (if available). In *TV & Cable Source* and *Radio Advertising Source*, there are useful rankings of Direct Market Areas and Metro Markets respectively.

Individual titles from SRDS's suite of databases may be purchased separately or as a package. Most of the SRDS suite is available only online, though print editions are still published for *Consumer Media* and *Business Media*. The database is searchable by title, keyword, and lifestyle or industry category. Results can be imported into documents and spreadsheets. The SRDS site also has a link to a Media Planning and Buying Calculators guide, available to nonsubscribers.

Media Market Guide (Local Edition). SQAD Inc. http://www.sqad.com/products/#media-market. $995/year; $297/single issue.

Media Market Guide (MMG) is a printed desktop reference of advertising cost projections for nationwide television, radio, magazines, and newspapers. SQAD is known for producing accurate rate forecasts for media buyers and ad agencies; its real-time transactional services are used throughout the industry. In libraries, it is a source for TV and radio advertising rates, though cable television is not covered in the print volume. It is useful for students who are studying "media math" and for business planners who are estimating an advertising budget. MMG serves as an adjunct to the descriptive listings in *SRDS Media Solutions*.

SQAD's information is generated by direct polling of advertisers, and estimates are based on three years of tracking data. For TV rates, MMG's Local Edition provides two listings. The first identifies the best geographic market for targeting a desired demographic group (e.g., Adults 18–34). Ranked tables of direct market areas (DMAs) give the cost-per-point (CPP) values for 19 demographic categories, and are sorted by "dayparts" (e.g., primetime, drive-time, early morning). The second table enables marketers to estimate the cost of TV advertising for a specific local area. It is an alphabetic listing of DMAs with cost estimates for dayparts and demographics. Similarly, radio rates are offered for metro markets and given for 26 demographic categories.

MMG is a professional source and it uses industry terminology and calculations, with some explanation. The tables are easy to use and clear. Published quarterly, individual issues of *Media Market Guide-Local Edition* are available, and library pricing is offered.

DEMOGRAPHICS AND GEOGRAPHIC SOURCES FOR TARGET MARKETING

As society responds to a restructured economy, there is renewed enthusiasm for small business, niche marketing, and entrepreneurship. In order to grow and prosper, businesses need to understand their customer base, both existing and potential. Marketers need information for customer analysis, market potential evaluation, retail site selection, price setting, advertising planning, and inventory decisions. As the need for demographic, geographic, and lifestyle information has grown, so has the number of sources for defining and locating the customer.

In a process known as "target market identification," business researchers use "income, demographic, and life style [*sic*] characteristics of a market and census information for small areas to identify the most favorable locations" (American Marketing Association 2010). Primary data from the U.S. Census is the foundation of demographic information on such population characteristics as gender, age, income, marital status, race, ethnicity, language, education, occupation, and housing. In its *Consumer Expenditure Survey* and *American Time Use Survey* (http://www.bls.gov/tus), the Bureau of Labor Statistics (BLS) publishes information about how Americans spend their money and use their time. These data are available on the web, and are utilized by every commercial publisher and market research firm as a benchmark for their proprietary research.

Most marketers desire the narrowest geographic level possible. ZIP-code-level data are routinely available and represent towns and communities. Sometimes even that is too broad for decisions at the neighborhood level, so ideally smaller Census Tract and Block data are available.

These fundamental studies are most useful when augmented with "lifestyle" and "psychographic" factors. Both terms refer to the "activities, interests, and opinions that shape consumer behavior" (American Marketing Association 2010). These elements include hobbies, personal interests, professional status, life stage, ethnicity, media choices, and social identification. Experian Simmons is one of the major providers of lifestyle data associated with buying habits, based on its *National Consumer Study* and other market research.

Customer segmentation systems give even more specificity to demographic and geographic variables. Markets are subdivided into "distinct subsets of customers that behave in the same way or have similar needs . . ." (American Marketing Association 2010.) The market could be a ZIP code, census district, or DMA (direct market area served by a unified broadcast signal). These intricate and expensive segmentation systems, once available only to nationwide firms, are valuable for decisions about product inventory, site selection, retail placement, and media buying at the neighborhood level. Segment categories are precise because of specific references to brand names, TV shows, magazine titles, car models, and other aspects of consumer and popular culture. Increasingly, library sources incorporate expert-level customer segmentation systems such as "PRIZM" from Neilsen Claritas (a worldwide leader in consumer measurement) and "Tapestry" from ESRI (the premier commercial publisher of geographic information systems [GIS] software).

Increasingly, databases offer mapping tools along with tabular reporting functions. Because demographics and geography are intrinsically linked, maps are an ideal way to display complex information so that it can be understood and synthesized. Labeled and colored maps greatly enhance the quality and readability of presentations for business plans, school reports, and bank-loan requests. Geographic information systems (GIS) software is well integrated in several library databases

American FactFinder. U.S. Census Bureau. http://factfinder.census.gov. Free.

The *American FactFinder* (AFF) web page disseminates a vast amount of demographic information collected by the U.S. Census Bureau, the baseline for all research related to target marketing. Within AFF, the Fact Sheet section is the essential starting point for local-level projects defined by city, town, county, or ZIP code. Fact Sheets incorporate results from both the decennial census, conducted every 10 years, and the American Community Survey (ACS), which is conducted on a five-year cycle. The ACS provides an average of population characteristics during the time period. By using sampling techniques, the ACS serves the needs of local planners for current information, even for small areas and population subgroups.

Narrative Profiles are linked to the ACS section of the Fact Sheet, providing an excellent adjunct for novice marketers, journalists, and grant writers. These textual summaries interpret the statistical tables in plain language with graphs and bar charts.

Census data are meticulously structured with specialized geographic and social terminology, and the AFF website also provides tools and explanatory resources for the general public. In addition to the Fact Sheets, AFF also links to other census products on business, industry, and government. Social science and economics researchers who wish to identify correlations between variables can use public-use micro-data samples (PUMS) or the census's extraction tool called DataFerret, available at http://dataferrett.census.gov.

Consumer Expenditure Survey. U.S. Bureau of Labor Statistics. http://www.bls.gov/cex/. Free.

The *Consumer Expenditure Survey* (CE) is an ongoing study of consumer buying patterns administered by the Census Bureau for the Bureau of Labor Statistics (BLS). Originally designed to benchmark the cost of the Consumer Price Index's "market basket of goods," it is the baseline data for the buying habits aspect of lifestyle, psychographic, customer segmentation, and geo-demographic information.

The CE survey provides detailed information on the real-world purchases and income of Americans. The data are published in annual tables sorted by various demographic characteristics. It covers routine items (e.g., food, toiletries, and alcoholic beverages), as well as large-scale installment purchases, such as vehicles, health care, vacations, and housing. There are tables for high-income brackets, singles, and Hispanic consumers.

The Survey uses the unique term "consumer unit," which can consist of a family, a person living alone, or shared households. The CE geography is regional, defined as Northeast, Midwest, South, or West. Additionally, totals for the national level and for Metropolitan Statistical Areas (MSAs) are published. Neither state nor local-level data are calculated but are available from public-use micro-data samples (PUMS).

American Time Use Survey. U.S. Bureau of Labor Statistics. http://www.bls.gov/tus. Free.

The *American Time Use Survey* (ATUS) tracks the amount of time individuals spend doing various activities, such as work, child care, volunteering, and socializing. Like the *Consumer Expenditure Survey*, its original impetus is economic, and the study was created to measure the value of unpaid work (including housework) and labor productivity. In addition, it has been used by other federal researchers and social scientists to make international comparisons about American life, and to study sleep deprivation, eating habits, geriatric well-being, and work-life balance.

The ATUS is important to target market researchers because it provides nationally comparable estimates for American lifestyles and product usage. The tables contain itemized data of "time spent in detailed primary activities" for weekdays and weekends, with percentages and by gender. There is a section of colorful bar graphs and charts on such special topics as students, leisure and sports, household activities, and older Americans. In the data files section of the website, there is an eating and health module with multiyear comparisons. Other items of special interest may be found in the "News Release" section (e.g., there is a table on "married parents' use of time").

The website is well supported by tools and documentation. In addition, in the Overview section there are links to published academic studies and journal articles that have cited ATUS data.

County Business Patterns. U.S. Census Bureau. http://www.census.gov/econ/cbp/index.html. Free.

County Business Patterns (CBP) is an annual statistical series about economic activity in small areas. Arranged according to the NAICS, it provides data on the number of establishments, number of employees, and total payroll dollars. Business planners use CBP to evaluate market potential, assess competition, manage sales territories, and plan advertising campaigns. Despite its title, data are not limited to counties. For local planning, statistics at the ZIP code and metropolitan area levels are useful. The information is presented in tabular form at the website and can be accessed from American FactFinder. In addition, downloadable files are available for time series analysis and other statistical operations.

Local Market Audience Analyst. SRDS Media Solutions. http:// www.srds.com. $695 /year and up.

The *Local Market Audience Analyst* (LMAA) is an online source for analyzing consumer markets and profiling customers. It provides demographic and lifestyle characteristics for geographic regions, utilizing powerful data from premier market research firms. It contains psychographic information on activities, purchasing patterns, and social behaviors organized into four research modules:

1. "Market Profile Reports," which provide demographic and lifestyle information on counties or DMAs
2. "Demographic Reports," which analyze by age, gender, income, and marital status
3. "Lifestyle Analysis Reports," which rank geographic areas and demographic categories according to the likelihood of participation in a behavior, hobby, or activity (e.g., gourmet wine or skiing)
4. "PRIZM Reports," which offer the proprietary segmentation system from Nielsen Claritas

The lifestyle and psychographic variables are extensive, using advanced Experian Simmons consumer behavior data. There are over 200 lifestyle designations such as "try new recipes," "go to yoga," "listen to Internet radio," and other similarly subtle attributes. In addition, the database incorporates PRIZM's extensive customer segmentation categories. This rubric categorizes DMAs according to social groups and life stages. For example, at one end of the spectrum there is Urban Uptown, which includes segments like "Young Digerati" and "Bohemian Mix;" at the other end is Rustic Living, with segments like "Golden Ponds" and "Back Country Folks." These colorful categories are expressive, and based on current sociology, popular culture, and economic conditions.

Results of searches can be printed or copied as tabular reports with maps. Despite the complexity of the data themselves, each module is well organized, using a step-by-step design that presents clear options. Importantly, the LMAA database features prominent instructions and help screens. At the overview level, there are "Info" icons and video tutorials that adequately explain how to create reports and interpret data.

Business Decision. CIVIC Technologies, Inc. http://businessdecision.info. $2,500 and up; listed prices are available.

Business Decision provides a demographic and lifestyles database with map and report functions for public libraries and their small and medium-size business clientele. It offers thematic graphical displays for essential marketing decisions such as identifying customers, locating retail shops, analyzing competitor locations, and designing media campaigns. The content is derived from the Census Bureau, other authoritative government agencies, and ESRI's Tapestry segmentation system. Data are regularly updated with current-year estimates.

Business Decision enables users to examine the marketing potential of specific geographic locations, including ZIP codes, DMAs, census tracts, and congressional districts. These options provide excellent neighborhood-level coverage. It is also possible to generate maps and reports that cross several standard geographic boundaries. Some examples include "ring studies" with business location information in concentric circles; "drive-time" studies, which measure distance by the time it takes customers to arrive; and "hand-drawn" shapes, which are useful for defining sales territories, service areas, or broadcast zones.

Business Decision offers the data elements and features of more sophisticated systems, yet it is especially easy to use for novices and onetime users. There is a selection guide indicating which map or report is most appropriate for a variety of business situations. Maps are generated by the software according to variables that the user selects in a familiar web interface. The standard subscription includes remote access for unlimited simultaneous users, and authenticated library patrons can create web-based reports and maps from any desktop. Subscriptions are affordably structured to meet the needs of public and small academic libraries.

SimplyMap. Geographic Research Inc. http://geographicresearch.com/simplymap. $7,195; small school and public library discounts are available.

Simply Map is an important web-based mapping and reporting application with a rich collection of local-level data sets. Its key value derives from the combination of an innovative interface and its data partnerships with high-level providers such as MediaMark, D&B, Nielsen, and Experian Simmons. *SimplyMap* offers extensive demographic variables from government sources such as the census and Bureau of Labor Statistics, plus additional material on business locations and media market profiles not typically found in other sources. Data can be retrieved for Tract and Block Groups, as well as for ZIP codes, counties, and states. The database provides an exceptional depth of information at the neighborhood level.

SimplyMap enables the novice or nonprofessional user to create complex and sophisticated maps and reports. The GIS-based interface is easy to learn, and maps can readily be exported to Word, PowerPoint, and websites. The software has tools for customizing reports, creating bar charts, and rankings.

New Strategist Publications. Ithaca, New York. Print and online reference books. http://www.newstrategist.com. For pricing information, contact the publisher.

New Strategist publishes several series of reference books that organize and synthesize vast quantities of statistics on demographics, buyer behavior, consumer spending, and time use in an attractive, easy-to-use format. Gathered from government agencies and some proprietary sources, the books answer such marketing questions as "who is buying?"; "what do they buy?"; "how much do they spend?"; "who makes up the population?" Published annually, the books present regional and national data. Their key strength is the presentation; each chart or table is displayed on its own page, accompanied by a succinct narrative and source notes.

The Consumer Series consists of 10 titles, including *American Attitudes*, *American Marketplace*, and *American Time Use*, which provide demographic, spending, and lifestyle data. The Who's Buying Series comprises 14 volumes with titles like Apparel, At Restaurants, By Age, and others. Derived from the Consumer Expenditure Survey, these volumes give detail on age, income, race, and marital status.

In addition to the print editions, New Strategist makes the content available electronically for PDF downloading or exporting to a spreadsheet. Multiuser subscriptions are offered, or users can access just a portion of the data on a pay-as-you-go basis.

MARKET RESEARCH REPORTS

Market research reports are prized for their comprehensive coverage, specificity, quantitative data, and succinct analytic narrative. Large amounts of current information from published secondary sources are synthesized with expert primary data. The best reports give context to marketing trends—customer demographics, purchasing patterns, media correlations, and market share—by incorporating elements of industry analysis such as economics, technological impacts, and regulatory trends.

Once available only to the corporate sector, market research reports ("MRRs") are now common in college and university libraries. Publishers offer versions of their databases for the academic market to support curricula in entrepreneurship and strategic marketing. Data and currency are valuable commodities, so MRRs remain an expensive component of the subscription budget. Unfortunately, although there is an equivalent interest in entrepreneurship and business planning in society at large, most market research report publishers do not offer versions for public libraries.

Some libraries might consider it effective to rely on the documents labeled as "market research" in *ABI/INFORM* and *Business Source*. *ABI/INFORM* (ProQuest) has some international reports, and also *First Research Industry Profiles* for the U.S. market. Intended to help sales and marketing teams understand the industry climate, these reports examine finance, regulations, sales, business challenges, and opportunities. *First Research* reports are about 10–12 pages long and updated quarterly. Similarly, *Business Source* (EBSCO) offers Datamonitor's industry reports. The *MarketWatch* series is a monthly service of industry news and opinion, but is not detailed market research. The lengthier reports in the *Industry Profile* series consist mostly of charts and tables geared to the investor or industry analyst, rather than to the small-business person or marketing manager. In both *ABI* and *Business Source*, these reports are listed by industry and by title as "featured content" or under special tabs, respectively. They are also retrievable with keywords. However, these alternatives may not be adequate to address the growing needs of entrepreneurship and strategic marketing programs. Thus, most academic libraries will consider such resources as *IBISWorld*, *Mintel Oxygen*, or *MarketResearch.com Academic*.

IBISWorld. http://www.ibisworld.com. $8,000/ per year and up.

IBISWorld is a good source for market research and industry analysis. The reports are lengthy, use a clear narrative style with many statistical tables and charts, and are updated on a predictable schedule. All reports share a standardized format so that readers can easily compare industries. *IBISWorld* covers performance and outlook, industry life cycle, products and markets, competitive landscape, and operating conditions. However, the reports include mostly aggregated discussion of consumer demographics and do not include psychographics or segmentation.

IBISWorld systematically analyzes more than 750 industry sectors across the whole spectrum of the economy. This breadth of coverage is invaluable in settings where students' business plans and marketing papers are driven by innovation, green business, or the latest extreme sports craze. With coverage of such topics as "party rentals," "wind power," or "swimming pool construction," *IBISWorld* fills a gap in available literature.

The database uses the NAICS codes as its primary navigational structure (searching by keywords and SIC Code numbers is also possible). The "drill-down" format makes the code system easy to understand, and thus supports business research skills. *IBISWorld* also offers an international option that includes China. Although other countries do not have individualized reports, the *Global Industry Research* series covers worldwide conditions, highlighting relevant countries and major companies.

Mintel Oxygen Academic. Mintel. http://www.mintel.com. For pricing information, contact the publisher.

Mintel is a top-tier producer of original market intelligence on consumer trends in household products, personal care, food and drink, financial services, media, retail, leisure, and electronics. The quality is unquestionable and the reports are substantive and detailed. Name-brand international corporations consult *Mintel* for marketing strategy and new product introductions because their insightful analysis is derived from a rigorous research methodology. However, *Mintel's* coverage of neighborhood-level enterprises (e.g., beauty care, lawn services, and coffeehouses) is limited.

Mintel Oxygen is a rich resource for target marketing and customer profiling. Its "Lifestyle" portfolio examines specific customer segments with reports covering such topics as "marketing to millennials," "senior purchasing decisions," and "green marketing." Reports integrate Experian Simmons data such as the Mosaic segmentation system and the National Consumer Study.

Mintel reports are easy to understand, with extensive but concise narrative, and are replete with attractive graphics and quantitative data. *Mintel's* primary search interface is a browsable list of categories, supported by a powerful "quick search" box.

MarketResearch.com Academic. http://www.academic.marketresearch.com. Subscription database. For pricing information, contact the publisher.

MarketResearch.com Academic (MRDC) is a premier source and the oldest market research service for academic libraries. Covering both major industries and niche markets, it aggregates reports from world-class researchers, including Packaged Facts (consumer goods), Kalorama Information (health sciences), Simba (media), and SBI (energy). Significantly, MRDC supports "green" curricula with extensive reports on sustainable technologies and renewable energy.

Full reports from MRDC are the most extensive and specialized available to the academic market. Written for corporate analysts, a typical report can be well over 100 pages and include forecasts, channel trends, demographics, psychographics, performance and challenges, manufacturing components, technology, regulations, and competitor comparison. The reports are made available to libraries at the same time as they are released to the private market. Interestingly, the corporate price is transparent so students can understand the true cost of valuable business information. The attractive interface is arranged in topical categories like consumer goods, demographics, heavy industry, life science, technology and media, and more.

In an ideal world, academic libraries might want *IBISWorld*, *Mintel*, and *MarketResearch.com Academic* to provide coverage of the complete economy, detailed lifestyle analysis, environmental technology, and multi-publisher scope. All are models of rigorous research, cogent writing, effective graphics, useable interfaces, and complete documentation. Considering budget limitations, most libraries will have to choose based on their curriculum and clientele. If their marketing projects are in the realm of entrepreneurship and small business, then perhaps *IBISWorld* with its coverage of all NAICS codes will be preferred. If the curriculum is focused on the disciplines of branding, advertising, new products, strategic innovation, and customer segmentation, *Mintel Oxygen* may be suitable. If the library needs interdisciplinary, comprehensive coverage of green energy, technology, health care, pharmaceuticals, and international strategies, then *MarketResearch.com Academic* might be ideal.

INTERNATIONAL TRADE

Export.gov. U.S. Department of Commerce, International Trade Administration. http://export.gov. Free.

Bringing products and services to the international marketplace is a mainstream activity in today's globalized society. Exporting is complex, requiring knowledge of foreign cultures, trade data, and a specific type of market research; often these data must be gathered from unpredictable sources. Exports are good for the U.S. balance of trade and therefore for the economy, so the U.S. Department of Commerce, through the International Trade Administration, offers *Export.gov* as a portal for international marketing information. Designed to meet the information needs of marketers and small business, this free site is compiled from contributions by 19 federal agencies, including the Export-Import Bank, Small Business Administration, and Foreign Agricultural Service.

Export.gov provides links to assistance, services, and information. The "Market Research Library" (MRL) is one of the most important features. Although free, this section requires registration and is restricted to use by U.S. companies, students, and researchers. The MRL provides industry and country-specific research reports such as market updates, regional snapshots, industry overviews, development bank reports, agricultural goods markets, business opportunity announcements, and product-oriented "best market" studies. There are trade guidelines, documentation requirements, technology updates, and analyses of market demand for specific products or services. Written by U.S. government overseas staff, reports include charts, tables, and narratives.

The *Country Commercial Guides for U.S. Companies*, known as CCGs, are useful reports for almost every aspect of an international marketing project.

Unlike other items in the MRL, they do not require registration. Co-titled "Doing Business in [country]," the extensive content is organized efficiently into 10 standardized chapters. CCGs describe a country's climate for commerce, investment, political risk, and economics; reports also discuss the selling environment, best export sectors, trade regulations, financing, business travel, trade events, and more. Updated annually, the CCGs provide material that is difficult to obtain in other sources. For example, Chapter 3 on "Selling" is indispensable for its descriptions of channels of distribution, advertising, pricing, and franchising. Although not available for every country, the CCG is often the only current source of secondary information for many countries in the world.

Export.gov is also useful as a newsletter for trade announcements, a handbook on legal issues, and a guidebook about trade regulations, licensing, documentation, and standards. The site has textbook material in its "Export Basics" tutorials, and a directory with Trade Leads and contact information for embassy officials. It is a one-stop portal and an essential starting point for any type of international marketing plan or project.

CONCLUSION

Business information is highly sensitive to changes in the economy and technology. There is no doubt that the core marketing resources described here will also undergo change. Some of these titles may cease, and new sources will be introduced; some titles will transition to online-only formats; and many will be redesigned or augmented with new features or new data sets. Libraries must be prepared to meet evolving information needs. They remain the ideal working laboratory for students and small-business people to find authoritative and practical information.

REFERENCE

American Marketing Association Marketing Power. 2010. "AMA Dictionary." http://www.marketingpower.com/_layouts/Dictionary.aspx. Accessed August 21, 2010.

7

Start-Ups

Chris LeBeau

INTRODUCTION

While England may have been known to Napoleon as the nation of shop-keepers, today the United States is characterized by entrepreneurship. It has captured the nation's attention from Main Street all the way up to the nation's capital. With the recession of 2008 and a record number of corporate job losses, strategists have repeatedly said that the economy will find salvation through our entrepreneurs. According to the Ewing Marion Kauffman Foundation's Kauffman Index of Entrepreneurial Activity, 2009 had the highest level of start-ups in 14 years (Ewing Marion Kauffman Foundation). Entrepreneurs are responsible for nearly 90 percent of the new companies. According to the Small Business Administration (SBA), there are 22 million small businesses employing close to 53 percent of the private workforce and contributing 47 percent of all sales in the country. Small businesses create two out of every three new jobs. And small businesses generally have a higher level of innovation than large firms.

What is entrepreneurship? Entrepreneurship is defined by people with innovative ideas for the marketplace, willing to take a risk on developing their ideas. The risks are high. According to the SBA only 50 percent of new employer firms survive 5 years, and only 25 percent survive 15 years or longer. Many new businesses are small businesses that are independently owned and operated, and do not dominate their field of operation (U.S. Small Business Administration, Office of Advocacy 2010a).

How small is small? The SBA has established maximum sizes that define small business. Their size standards vary and are based on the North American Industry Classification (NAICS) codes because different industries have different levels of costs and revenues. So, "small" is relative to the rest of the industry and to other industries (U.S. Small Business Administration 2010b). In developing size criteria, the SBA looks at factors including "average firm size, average assets as a measure of start up costs and entry barriers, industry concentration and size distribution of firms" (U.S. Small Business Administration 2010c).

The SBA has two common maximum size categories. For manufacturing and mining the criteria are 500 employees, and for nonmanufacturing the criteria are $7 million in gross revenue. These size definitions are probably larger than many readers expect. Some argue that the size criteria are overly comprehensive. On the other hand, there are thousands of sole proprietorships with no employees making well under $50,000 per year. It is the larger "small business" that generates jobs. These are the businesses that get financing and investment (Shane 2010).

There are a number of resources that can prove useful for the multiplicity of entrepreneur and small-business needs. These business owners and developers must assemble business plans. This requires financial and market information. Business owners need to demonstrate their knowledge of the marketplace; they must know their competitors. They must have a good concept. They must have a financial plan and identify their expected revenues, cash flows, and operating expenses. Entrepreneurs may need patent and trademark information. If their product is manufactured, they must have a reliable production process. Their processes may have technological advantages that set them apart. They need to be knowledgeable about the barriers to entry and to convince investors that they can meet those successfully. Small businesses and entrepreneurs need to find suppliers and develop good supply chains and logistics. They need help with managing a business, human resource management, legal advice, accounting, and taxation issues. They need to understand the demographics of that marketplace, potential customers, and their wants and needs, lifestyles, and behaviors. In other words, they need marketing advice. Professional and trade journals are of interest, as are trade organizations, conventions, and trade shows. The needs are daunting, yet day after day, entrepreneurs dive into the oceanic marketplace, ready or not.

Many of the sources mentioned in the other chapters of the *Basic Business Library* answer some of these questions. Following are some core resources. References are made to other chapters when appropriate. It is difficult to categorize resources into neat boxes because a number of databases serve multiple needs. It is indeed unfortunate, too, that some of these resources are extremely helpful to small business and entrepreneurs, yet unavailable or carry limitations for public library purchase. Some academic resources often come with limitations for commercial use. While a list of resources is essential for a library, librarians should also become familiar with their local and state small-business development centers created to actively support small business and entrepreneurs.

GENERAL COMPREHENSIVE RESOURCES

There are several resources that provide a comprehensive mix of information, guides, how-to resources, and forms. These are good places for entrepreneurs to begin their work. Some are proprietary resources while others are free government sites.

AllBusiness. Short Hills, NJ: Dun and Bradstreet. http://www.allbusiness .com/. Free, with some content for sale.

AllBusiness covers the finer aspects of starting and operating a new business, and it does so in a very consolidated way. The Dun & Bradstreet site offers tools for the new business owner, short multimedia clips covering tips, and more than 5 million journal articles written by in-house staff and by the Gale Cengage Learning staff. While the main body of content is free, there is much for sale on the site offered through memberships. One must wind a path through the advertising of related products such as forms.

An entire section is devoted to franchises. The franchise directory lists several hundred franchise opportunities. Franchise entries give brief information, including required investment amounts, business descriptions, an all-star ranking, and the number of employees needed to operate a franchise. Entries also include a three-year growth rate based on the numbers of units, the franchise and royalty fee, the net worth and capital requirements, and franchise-sponsored financing. *AllBusiness* runs an all-star ranking of 300 listed franchises. All of this is accompanied by feature articles with tips for buying, growing, and franchising a business. The franchise directory is a particularly good addition to this well-organized site, packed with valuable content for the new business owner.

ProQuest Entrepreneurship. Ann Arbor, MI: ProQuest. http://www .proquest.com. Call company for pricing.

The audience for *ProQuest Entrepreneurship* spans the needs of the practitioner to the educator and student. This well-designed database features menus with major business concepts the average entrepreneur or small-business owner would seek. The topical approach lists sources for start-ups, management, legal issues, marketing and sales, operations, product development, and profit and financial management. Topic links connect searchers to 115 journals, 50 trade publications, working papers, conference papers—in all, a little over 400 sources are included.

The practitioner or business planner has access to forms, tips from successful business owners, and start-up toolkits and guides. The basic search screen walks searchers through topics such as product development and design, innovation, business planning issues, marketing, advertising, pricing, sales, cash flow, purchasing, and technology use. Expectedly, there is a topic heading for "start-ups." Start-up information covers idea creation, feasibility, and industry and competitor analysis. It also includes forms of ownership and franchising. Users can find business models, as well as location and planning resources. A special section is devoted to family-owned business, women-owned and minority-owned business, web-based business, and native and aboriginal business.

Market research sources round out the database. *BizMiner* is a major supplier of *ProQuest Entrepreneurship*'s market reports. Users will find *BizMiner*'s Local Market Vitality Profiles, Industry Financial Profiles, and US Market Research reports among results. New Strategist contributes some of its publications, as does *Hoover's*, which adds its In-Depth records. Freedonia, First Research, Snapshot Series, and JUST also supply industry and market research reports.

But there is even more content. The database also includes approximately 60 books such as *Business Plans That Work, Entrepreneurship for Dummies, How to Grow Your Business*, and a number of additional titles from the Dummies series. ProQuest adds some of its *Annual Report* content. Journals include titles such as: *European Journal of Innovation Management, Journal of Small Business and Enterprise Development*, and *Minority Business Entrepreneur*. The database offers the "Starting a business in . . . " series. Also included are very short video clips on topics such as business valuation, exit strategies, and promotion. These come complete with a text copy of the video. A future enhancement will be the addition of 400 business plans from the University of Texas–Austin's Business Plan Competition.

Small Business Resource Center. Farmington Hills, MI: Gale Cengage Learning. http://www.gale.cengage.com/SmallBusiness/. Call company for pricing.

This database is another all-inclusive mix of sources for the small-business owner or entrepreneur. The *Small Business Resource Center* covers all major areas of starting and operating a business, including accounting, finance, human resources, management, marketing, tax, and more. It covers nearly 190 journal and magazine titles suited to small business and some key newsletters. It also contains some of the famous Gale reference publications such as *Business Plans Handbook, Encyclopedia of Major Marketing Campaigns, Encyclopedia of Small Business*, and *Small Business Sourcebook*. Users will find more than 10 years' worth of business plans from *Business Plans Handbook*, plans for everything from bed-and-breakfast accommodations to microbreweries.

The *Small Business Sourcebook*, although included, is quite disassembled to make its contents searchable. Alone it offers a wealth of resources for the entrepreneur. By entering a type of business and limiting to this source, users will find business start-up information, the best associations and trade organizations, reference and statistical sources, the best trade journals for a line of business, trade shows and conventions, consultants, computerized databases, videos, and libraries to refer to.

The database is searchable a number of different ways, but it also is designed to suggest quick paths to needed information. In addition to business plans, there is a lengthy list of "Business Topics" including everything from handling brand image to tax planning. The "Types of Businesses" section lists several dozen commonly researched lines of business. Once one is selected, the searcher finds information organized into sections for business plans, articles, an overview of the business type, and reference directories. Another special section is labeled "How To . . . ," featuring helpful guides: "How to Start A Small Business," "How to Write a Business Plan," "How to Buy a Business," "How to Finance Your Business," "How to Grow Your Business," and "How to Locate and Expand Your Business."

The database includes some well-chosen books including titles like: *How to Incorporate: A Handbook for Entrepreneurs and Professionals, How to Start Your Own 'S' Corporation, Specialty Shop Retailing: How to Run Your Own Store, SBA Loans: A Step-by-Step Guide, The Unofficial Guide to Marketing Your Small Business*, and *Attracting Investors: A Marketing Approach to Finding Funds for Your Business*.

SBA.gov (U.S. Small Business Administration). Washington, DC: U.S. Department of Commerce. Small Business Administration. http://www.sba .gov. Free.

The Small Business Administration (SBA) was established through an act of Congress back in 1953. It has served in its capacity as an independent agency of the federal government for over half a century. There are now 10 regional offices and 70 district offices, most of which support several local offices throughout each state. The purpose of the SBA is to assist the growth of small business, which it does through loans, counseling, and other types of assistance. It provides resources that help businesses manage all facets of their operations, from start-up to the sale of a business, or even through bankruptcy. The SBA guides small business through contract procurement. It offers targeted assistance for businesses owned by women, minorities, veterans, Native Americans, young entrepreneurs, and even entrepreneurs past 50. Assistance on the website is available in 13 different languages. The SBA sponsors the Office of Small Business Development Centers, which pulls together state, local, and private resources to offer assistance in every state. SBA also sponsors the Office of Women's Business Ownership, which emphasizes the needs of economically and socially disadvantaged women business owners.

For small businesses involved in international trade, the agency provides a linked connection to *Export.gov*, a U.S. government website to assist businesses with conducting business overseas. Lastly the SBA provides help to any size businesses that have been impacted by natural disaster. The SBA offers free newsletters and publications, free online training, and free podcasts and multimedia resources.

USA National Innovation Marketplace. Washington, DC: Department of Commerce and National Institute of Standards and Technology. http://usainnovation.planeteureka.org/marketplace/usa/. Free

In 2009 Vice President Biden announced the National Innovation Marketplace, which is a service of the National Institute of Standards and Technology and an outgrowth of the Department of Commerce's Manufacturing Extension Partnership (MEP). The hope for this "marketplace" is to add new fuel to American manufacturing innovation and to provide a marketplace where the ideas of innovators might be matched with the needs of manufacturers. As technologies progress and products evolve rapidly, manufacturers and innovators need to know where the next new developments will be. Many innovators seek partners in the areas of manufacturing, research and development, distribution, licensing, or other aspects of product development.

This site uses a tool known as Merwyn, which acts as a business marketplace simulator. Innovators and inventors use Merwyn for a fee to test the market for their products. The simulator generates a four-page report that gives a product description, several scenarios of sales forecasts for a product, the development status of the product, the number of patents and protection status, the remaining time and cost to first sale, the fair market royalty projections, and an overall concept score. Companies in need of an invention may search the website to locate an invention or entrepreneur.

BUSINESS PLANS

Most entrepreneurs must write a business plan if they intend to seek financial support in the form of a bank loan, an initial public offering, or private equity funding. Business plans are generally good practice. They force an entrepreneur to organize his or her plans, crystallize his or her mission and goals, lay out a cost structure, and plan revenue streams. A business plan requires the entrepreneur to address human resource needs and costs. The entrepreneur will have to design a growth strategy and demonstrate his or her knowledge of the marketplace. Only when the plan is accomplished successfully, assuming other market conditions are optimum, will the entrepreneur secure funding. There are many sources on the web where entrepreneurs may purchase business plan software and templates. Below are some sources with free business plan templates for entrepreneurs to follow.

Bplans.com. Eugene, OR: Palo Alto Software. http://bplans.com. Free.

Palo Alto Software claims to have the largest collection of free sample business plans anywhere. They list more than 860 business plans on their website. The site's abundant materials create a complete resource for the entrepreneur. In addition to sample plans, the site has created sections for business planning, a "how-to" section for starting and growing a business, and a resource section with calculators and tools. The site also engages the user with videos, advice blogs, and attention grabbers like "common business plan mistakes." The business plans span industry many sectors— manufacturing, retail, service, wholesale, recreation, transportation, construction, real estate, and the nonprofit sector.

The business plans available through this site are extremely thorough. They are structured with a company summary, market analysis, strategy and implementation, management summary and a financial plan. Planners will find examples of how to present start-up expenses and funding, market segmentation, market needs, some simplified competitive market strategies, keys to success for the different industries and businesses, some sales strategy and forecasts, a personnel plan, breakeven analysis and projected profit and loss, and industry ratios. Appendices provide good models of financials displaying monthly data for sales, personnel, cash flow, and related expenses. Although many plans are actual business plans, users are advised not to use the data found in the plans. *Bplans.com* has expanded its offerings with marketing plans.

Bplans.com has won several awards as a valuable "plain talk" resource. The purpose of the site is to sell Palo Alto Software business-planning software, and the plans are sprinkled with ads. Although the ads may deter certain users, the well-drawn plans are worth the effort it takes to bypass the ads.

Business Plans Handbook. Farmington Hills, MI: Gale Cengage Learning. Volumes available in print and e-books; see http://www.gale.cengage.com/. Price: $299/volume for the e-book version; $212 for print. Also available as part of Gale Virtual Reference Library; see http://www.gale.cengage.com/gvrl/.

Most new business owners must create business plans in order to seek financing and support for their new business venture. This handbook series, issued in three volumes per year, offers a collection of actual business plans. Business owners or entrepreneurs can adapt these plans for their own needs. Each volume has approximately 20 business plans from the manufacturing, retail, and service industries.

A typical business plan includes a statement of purpose; an executive summary; a description of the business or business concept; some market analysis including an analysis of the competition; a description of the product or service and possibly the production process; growth strategies, risk factors, and names of those in management; and a financial statement showing expected revenues and expenses for a minimum of one year. Examples of the kinds of business plans in the series include: advertising agency, art gallery, beekeeping, computer training service business, flower shop, interior renovation, tattoo and body piercing, vending machine operation, and website designer. The online version of the *Business Plans Handbook* has additional material: a business plan template, a list of organizations, agencies and consultants, and a glossary of small-business terms. The e-book version is available through the Gale Virtual Reference Library and the *Small Business Resource Center*.

Conversely, the print version contains some material not found in the online version. This bonus material includes a listing of associations, a list of SBA Regional Offices and Small Business Development Centers, a listing of offices for the Service Corps of Retired Executives (SCORE), Venture Capital & Financing Companies, and an updated bibliography. Although some of this material is readily available on the web, it is a convenience to have it included in the resource.

Note that the *Small Business Administration* (covered above) also offers sample business plans and advice on writing them.

PROFESSIONAL ORGANIZATIONS AND TRADE SHOWS

There are a number of organizations available to assist the entrepreneur. Among these organizations are trade associations, which offer a wealth of advice, training, support, and data to support the new business owner's efforts. Some sources are print, some are online, and some are actual organizations entrepreneurs would want to contact.

Edward Lowe Foundation. Cassopolis, MI. http://www.edwardlowe.org/index.elf. Free.

This private foundation essentially owes its existence to Kitty Litter and the entrepreneurial skill of founder Edward Lowe of Cassopolis, Michigan. The foundation supports second-stage entrepreneurism, using a strategy of "economic gardening." This approach creates the right environment for the company to thrive. Second-stage companies have survived the start-up period, but are not yet considered to be mature companies in the growth cycle. The foundation defines second-stage companies as having between $750,000 and $50 million in revenues and between 10 and 99 employees. Rather than serve as a grant-making vehicle, the foundation conducts its work by developing programs to meet the needs of entrepreneurs, particularly through peer support programs and collaborations with the nonprofit and public sectors. Program support is wide ranging and encompasses management, finance, human resources, marketing, law, technology, and operations. The website also provides some good online resources including essentials like the key indicators of financial health, inventory control techniques, and tips on delegating authority.

Entrepreneurship.org. Kansas City, MO: Ewing Marion Kauffman Foundation. http://www.entrepreneurship.org/. Free.

The Kauffman Foundation has long been involved in entrepreneurship. The Foundation has a tradition of collaboration with government entities. In the past, it has collaborated with the SBA. Now it is partnering with the U.S. Commerce Department's International Trade Administration to promote best practices in entrepreneurial leadership to advance economic growth on a global scale. The partnership plans to create ways for entrepreneurship to thrive in all nations, and to show people the way toward operating businesses, creating wealth, and employing people.

The major part of the website is the Global Content Repository, which offers advice, tips, and stories on the major business functions: accounting and finance, human resources, sales and marketing, products and services, and operations. The site features videos and podcasts from government officials, authors, business leaders like Mark Zuckerberg, and other experts talking on topics ranging from angel investors to innovation. The site also tracks conferences and events of interest to the entrepreneur. One unique feature of this site is the space devoted to public policy and its impact on business. Another section is devoted to legal aspects including a list of universities that offer legal clinics to help entrepreneurs. Other topical sections of the website cover community economic development, sustainability, women entrepreneurs, and social entrepreneurship.

National Trade and Professional Associations of the United States. Washington, DC: Columbia Books. Price: $299.

This book lists nearly 8,000 trade organizations and associations, giving contact information, convention and trade shows information for future planning purposes, association budget figures, training and certification information, names of key executives, and other details about the organizations.

Service Corps of Retired Executives (SCORE). http://www.score.org/. Free.

SCORE started its work of mentoring and counseling small-business owners and entrepreneurs back in 1964. The organization offers workshops, seminars, and one-on-one counseling on a variety of topics such as business formation, financing, management, and operations. The SCORE website offers tools and tips, business-planning templates, sample cash flow statements and sales forecast sheets, financial tools, business assessments, podcasts on marketing, estimating expenses, and much more. SCORE assists as many as 20,000 businesses annually and has a good track record assisting women- and minority-owned businesses. Entrepreneurs can find SCORE in 350 offices nationwide.

U.S. Sourcelink. Kansas City, MO: Small Business Administration, Kauffman Foundation of Entrepreneurship, and the University of Missouri–Kansas City School of Management. Free.

U.S. Sourcelink grew out of a service known as *KCSourcelink* in Kansas City, Missouri. The KCSourcelink began as a collaboration between the Ewing Marion Kauffman Foundation (Kansas City), the Small Business Administration, and the University of Missouri–Kansas City Henry W. Bloch School of Management. Founders observed a multitude of nonprofit resources in the region ready to help entrepreneurs. An organization was needed to bring entrepreneurs and resources together.

Since its inception in 2003, *KCSourcelink* has matured into a groundbreaking and successful resource for entrepreneurs. The service is a network of 140 nonprofit services and organizations available to help the start-up business owner. The success of *KCSourcelink* led to the growth of other city and state "source links," under the umbrella of the national *U.S. Sourcelink*. *KCSourcelink* is being replicated around the country. There is a *Missouri Sourcelink*, *Alaska Sourcelink*, *Arkansas Sourcelink*, *St. Louis Sourcelink*, and *Tulsa Sourcelink*, and the model is being replicated in Europe.

People seeking assistance fill out a short questionnaire, which asks for the business location, business stage, industry, minority or female ownership, stage of the business plan, and the sort of assistance the person needs. The types of assistance available cover 22 possible selections including business planning, economic and property development, financial resources, freight and distribution, human resources, import and export assistance, legal assistance, libraries and research, management and training, manufacturing and high tech, marketing, product development, tax service, and more. There is advice for the entrepreneur on topics such as protecting intellectual property, developing a business plan, hiring employees, insurance, and applying for grants and loans. The regional organizations also advertise local business classes that help entrepreneurs learn about networking, marketing, managing, business credit, and raising capital. In addition, one can get information about local business incubators. This is an essential resource for economic growth in the region.

VENTURE CAPITAL, PRIVATE EQUITY FUND SOURCES, AND VALUATION

Many entrepreneurs go in search of venture capital to finance their commercial ideas because they cannot secure traditional bank financing, or at least not enough of it. Nor can they obtain financing through public offerings, and in some cases this may not be desirable. There are several resources that list venture capital and private equity funding sources. Firms willing to provide funding often are interested in funding only at certain stages in the product development cycle or business's life cycle. There are a number of stages for which a private equity firm may choose to involve itself. The stages are: seed financing, research and development, start-up, first stage (just beyond start-up), second stage (working capital), third stage (mezzanine or expansion), bridge financing, balanced, acquisition financing, management buyouts, leveraged buyouts, industry rollups, late stage, recapitalization, fund of funds, generalist, and turnaround. According to *Pratt's Guide to Private Equity and Venture Capital Sources*, businesses seeking venture capital funding have only a "15% change of being seriously considered seriously for investment" and about a "three percent chance is securing funding" ("Characteristics of a Successful Entrepreneurial Management Team" 2008, 17).

The following sources are useful for both the seekers of funding and funders for new business ventures. There are several sources a library might wish to consider. Some resources are not practical for library subscription; however, librarians may wish to know about resources to which they can refer patrons.

The most common type of information found in these sources is a listing of firms, including description of both private equity firms and venture capital firms. These resources typically give the total amount a funding source has committed to a project. Harder to find are the specifics of the funding deal. Deal details users want are not only the cash amounts of the deal, but the percentages of ownership and exit details.

The Directory of Venture Capital & Private Equity Firms. Amenia, NY: Grey House Publishing. http://www.greyhouse.com/. Call company for pricing.

Grey House has supplied libraries for several decades with quality reference titles. The publisher has taken its titles online with its GOLD product, Grey House OnLine Databases. One title of interest to entrepreneurs is the *Directory of Venture Capital & Private Equity Firms,* which lists 2,300 venture capital firms. Entries provide contact information, names and information about the managing partners, average and minimum investments, investment criteria and funding stages (i.e., seed, start-up, first stage, buyout), the fund size, geographic preference, industries in which the fund invests, and a list of the fund's portfolio of companies. Searches can be structured by keyword, organization name, domestic or international fund, city, state, country, ZIP code, and area code.

Dow Jones VentureSource. New York: Dow Jones. http://www.venture source.com. Call company for pricing.

Many entrepreneurs rely on venture capital for various stages of funding. *VentureSource* is a resource that pulls together 30,000 venture-backed companies and 8,000 private capital firms from the United States, Europe, Israel, and China. Entrepreneurs can use this database to find and research investors. *VentureSource* gives aggregate funding and funding stage details. It is possible to evaluate which industries receive the most funding. The resource can also be used for investment benchmarking. Company records give details about the executives and board members, the target markets of the fund or private equity firm, the region in which they operate, their products and financial status, the funding stages offered, a record of financing, past investments, types, and dates. The source can be used not only to identify funding but also for competitive intelligence purposes.

Pratt's Guide to Private Equity and Venture Capital Sources. Toll, David. New York: Thomson Reuters. 2010. Price: $995.

Pratt's Guide has been around since 1984 serving as a reliable source of private equity funding. The resource covers nearly 20,000 privately-owned firms, small-business investment companies (SBICs), and public and private company subsidiaries. Entries for funding sources provide the address of the main office and branch locations, names of the management staff, the type of firm and its association memberships, its project preferences, the type of financing preferred, the size of investments the firm will consider, the firm's geographic preferences, its industry focus for funding, and the year founded. Entries also indicate the spread of allocation support with percentages invested in different areas. The resource lists predominantly U.S. firms, but is not restricted to the

United States. The print version of *Pratt's Guide* has several helpful chapters written for the funding seeker. There is a chapter explaining private equity, a chapter on financing "high technology," and a chapter on choosing a venture capital firm, approaching the firm, and how to structure financing. Another chapter includes other sources of possible financing such as corporate investors and bank financing. ThomsonOne.com features an online version of this resource, the Private Equity module, which is much more extensive.

Pratt's Stats. Portland, OR: Business Valuation Resources, LLC. http://www.bvresources.com/. Price: Call company for subscription pricing; also individual pay-per-view option (pay-per-view Pratt's Stats $219; pay-per-view BizComps $129; pay-per-view Public Stats $129).

This database is a place where entrepreneurs can find private transaction data for sales of privately and closely held companies. This kind of data is commonly referred to as "comps" or comparables and market data. The database collects information on up to 88 data points (valuation multiples and financial ratios) for the financial and transactional details of the sale of a business, which help an investor calculate the financial value and fair price. Searches are relatively easy to conduct by the novice. Data are sourced from a number of "intermediaries" as well as from SEC filings.

Business Valuation Resources offers two similar products, Bizcomps and Public Stats. The first gives transaction data for very small "main street" companies, and the latter gives sales transaction data for public company sales transactions.

Valuation & Deal Term Database. Shreveport, LA: VC Experts Inc. http://vcexperts.com/vce/.Price: $125/user/month or $995/user/year; the *Encyclopedia*: $59/user/month; for academic institutions: $5,000/year for five logins, includes complimentary access to the *Encyclopedia*.

VC Experts is a major provider of commentary, data, and analytics for those entrepreneurs and investors in private equity and venture capital circles. This resource gives valuation and deal term data on thousands of privately held U.S. companies. Entrepreneurs can identify funding sources that suits their needs, and investors and entrepreneurs alike can use this information to negotiate better valuations, deal terms, and exit strategies.

The resource has three parts. The *Valuation and Deal Term* database details more than 2,800 privately held U.S. companies. Unlike other similar resources, this database includes analysis of 13 individual deal terms on more than 3,700 private financing transactions, with comparisons to national and regional averages. Also featured are postmoney valuation estimates on more than 2,000 private financing transactions. "Postmoney" is a term referring to the situation or number of shares after a deal is made. Search criteria include company name, industry, region, financing round, investor, and individual deal term. Valuations and deal terms come from the offices of secretaries of state. There is also a Portfolio Company Analysis tool to model financing and payouts. The third part is *The Encyclopedia of Private Equity & Venture Capital*, covering all aspects of raising and investing money in these ventures with expert commentary. The database may be purchased with or without the *Encyclopedia*.

Venture Deal. Menlo Park, CA: Venture Deal. http://www.venturedeal .com/. Price: $25/month.

This is a low-priced way for investors and entrepreneurs to follow the funding and trends in the venture capital markets. *Venture Deal* maintains a database of deals of start-up companies, venture capital firms, and company financings, dating back to 2003. Information is updated on a daily basis. Funding range, venture capital, private equity, angel groups, corporate lenders, hedge fund, and public market investors all can be identified with this resource. Areas for funding include everything from agriculture to banking to technology. Searches can be tailored to the major regions of the country. One of the most common search modes is "transaction type." In this search mode, searches may be run for technology companies, venture investors, transactions, and executives. In venture capital jargon a "series" is a funding round of which there are a number of levels. *Venture Deal* offers search criteria for Series A–F funding rounds, IPOs, and an "undisclosed" category.

A venture investor detailed record includes the focus area of the deal, and brief information about the investors. Records also include the activity level of the investor company, which is the number of deals currently in progress. Records include a transaction history displaying the recipients of funding and the amounts. This is valuable information for the funding seeker and for a competitor as well.

INDUSTRY AND MARKET ANALYSIS, AND DEMOGRAPHICS

Knowledgeable entrepreneurs will need to research the industry and marketplace for their start-up businesses. They need to understand how their industry operates, average benchmarks, market and product segmentation, product lifestyles, key success factors, competitive environment, best uses of technology, best practices, and a host of other information. They also need to understand the consumer of the product and how consumer behavior may impact their success. The following resources assist entrepreneurs with all of these questions.

BizMiner. Camp Hill, PA: The Brandow Company. http://www.bizminer .com/. Price: $1,000 and up; Academic Standard and Academic Premium plans are offered. Public libraries may also subscribe; $.01-$.02/covered person, or librarians can refer patrons to BizMiner directly from which they can purchase individual reports for a reasonable price, most for under $100. Commercial subscriptions begin at $995 for one user.

BizMiner is a unique resource for industry research and planning needs. BizMiner's industry-reporting series offers detailed business trend reports on the local, state, and national levels for a wide array of industries. The product has two major series of reports—Industry Financial Analysis and Industry Market Analysis—organized by the North American Industry Classification System (NAICS) or the Standard Industrial Classification (SIC) system. A unique aspect of Bizminer is the industry and market data specific to start-ups, sole proprietorships, and small business. Entrepreneurs have ample data to evaluate the market for their product or service as well as benchmarks for operating their businesses.

The first series of industry financial reports aggregates financials, ratios, and cash flows for 5,500 lines of business. Financial tables include items such as average annual revenues and income, home office expense, rent, advertising expense, average salary, wages, and benefits. One other industry series is the Micro Firm Profit & Loss Profiles, which cover 4,000 lines of business.

BizMiner's Industry Market Analysis series includes industry-specific metrics and market-specific start-up and small-business operational data for more than 6,500 lines of business in 300 U.S., state, and metro areas. Research is not confined to small businesses; very large sales classes are included as well. The market reports include industry market volume, market share for all sales classes, average annual company sales, employment levels, sales per employee, failure rates, and entrepreneurial activity rates. Failure rates, in particular, are of interest to entrepreneurs.

The market analysis also features micro market industry reports with data from counties and ZIP codes for more than 1,000 industries. One other useful report is the Competitive Market Analyzer, enabling users to compare 6,000 lines of business in state, metro, county and ZIP code market areas. Market reports cover competitive indicators, market volume, and growth projections. Like the financial and market research reports, the Competitive Market Analyzer narrative is exportable into business planning, market research, and other strategic documents. Like BizMiner's financial series, the Analyzer offers input tools to customize individual firms' benchmarks within the narrative analysis.

All data can be downloaded into reports in PDF, HTML, or CSV formats.

First Research Industry Profiles. New York, NY: Dun & Bradstreet. http://www.dnblearn.com/index.php?page=hoover-s-first-research. Call company for pricing. There are a variety of subscription options including à la carte pay-per-view.

First Research is a resource with 900 industry profiles. It was acquired by Dun & Bradstreet in 2007. *First Research* profiles serve the varied needs of the researcher, the business planner, and the business marketer. The reports facilitate market analysis with industry overviews. The report sections include: the competitive landscape, the products, operations and technology, sales and marketing, finance and regulation, human resources, industry indicators, and industry update. Industry challenges, trends, and opportunities are also covered. The section on executive talking points raises a number of valuable questions that new business owners should consider. Reports end with an opportunity ranking, a list of industry acronyms, and a list of valuable free industry websites. If small businesses constitute a large part of an industry, data for small business will be displayed apart from the overall aggregate industry data.

Reports draw data from third-party providers: valuation multiples, which are used in business valuations for acquisitions, are provided from Business Valuation Resources. Fintel supplies the benchmarking financial ratios for private companies. Inforum provides industry forecasts.

First Research reports appear in ProQuest's *ABI/INFORM* and in *MarketResearch.com*. *First Research* can also be linked to D&B's *Hoover's* database for libraries that subscribe to the latter.

IBISWorld. Santa Monica, CA: IBISWorld. http://www.ibisworld.com/. Price: $9,000 and up to academic libraries only; anyone may purchase individual reports from the *IBISWorld* website for $750.

IBISWorld got its start in Australia in 1971. Focused on the business market for years, *IBISWorld* opened up its product to academic libraries in 2005. This database covers more than 700 industries. From auto manufacturing to shoe repair, entrepreneurs will find industry overviews mixed with a combination of good detail and national-level data. Although one will find some regional charts for such functions as sales, this database does not provide much regional-level data. *IBISWorld* provides the "big picture" industry view. Reports run 25–30 pages in length. The service may be purchased in modules or as a comprehensive product. The five modules are Industry Market Research, Global Industry Research, Industry Risk Ratings, Company Research, and Business Environment. At least half of the industry reports are updated three to four times per year.

Industry market reports examine industries from a number of perspectives. Reports include industry performance, external drivers, an industry outlook projecting five-year growth trends, industry life cycle, demand determinants and market segmentation, a brief assessment of import and export trade, products and markets, competitive landscape, key success factors and cost structure, as well as barriers to entry and globalization issues. Reports also cover industry operating conditions and analyze structural risk, investment requirements, growth strategies, the use of technology, revenue volatility, and regulatory and taxation issues. Ratios and benchmarks are an important element of the reports. The key ratios are not the usual ratios frequently found in the standard sources. These ratios typically include imports as a percentage of demand, exports as a percentage of revenue, wages as a percentage of revenue, employees per establishment, and average wages. Although this is primarily an industry database, there are 8,000 companies mentioned in the reports. *IBISWorld* has added global reports, including more than 100 China industry reports as well as a UK report module.

IBISWorld's business environment reports provide 300 key economic indicators that explain how the external environment impacts businesses. The Industry Risk Ratings look at operational risk of an industry. Operational risk includes the risk arising from within the industry referred to as structural risk; growth risk is assessed by the expected future performance; "external sensitivity risk" stems from external forces outside the industry. The Company Research module is the place to find personnel, company financials and business segments, key competitors, market share, and industry outlook.

Searches for American companies can be organized by 1997, 2002, or 2007 NAICS codes or SIC. The database is also keyword searchable, making it simple to locate the mentions of individual companies. A very handy feature is the ability to keyword search individual reports. These industry reports support business plan creation, business valuation, benchmarking, market analysis, and more.

Plunkett Research Ltd. Houston, TX: Plunkett. Print and e-book: $299.99 each. Online database: for public libraries: $2,295/year for small libraries; $2,995/year for midsize libraries; $3,995–$9,995/year for large libraries, branches extra. For academic libraries: $2,795/year for small campuses; $3,495–$3,995/year for midsize campuses; $4,995/year and up for large campuses.

Plunkett has been supplying libraries with industry data since 1985. While their print product is still available, Plunkett offers an attractive online bundle of their books and data. Plunkett Research has expanded its industry coverage to 32 industry sectors, which is fewer than some other industry sources, but the product is offered at a more affordable price for many libraries. Each industry section has the same layout, covering market research and trends, company profiles, statistics, contact information, a list of related associations and organizations, some export organizations, a glossary of terms for the industry, and a video for those who enjoy the addition of multimedia to screens of data. Data are compiled from a number of government sources as well as from some private industry trade associations.

In addition to industry coverage, the product adds 250–500 company profiles for each industry, for a total of 8,000 companies. Companies are both domestic and international; 20 percent are private. Company profiles may be seen in total, or searches may be filtered by sales and employee counts, region of the country, public or private ownership, and a few specialty business activities, mostly logistical.

Other than researching industries, users may use this information to create business plans and market plans, analyze emerging technologies, gain company intelligence, make sales prospect lists, and job search. Plunkett is suitable for all types of libraries. Access may be also purchased for the online version of a single title in PDF format.

Data may be exported into Excel or into PDF format; industry report updates are posted on the opening screen. Build-a-report allows users to pack together a variety of smaller reports from an industry into one PDF folder. Plunkett also offers customized research for a fee.

Standard & Poor's Industry Surveys. New York: Standard and Poor's. 2010. http://www.netadvantage.standardandpoors.com/.

Standard & Poor's (S&P) is one of the legendory names in business publishing. Its *Industry Surveys* has held a place on thousands of library shelves for decades. The work is found online through S&P's NetAdvantage product. *Industry Surveys* analyzes 55 major North American industries or sectors and *Global Industry Surveys* follow 28 global industries covering European, Asian, and Latin American markets.

Every survey begins with the current environment of the industry. Other content includes industry trends, how the industry operates, key industry ratios and statistics, glossary, trade journals and trade associations, and comparative company analysis. Surveys contain excellent tables of data, charts, and graphs to illustrate trends. Often the top companies in the industry are listed, and frequently this is a good place to find market share. Another section of each survey discusses the industry and management structure. A special feature is the insert with an explanation of how to assess the creditworthiness of firms in the industry. The comparative company financial data help users get perspective on the firms in the industry.

While strategic planners, investors, students, and faculty may get more use from this source, entrepreneurs may find the industry overviews very informative. Unfortunately, the source is limited in the number of industries it includes, covering only the largest and most prominent industries. *Industry Surveys* is issued quarterly.

MARKET RESEARCH

While there is a chapter in this book on marketing resources, a few are mentioned here for the entrepreneur. Basic demographics are easy to find at the U.S. Census website. Geospatial mapping is one of the latest tools for market research. Geographical information systems (GIS) use basic government-gathered demographic data for their geospatial mapping. There are several desktop products available for the library market that give not only demographic data but also some additional market and consumer data.

American FactFinder. Washington, DC: U.S. Census Bureau. http://www.census.gov. Free.

American FactFinder is the place to find basic population and housing data. This Census site holds the decennial census data as well as the more up-to-date American Community Survey (ACS) and population estimates. A quick city or town search will generate social, economic, housing, and population data revealing age groups, sex, race, language spoken at home, foreign born, levels of education, housing data, median household incomes, and more. Decennial census data from Summary File One is comprised of 100 percent data, that is, data represented by the full census count. Data for very small groups can be found in Summary File One, and data are provided from the national to the block level. For a wider variety of data, the decennial census Summary File Three is comprised of sample data from the long form, which is data collected from 5 percent of the population. Data are provided down to the block group level. The ACS one-year estimates give data for places larger than 65,000 population and goes down to place, congressional district, or school district level. Unlike some of the commercial products, private identities are protected; no names are given in the U.S. Census data.

Business Decision (Library Edition). Pasadena, CA: CIVICTechnologies. http://www.businessdecision.info/. Price: $2,500+ (academic and public). This product has pricing tiers based on library type and geographic content coverage.

Business Decision is a desktop geospatial mapping tool. It integrates social behavior and consumer buying behaviors. The product is designed as a tool for small business, entrepreneurs, nonprofits, and students to analyze geographic areas and perform basic market analysis. This system is fueled with data from the highly regarded ESRI company. The interface steps users who have no GIS experience through the map creation process. Geographic search selections are based on census geographies—city/town or CBSA (core based statistical area), county, county subdivision, state, ZIP code, Congressional district, census tract, and DMA (designated market area). Geographic searching is enhanced with specific address searching, ring mapping, hand-drawn mapping, and Nielsen designated market areas (DMAs). Users may also upload their own data in CSV format.

ESRI Tapestry segment data set this product apart. Tapestry market segments are developed on a neighborhood concept, using socioeconomics and demographics. Tapestry consists of 65 market segments. Within the segment structure are 12 Lifemode and 11 Urbanization groups. Furthermore, there are 60 attributes describing demographics, socioeconomic background, residential characteristics, and consumer buying habits.

Business Decision provides as many as 29 reports with past and current Census data and ESRI projections. There are demographic reports, disposable-income reports, consumer expenditure reports, and Tapestry reports for every locale. There are also housing, market, and network profiles for locales. Some reports make good use of colorful charts. The database product offered for public libraries carries fewer of the detailed reports.

A market profile report includes a combination of data about household income, median home value, per capita income, median age, total household income, owner-occupied housing value, housing units with rent, population data, school enrollment, educational attainment, marital status, employment status, labor force employment rates, employed population by occupation, means of transportation, and consumer spending on broad categories. Market profiles also include a buying power index and consumer expenditure data. Geographic comparison tables are a great feature for users seeking to compare market areas.

Among the best uses of this product for the small-business owner are analyzing areas for trade, identifying target markets for sales, marketing, and mailings, running competitive analyses, evaluating market penetration, and finding the best locations for new retail establishments. Tapestry segment data can help business owners target areas in which to place ads and the types of ads that might work best in a given neighborhood. The data are also good for site selection. Work space may be saved for ongoing projects. Users can add small amounts of their own data.

DemographicsNow (Library Edition). Farmington Hills, MI: Gale Cengage Learning. http://library.demographicsnow.com. Price: $3,628 and up.

DemographicsNow is another desktop database that gives libraries basic access to Census data and geospatial mapping. Demographic data is supplied from Experian/Applied Geographic Solutions. *DemographicsNow* is a user-friendly application incorporating 1,000 demographic variables with Census-defined geographic variables including state, county, census tract, block group, place, Metro CBSA, and ZIP code plus DMAs. Areas can be ranked based on a selected demographic or income-based variable. Consumer expenditure data have been added to show consumption for basics such as apparel, auto and transportation, food and beverage, health care, furnishings, restaurants, and shelter.

The interface guides the novice user through a search beginning with geography and followed by the choice of map type: summary, comparison, ranking dynamic map. Comparison reports are helpful to compare market areas, and *DemographicsNow* allows comparisons of up to 16 geographical areas. A business owner can compare the percentage change in demographics, the average, median, and per capita income in geographic areas, and the percentages of ethnic groups in the selected cities. A business owner can find numbers of households and five-year projections to guide new store locations or to help determine product lines. It is possible to compare the retail potential for household items based on geography. Demographic trend data give business owners indicators of growing or shrinking market areas.

For the times when superimposed geographic borders do not satisfy a user's needs, ring mapping might be just the thing. With ring mapping, users can plot specific variables in a given radius centered on an address. Results are downloadable into Excel, Word, HTML, or PDF. This product may be best suited for site analysis, economic development, and researching disposable income. Libraries may purchase national- and/or state-level data.

SimplyMap. New York: Geographic Research. http://www.geographic research.com/. Price: $7,195 and up; discounts available for smaller public libraries (serving populations below 100,000). Some modules not available to public libraries.

SimplyMap is a web-based, geospatial mapping application that finds a multiplicity of uses. It is a sophisticated product with a reasonable learning curve. Users need to know little or nothing about GIS software in order to create thematic maps and reports. Subscribers choose from a variety of data sets, which determine the price. One option is to use the product with only Census data—historical census, plus 1980, 1990, 2000, and estimates and projections. Another option is to add the subscription module for Experian/Simmons market data with 80,000 market data variables, and Experian Simmons LOCAL with its 60,000 data variables and 8,000 specific brands for 210 market areas. Another option is the Nielsen Claritas's PRIZM data, offering 66 demographic and behavior types, attitudes, lifestyles, and preferred brands. Or Subscribers may also choose Mediamark Research (MRI) data. MRI supplies the Survey of the American Consumer—quality-of-life, market segments, and life stages data. Other data partners include Dun & Bradstreet (D&B), EASI (Health Data and Life Stage Clusters), and Envonics. D&B supplies over 4 million points of interest, allowing users to plot locations for specific businesses and organizations. Also available are health care and illness data with vital and health statistics from the Centers for Disease Control and Prevention.

Researchers select census-designated areas, then choose from hundreds of variables to be mapped. Maps can be downloaded as image files in GIF or PDF format. Reports can be generated in Microsoft Word or PDF. Data can also be downloaded in report form. The product does not, however, bundle reports for locales as some other GIS products do.

SimplyMap gives small businesses and entrepreneurs a way to gather market intelligence, and to plot market and demographic data without spending the big dollars for market research and without investing the time commitment to learn more complex programs like ESRI's ArcInfo. Product support is excellent.

MARKET RESEARCH REPORTS

MarketResearch.com. Rockville, MD: MarketResearch.com. http:// www.marketresearch.com. Price: $5,000 (academic pricing—nonembargoed, but limited number of report providers; there are modest discounts for academic libraries wishing to purchase reports not included in their plan). Public libraries may be offered an embargoed version of the database; special pricing is available for small-business development centers. Individual report prices not purchased through a subscription plan vary from under $100 to $35,000.

The database is one of the larger report aggregators, carrying some 300,000 market research reports from more than 700 publishers. These market research reports provide expert analysis of dozens of industries and include market data, trend analysis, qualitative and quantitative material, and socio-demographic data. Reports often include information about the industry as well as the market. The reports offer extensive and excellent coverage.

The database is divided into major industry groups including consumer goods, food and beverage, heavy industry, life sciences, service industries, technology, and media. Reports are aggregated from analyst services including Kalorama Information, Euromonitor International, BCC Research, Mintel International Group, Datamonitor, Snapdata International Group,

Packaged Facts, Icon Group International, Frost & Sullivan, Paul Budde Communication, Compass Intelligence, Freedonia, Gartner, and Simba. Market research firms often specialize. Kalorama, for example, specializes in life sciences, while Packaged Facts' strength is demographic research.

Reports typically follow a common format: an executive summary including market size and global trends, market trends and composition of the market, products, market forecast, market size and growth, competitive analysis, factors influencing growth, some corporate and competitor profiles, challenges, opportunities, and strategic recommendations. Reports tend to contain a good mix of tables and graphs.

The database includes hundreds of country reports from publishers such as Economist Intelligence Unit, Datamonitor, Business Monitor International, GlobalData, Global Demographics, Gobi, and others. Company reports are provided by Datamonitor, SGA Lists, World Market Intelligence, and others. Subscribers will want to note possible overlap with EBSCO and Gale databases (among others).

Reports are searchable by title, abstract, publisher name, and keyword. Searches can be limited by region, price, and date. Business planners can view an extensive table of contents before downloading or purchasing individual reports. The size of reports ranges from 10 to 1,000 pages.

ReferenceUSA U.S. Consumers/Lifestyles. Omaha, NE: Infogroup. http://www.referenceusa.com/. Call company for pricing.

This is a relatively new addition to the Infogroup's ReferenceGroup database lineup. Similar in look and feel to ReferenceUSA's *U.S. Standard White Pages*, the *U.S. Consumers / Lifestyles* database includes 203 million consumers, their addresses, and their interests. For individual names, entrepreneurs can find consumers who are interested in apparel, wine, books, magazines, hobbies, fitness, home improvement, motor vehicles, personal finance, pets, photography, politics, religion, sports, technology, or travel. Records may indicate an individual's purchase behavior such as "bargain seekers," "catalog shoppers," or "Internet purchasers." Consumer preferences are drawn from sources such as magazine subscriptions, product registrations, and store consumer cards.

SRDS Local Market Audience Analyst. Des Plaines, IL: SRDS. http://www.srds.com/portal/servlet/LoginServlet. Price: $695 and up.

SRDS (Standard Rates and Data) is best known for publishing media rates used by advertisers and marketers. While media rates are helpful for entrepreneurs ready to advertise products, SRDS offers another product that can be useful to the entrepreneur. *The SRDS Local Market Audience Analyst* provides market research by indexing demographics and lifestyles to give the entrepreneur better insight into market venues. The product covers 210 DMAs and 3,000 U.S. counties. The market research data are supplied from Experian Simmons and include 200 lifestyles. The Experian Simmons data give the entrepreneur geographic information about consumers such as market areas that have a high number of people who like to eat foreign foods, or who spend more than $400 year on children's clothing, or those who do on-line banking. Nielsen Claritas supplies the product with its PRIZM market segments of social and lifestyle groupings.

The *SRDS Local Market Audience Analyst* interface offers four types of reports. Demographics Reports give the entrepreneur a look at the 20 demographic variable groupings for population, housing, ethnicity, occupation, and travel time to work. The entrepreneur can compare any of these variables across all the 210 DMAs to find the best target markets for a product or service.

The Market Profile Reports give the entrepreneur a way to explore market areas through the use of demographics combined with high-indexing behaviors. The entrepreneur can see which lifestyles are above or below national norms by county or DMA.

The Lifestyle Analysis Reports give entrepreneurs an opportunity to correlate individual lifestyle behaviors, such as dressing conservatively, to various lifestyle categories. Taken a step further, the entrepreneur can examine related behaviors to identify cross-selling opportunities and market potential. This is helpful for proper placement of new product developments, for developing advertising campaigns, and for cross-mix channels in advertising. The market potential reports index a specific behavior across the DMAs.

PRIZM Reports allow the entrepreneur to do two kinds of reports. With the Concentration Report, users can align PRIZM groupings to DMAs, providing insight into the household makeup and lifestyle traits of selected target audiences. Reports provide the actual numbers and percentages of residents constituting the groups in the DMAs. The other type of report, the Group Lifestyle Report, combines a PRIZM group with a lifestyle category, displaying the dominant lifestyles, from high to low, for that group.

PRIZM social groups categorize people into an assortment of 14 urban, suburban, and rural clusters, as well as wealth. PRIZM life stage groupings list 11 categories identifying family composition and wealth. An example of a PRIZM social group is the "urban core," and within the "urban core" there are four subcategories or urban social types.

The product's demographic data contains the last two decennial censuses plus Census estimates and projections, taking the user 15 years beyond the latest decennial data.

COMPETITORS AND SUPPLIERS

Entrepreneurs need to establish a list of suppliers who will provide them with raw materials and services. Coincidentally, the sources that provide this information also can serve as a resource to identify competitors in the marketplace.

D&B Global Directory. Short Hills, NJ: Dun and Bradstreet. http://www.dnb.com/us/. Price: $3,590 and up.

Dun and Bradstreet has been a leader in providing business information since 1841. The company's initial purpose was to serve as a reliable source of company credit information. D&B began publishing the *Million Dollar Directory* in 1959. Libraries have carried this well-recognized series for decades. The *Million Dollar Database* now includes 14 million public and private domestic company records. The D&B *Global Directory* expands on that longstanding title to include global companies. The resource can be purchased in five levels or slices. Slices are delineated by one of the following criteria: sales dollar, number of employees, or the employee size of branches. The database is updated once a month.

The very largest companies constitute the "Series" level of companies with more than $9 million in sales or 180 total employees or branches with at least 900 employees. The *Million Dollar Database* level is defined by businesses with at least $5 million in sales or at least 100 employees. The Plus level is made up of companies with more than $3 million in sales or at least 50 employees or branches with 500 or more employees. The more comprehensive Premier level contains companies with at least $1 million in sales or at least 20 employees or branches with 50 or more employees. The Total level gives the full listing of companies.

The *Global Directory* lists 23 million international businesses representing 200 countries. Slices may be purchased for each continent and then refined by employee size criteria and sales. There are records for headquarters, single locations, and branch locations; the database provides all levels of corporate family tree linkage.

A host of different searches is possible with the 35 searchable fields. One search category is devoted to geographic areas, including continent, country, state, county, ZIP code, MSA, and area code. Other major categories include size criteria and industry description criteria. While sales figures are included, users will not find financial statements in this product. This database is strictly expanded directory information.

The entrepreneur or small-business owner is able to create business-to-business contacts, find sales prospects, identify potential suppliers, discover the competition in an area, and assess the credit risk of firms. Buyers and sellers can identify the headquarter locations of business entities, and determine the size of a business. Employee size might be important for any firm targeting companies of a certain size. Plant or facility size may be useful to sellers of services and products, but it may also be an interesting bit of business intelligence about a competitor. Several other useful search criteria are minority-owned businesses, women-owned businesses, and importers/exporters.

Records give the year founded for each company, so searchers can create of list of new business locations. Many company records also provide a list of executives and biographies for half a dozen of the top executives. SIC codes and NAICS codes are listed and the primary codes are noted, which is no longer the case with so many business resources. Often records will include a list of products, but not brand names.

The corporate family tree is linked to the main record. Expanding the family tree brings up a list of the individual branches and subsidiaries. A map link from the main record clicks into Mapquest. The database integrates with another D&B product, *Hoover's* company reports, for comprehensive company information.

ReferenceUSA U.S. Businesses. Omaha, NE: Infogroup. http://www .referenceusa.com/. Call company for pricing.

Reference USA's *U.S. Businesses* bears similarity to D&B's *Million Dollar Database*, and the two competitors continue to add new fields of information in an attempt to outshine each other. *U.S. Businesses* is a database of 14 million businesses that can be put to different purposes for the entrepreneur and small-business owner. Many of the same fields that are found in the Dun & Bradstreet product are found here. Company records display company name, address and contact information, executives' names, titles and gender, type of business (SIC code or keyword or major industry), geographic areas, number of employees and sales volume, type of ownership (headquarters, foreign parent, home-based, and public or private), stock exchange and ticker symbol, credit ratings, and links to purchase a full credit report on business expenditures. The database also offers an expanded six-digit SIC code and an expanded eight-digit NAICS code for more precise searching.

For private companies, sales figures are either verified by phone or estimated through modeling based on public information and on sales per employee for various SIC codes. The database also has some "special selects," which include yellow page ad size, number of years in the database, year established, and square footage. Other unique fields are brands and products, foreign parent, home-based businesses, business expenditures, and number of PCs. ReferenceUSA's *U.S. Businesses* features radius searching, which enables an entrepreneur to scope out information on businesses in all directions from a specific point. Not all of this information shows up in every company record.

Business expenses allow business owners a way to compare their expenses with other businesses. An entrepreneur is able to establish benchmarks for items such as accounting, contract labor, legal, office supplies, payroll, rent/leases, telecommunications, advertising, insurance, management, package/container, purchase print, technology, and utilities.

The database has been enhanced with historical data and graphs of sales volume and numbers of employees over four to five years. Public company records link to previous annual reports, 10-Ks, and Google Finance. Records also link to global citizen reports (corporate responsibility), and public filings such as tax liens, civil filings, judgments, and bankruptcies. Associated Press and BusinessWire supply news stories. One newer feature is the list of competitors report.

ReferenceUSA provides continuous updates to the database from 5,000 sources of information; much of the information is updated by phone calls and from public data.

ThomasNet.com. New York: Thomas Publishing Company. http://www.thomasnet.com/. Free.

ThomasNet is a free resource for buyers and suppliers of manufactured goods and services. From structural beams to high-pressure valves to insect cages, ThomasNet helps business owners locate sources for these products. Business owners can find contact and product information for manufacturers, custom manufacturers, service companies, and distributors of thousands of products in the United States and Canada. Entries include product details and often CAD drawings. Products are categorized as well as any cataloging librarian could devise. Many companies include links to their product catalogs to enable users to view the full array of products and specifications. The database is searchable by product, service, company, brand, or even CAD drawing. *ThomasNet* features product news and some white papers, such as the latest news on laser scanners or barcode readers. Searches can be narrowed to women-owned, minority-owned, or veteran-owned companies. Some records display links to request quotes.

TREND FOLLOWING AND MARKET WATCH

Business and Company Resource Center. Farmington Hills, MI: Gale Cengage Learning. http://www.gale.cengage.com/BusinessRC/. Price: $4,995 and up.

The *Business and Company Resource Center* draws from the inventory of Gale's 5,700 full-text journals, magazines, newsletters, newswires, newspapers, and country reports to create a business portal. The portal content is enhanced with the addition of some of Gale's noted business reference titles like *Business Rankings Annual, Brands and Their Companies, Encyclopedia of American Industries, Encyclopedia of Associations, International Directory of Company Histories, Market Share Reporter,* and *Ward's Business Directory of U.S. Private and Public Companies.* This pooled content enables Gale to create company profiles that give a comprehensive overview of not only a company, but of the industry and the marketplace. A search on a company will yield basic company information, financials, brand information, business rankings, market share, investment reports, and a company history. Periodical content retrieved from a company search is faceted into categories for legal issues, management, operations and technology, sales, marketing, strategy and planning, and much more. Industry information is another feature of the portal. The database also incorporates a financial dashboard to monitor financial markets, securities, and mutual fund performance. Financial data is supplied by third parties, such as Mergent and Telekurs.

Entrepreneurs and franchise owners may use this resource to explore industries or lines of business, some as small of "Juice Bars" or "Cybercafes." Entrepreneurs can check out the top franchises or businesses in a given sector, or they might check *Market Share Reporter* for the leading chains. BCRC also offers users the ability to scope out business ideas that have already come to the marketplace. For example, a search for a new venture for electric bicycles will result in articles from newspapers, trade journals, and business magazines on this trend, as well as define the market drivers for this product. Every industry search leads the searcher to a list of related trade associations from listings in Gale's *National Organizations of the U.S., Regional, State and Local Organizations of the U.S.,* and *International Organizations.* Trade associations are often a good source of industry data found nowhere else. The small-business owner or entrepreneur will be able to use this hybrid resource in a multitude of ways.

Business Source Premier. Birmingham, AL: EBSCO. Call company for pricing.

Business Source Premier fills the need for access to general business journals, magazines, and trade journals. Its 3,300 titles cover the fields of marketing, management, MIS, production, operations, accounting, finance, and economics. A little more than 50 percent of the titles are academic, one-quarter are trade titles, and the remainder are business magazines. The database has expanded its content to encompass nearly 100 books, including the Blue Ibex "Doing Business in . . . " series, case studies mostly from Datamonitor, country reports from sources including Business Monitor International, ICON Group International, Country Watch, Economist Intelligence Unit, and the

Superintendent of Documents, domestic and international industry reports from Datamonitor, and company profiles containing SWOT analyses. Market research reports are dated and very limited. *Business Source Premier* carries some unique titles, particularly *Harvard Business Review*.

LexisNexis Academic. Dayton, OH: LexisNexis. http://www.lexisnexis .com. Call company for pricing.

This resource is one of the hybrid databases that leverages all its publications to create a "dossier" of company information. Its scope covers domestic and international companies, both public and private. *LexisNexis Academic* Company Dossier creates company snapshots that include the executives, stock performance, competitors, a few news items, industry classification codes (NAICS and SIC), extensive financial data going six years back, extensive lists of company ratios, and recent financial analyst reports. The Company Dossier is an aggregation of information pulled from a number of sources and publishers such as *Hoover's, CoreData, Standard & Poor's, Disclosure, WorldScope, Vicker's, Nelson,* and *Zacks*. Other notable sources cannot be searched directly, yet find their way into search results: *Standard Directory of Advertisers, LexisNexis Corporate Affiliations,* and *Zoom Information*. The database's tie-in to the legal portion of the LexisNexis system gives the researcher the ability to research legal matters and lawsuits that may impact company performance. While easy to identify private companies, private company details are always scarce.

Entrepreneurs can use this source to find competitors (by searching industry codes). They can also find out the sales figures or estimates for private companies. Another reason to use this resource is to scan the trade journal news, newswires, magazines, and newspapers for mentions of new product launches. Not only can entrepreneurs discover new products coming to market, they can read about how the products are received. New products often find their way to new markets outside the United States. Scanning the literature reveals where those new markets are opening up.

In a more recent development, LexisNexis now markets a version of its database for public and government libraries. The product is *Library Express*. This database contains much of the same content—business, biographical, news, and patent—and the legal content is somewhat reduced.

ProQuest ABI/INFORM Global. Ann Arbor, MI: ProQuest. http://www .proquest.com. Call company for pricing.

This database complements the *ABI/INFORM Trade and Industry* database. It offers the entrepreneur access to 3,380 publications, two-thirds of which are full-text. Coverage includes business conditions, management practice and theory, business trends, corporate strategy, marketing, and the competitive landscape. Content has been expanded to include *EIU: ViewsWire*, business dissertations, and the *Wall Street Journal* back to 1984. One particular source entrepreneurs will come to appreciate is the addition of *First Research* industry profiles. Approximately 60 percent of the titles are scholarly publications and 30 percent are trade publications. The remainder encompasses working papers, magazines, a few conference proceedings, and some books. The few entrepreneurship-oriented journals are mostly research journals rather than practitioner titles.

ProQuest ABI/INFORM Trade and Industry. Ann Arbor, MI: ProQuest. http://www.proquest.com. Call company for pricing.

With *ABI/INFORM Trade and Industry*, business planners can stay abreast of industry trends and developments by reading the latest trade journals. *ABI/INFORM Trade and Industry* provides users with product development, marketing trends, and a wide variety of other topics necessary to stay competitive. The database contains publications on dozens of industries such as advertising, construction, energy, finance, insurance, pharmaceuticals, telecommunications, and transportation. As the title implies, this database is light on scholarly journals. *ABI/INFORM* Trade and Industry carries just over 2,000 publications, the majority of which are full-text. Trade magazines and journals include titles such as *American Spa, Computer Dealer News, Construction Bulletin, Financial Planning, Homecare Magazine,* and *Textile World.*

Business Monitor International populates the database with more than 600 country and commodity forecasts and market and industry research reports. The Economist Intelligence Unit (EIU) provides country data and forecasts. ProQuest has also added annual reports and 10-Ks from its collection back to the mid-1980s. The database is not a place to find newspaper coverage.

ReferenceUSA New Businesses. Omaha, NE: Infogroup. http://www .referenceusa.com/. Call company for pricing.

This database from Infogroup contains 4 million new businesses. It is updated weekly from data obtained from sources such as post office and utility company records. Records are searchable by company name, yellow page listing, SIC or NAICS code, or major industry group, and newness to the database. Searchable geographic criteria includes state, ZIP, county, MSA, city, area code, street address, or neighborhood. The database features radius searching. Businesses listed have been around for up to one year. Business entries do not give the date they were entered or date opened. Records are often missing some fields of information due to the rapid way the database is compiled. Searchers can use this database to discover new businesses that might be competitors, and buyers or suppliers in the same market area.

FRANCHISES

Franchises are a growing part of American business. They offer the entrepreneur a way to start a business, or jump-start a business, with many of the business development issues already solved. A franchise offers the new business owner a recognized brand, site location guidance, marketing plans and materials, advertising, training, and some degree of financing. The U.S. Census Bureau issued its first comprehensive report on franchises in 2010, the *2007 Economic Census Franchise Report*. The report counted only employee-based businesses, not nonemployer businesses, so the number of franchises is larger than even reported. The Census Bureau found that franchises account for 10.5 percent of all businesses with paid employees. These businesses amass sales of $1.3 trillion and have payrolls amounting to $153.7 billion. There are a number of sites on the Internet appealing to the entrepreneur in search of a franchise opportunity. Most give scant information and serve to advertise the franchise to franchisees or to sell a franchise rather than to seek franchisees. The SBA approves franchises for the purpose of facilitating business loans. Fifteen states require franchises to file presale disclosures known as the Franchise Disclosure Document (FDD). These states are: California, Hawaii, Illinois, Indiana, Maryland, Michigan, Minnesota, New York, North Dakota, Oregon, Rhode Island, South Dakota, Virginia, Washington, and Wisconsin. This section will focus on just a few franchise sites.

Entrepreneur.com. Newburgh, NY: Entrepreneur Press. http://www .entrepreneur.com/. Free.

For 31 years *Entrepreneur* magazine has been publishing *Entrepreneur's* Franchise 500, a ranking of franchises based on objective metrics. Entrepreneurs who choose the franchise route can find the top franchises, the fastest-growing franchises, low-cost and home-based franchises, as well as global franchise opportunities. *Entrepreneur.com* uses criteria requiring a franchise to have a minimum of 10 units with at least one based in the United States and it must be seeking new franchisees in the United States. Franchises are analyzed for financial strength, growth rates, size of their system, the start-up costs, and the number of years in operation. Entrepreneurs can find franchises grouped by categories such as automotive, children's products, health care, and pet businesses. Visitors to the site can find details about start-up fees, royalty rates, total investment required, training and support, founding year, contact information, suggested territory size, and types of financing.

Entrepreneurs can find quantities of other relevant information about franchising at this site. There is helpful advice for business planning, how to evaluate a franchise opportunity, managing a company's online presence, marketing, how-to guides, human resources tips, how to work from home, financing hints, and much more. The site is replete with ads, as one might expect.

Franchise.com. Portsmouth, NH: Franchise.com. http://www.franchise .com. Free.

Franchise.com is one place to find the SBA-approved franchise opportunities. Entrepreneurs will find several ways to search the maze of franchises representing 75 industries. Users will find franchises of interest to women, veterans, and minorities. There is a category for low-investment franchises, SBA-approved franchises, and master area franchises, which would appeal to business owners with great resources than average who seek to develop a pilot franchise in new territory. This site also features a top 25 list of franchises. Opportunities can also be searched by company name, industry, state, required investment, and even those with a lifestyle appeal.

International Franchise Association. Washington, DC. http://www .franchise.org/. Free.

The IFA has been in existence since 1960. It is a membership organization, 30,000 strong, comprised of franchisors, franchisees, and suppliers. However, one does not have to join to use the website search engine. Entrepreneurs can search 1,100 franchises in 35 different industries. There is also a search interface where users can keyword search and limit by required start-up cash or investment, or seek franchises that have financing options. Searches may also be narrowed by domestic or international locations or limited to a specific state. Much like *Entrepreneur.com* entries, these business entries give contact information year the business and franchising began, number of franchised units, start-up costs, total investment, and some brief training information. The site features a number of pages covering franchising basics from finding the right franchise to handling taxes for franchises. The organization makes a special appeal to veterans. The Association also publishes its *Franchise Opportunities Guide* along with articles and a number of other publications to facilitate the development, purchase, and sales of franchises.

Small Business Development Center—National Information Clearing-house. San Antonio, TX. http://sbdcnet.org/SBIC/franchise.php. Free.

This Clearinghouse is funded by the SBA and the University of Texas at San Antonio. Their website has a section devoted to franchising. The entrepreneur will find several portals of franchise opportunities including the *Franchise Directory* (also known as the *Franchise Handbook*), links to sites that help entrepreneurs evaluate franchise opportunities, information on how to recognize a franchise scam, as well as legal information for buyers and sellers. The directory of most interest is the *Franchise Registry*, which is the directory of franchises approved by the SBA for which franchisee applicants will receive expedited loan processing.

REFERENCES

"Characteristics of a Successful Entrepreneurial Management Team," *Pratt's Guide to Private Equity and Venture Capital Sources*. New York: Thomson, 2008.

Ewing Marion Kauffman Foundation. "Despite Recession, U.S. Entrepreneurial Activity Rises in 2009 to Highest Rate in 14 Years, Kauffman Study Shows," May 20, 2010. http://www.kauffman.org/newsroom/despite-recession-us-entrepreneurial -activity-rate-rises-in-2009.aspx. Accessed June 9, 2010.

Shane, Scott. 2010. "The Term 'Small Business' Is Baloney," *Bloomberg Businessweek*, May 14. http://www.businessweek.com/smallbiz/content/may2010/sb20100513 _562175.htm. Accessed June 13, 2010.

U.S. Small Business Administration. Office of Advocacy. 2010a, "Frequently Asked Questions." September 2010. http://www.sba.gov/advo/stats/sbfaq.pdf. Accessed October 5, 2010.

U.S. Small Business Administration. 2010b. "Guide to SBA's Definitions of Small Business," n.d. http://www.sba.gov/idc/groups/public/documents/sba_homepage/ guide_to_size_standards.pdf. Accessed June 5, 2010.

U.S. Small Business Administration. 2010c. "FAQ," n.d. http://www.sba.gov/con tractingopportunities/officials/size/faq/index.html. Accessed June 5, 2010.

8

Deep Business Research:
Resources for In-Depth Academic Research in Business

Gary W. White

INTRODUCTION

Although Chapter 1 of this book serves as a checklist of essential business information sources for any type of library that serves a business clientele, this chapter is designed to provide an overview of business resources that are particularly useful to the high-level academic researcher. Generally, although any of the resources covered in this book can be of potential value to an academic business researcher, there are also many specialized products available that go beyond what an undergraduate student or a nonacademic business researcher would typically need for research purposes. Faculty, MBA, and doctoral students in business typically need access to a variety of business information products, including those providing access to the scholarly literature in business and related disciplines; those that provide in-depth company, industry, and market research analysis; time series of historical business data or other types of economic or financial data sets; and very specialized data and information resources that support research in both specific niches as well as interdisciplinary areas of study. The number of potential business resources and data sets that might be in demand by an academic researcher is far too large for this chapter to be all-inclusive, and every academic institution has very specialized faculty with specific research needs that will likely fall outside the scope of what may reasonably be included in this discussion. Instead, this chapter will cover those resources that are typically available in many of the top-ranked business schools/MBA programs, and are therefore used more frequently by high-level researchers than by undergraduate students or nonacademic researchers. In preparing this chapter and in the selection decisions for items to include, I relied heavily on the Academic Business Library Directors (ABLD) group, a network consisting of the business library directors of the top 50 ranked business libraries in North America (http://www.abld.org/). I would like to acknowledge the work of this group and the assistance of individual members in reviewing drafts of this chapter, both of which have been invaluable in the compilation of the resources in this section.

SCHOLARLY LITERATURE AND CITATION DATABASES

Access to scholarly literature is of utmost importance to academic researchers. In business, two of the primary databases are ABI/INFORM and EBSCO's Business Source products, both covered extensively elsewhere in this book. In addition to these two core databases, academic business researchers may rely on many other potential sources for scholarly literature, depending on the specifics of their research. Included in this section are *EconLit*, a database providing access to economics literature, as well as citation databases and databases specifically designed for the sharing of academic research. Additionally, there are a number of resources used to access electronic journals, such as JSTOR, ScienceDirect (SciVerse), and Wiley Online Library, which are not included in this chapter (see Chapter 2: "Business Literature").

Google Scholar. http://scholar.google.com/. Price: Free.

Google Scholar has quickly established itself as the first stop for many academic researchers because it is a free web search engine that provides access to content (some full text) of scholarly literature across an array of publishing formats and disciplines, including journals and working papers. Originally released in November 2004, the Google Scholar index includes many peer-reviewed journals from U.S. and global scholarly publishers. Libraries are able to link their licensed full-text content to Google Scholar. The "cited by" feature provides access to abstracts of articles that have cited the article being viewed, thus making Google Scholar a viable alternative to the commercial Web of Knowledge and Scopus products, although the functionality is limited in comparison to these proprietary databases. Also, full-text content is generally not available unless through subscriptions at affiliated academic institutions.

Social Science Research Network (SSRN). http://www.ssrn.com. For pricing information for the alerts service(s), contact the vendor.

The Social Science Research Network began in 1994 as a way for scholars to share their research in a timely manner before articles are able to go through the journal refereeing and publication process, and it is thus a favorite means of access to working papers. Academic papers can be uploaded directly to the site by authors as PDF documents, and all of these author-uploaded papers are available for free downloading—often from multiple sites. Institutions or individuals can also subscribe to the database or one of its disciplinary sections for services such as alerts. The SSRN database consists of two parts: an Abstract Database containing abstracts on over 300,000 scholarly working papers and forthcoming papers, and an Electronic Paper Collection currently containing over 250,000 downloadable full-text documents in Adobe Acrobat PDF format. SSRN is also subdivided into segments by discipline, and is searchable by author, subject, title, or journal name.

EconLit. American Economic Association. http://www.aeaweb.org/econlit/. Price: $2,500/year institutions/single user; contact vendor for additional information.

EconLit, produced by the American Economic Association, is the premier database for economics literature, and it should be considered the first choice for anyone conducting academic economics research. Dating back to 1969, *EconLit* is a comprehensive index of journal articles, books, book reviews, collective volume articles, working papers, and dissertations. Libraries can license *EconLit* through a number of platforms, including those offered by EBSCO, CSA, and Ovid, all of which provide the capability of full-text linking. Journal lists and other information may be found at the *EconLit* website.

ISI Web of Knowledge. Thomson Reuters. http://wokinfo.com/. Contact the vendor for pricing information.

ISI *Web of Knowledge*, an online database owned by Thomson Reuters's Institute for Scientific Information, consists of a number of citation databases used by academic researchers to provide searching capabilities and citation analysis services. Component databases of *Web of Knowledge* include: *Web of Science* (including Science Citation Index [SCI], Social Sciences Citation Index [SSCI], Arts & Humanities Citation Index [A&HCI], and Journal Citation Reports, among others. With *Web of Knowledge*, users can analyze cited reference data to move both backward and forward in time to track and determine the research influence of a particular work or author. The database can also be used to find high-impact authors and institutions within particular fields, and to analyze citation trends over time. *Web of Knowledge* allows easy linking to full-text content, offers individual customization and alerts, and provides easy exporting to EndNote. *Web of Knowledge* is a competitor with *Scopus*.

Scopus. Elsevier. http://info.scopus.com/. For specific pricing information, contact the vendor.

Scopus bills itself as "the largest abstract and citation database of peer-reviewed literature and quality web sources with smart tools to track, analyze and visualize research." A direct competitor with *ISI Web of Knowledge*, *Scopus* (owned by Elsevier) as of this writing includes over 16,500 peer-reviewed journals and is especially useful for scientific research. *Scopus* offers citation searching and tracking, alert services, RSS feeds, seamless linking to full-text content, and data export via bibliographic management tools including RefWorks and EndNote. Subscription pricing is based on FTE.

U.S. PUBLIC COMPANY/INVESTMENT INFORMATION AND REPORTS

Business researchers regularly need access to data from a variety of public company reports. Although many researchers access company information via the Securities and Exchange Commission's (SEC) free EDGAR database (http://www.sec.gov/edgar.shtml), or databases such as Hoover's Online (covered elsewhere in this book), advanced business researchers may also need access to proprietary investment reports and historical data about companies. This section and the "Business Data/Time Series" section discussed later cover many of the advanced sources for textual and numeric company information.

Bloomberg Professional. http://about.bloomberg.com/product.html. Price: One license/seat, $1,900/month. Discounts with multiple licenses; contact the vendor for information.

The Bloomberg system is one of the most popular sources for current and historical financial information on individual equities, stock market indexes, fixed-income securities, currencies, commodities, and futures, for both international and domestic markets. Bloomberg also provides company profiles and financial statements, investment reports, analysts' forecasts, news on worldwide financial markets, and audio and video interviews and presentations by key players in business and finance. Although the service has traditionally been accessed by means of a dedicated computer terminal consisting of dual monitors and a specialized keyboard, Bloomberg recently began to offer access via mobile devices, through its Bloomberg Mobile service. Most of the top business schools and libraries provide access to Bloomberg as a training tool for students in finance and investments.

Thomson Reuters. http://thomsonreuters.com/.

Thomson Reuters is one of the leading providers of business information data, investment reports, and business news. Thomson started business in the 1930s in Canada, operating primarily in the news and media, gas and oil, and airline industries. Thomson became a public corporation in 1977. Starting in the late 1980s and early 1990s, Thomson decided to focus on the publishing and information sectors. Among its significant acquisitions were Research Institute of America (1989), Institute for Scientific Information (1992), West Publishing (publisher of Westlaw, 1996), Information Access (1994), Macmillan Library Reference (1999), The Financial Times Group (1999), Dialog Information Services (2000), Primark (2000), First Call (2001), Biological Abstracts Inc. (2004), Peterson's (2006), K. G. Saur (2006), and Reuters Group (2008). Through its aggressive acquisitions and growth strategy, Thomson Reuters is now one of the largest information providers in the world, offering 75+ separate business and finance databases alone. Among the leading business databases for business school faculty and graduate students are **Datastream, First Call, I/B/E/S, GSI Online, ISI Web of Knowledge, SDC Platinum**, and **Compact D/SEC (Disclosure)/** *Worldscope*, all discussed separately in this chapter.

Many top business schools access Thomson information via the **Thomson One Banker** platform. **Thomson One Banker** draws data from a variety of Thomson products, providing access to company overviews and financials, stock quotes, earnings estimates, SEC filings, ownership information, mergers and acquisition deals, private equity information, press releases, and equity analyst reports (formerly **Investext**) on companies and industries. Contact the vendor for pricing information on any of these products. Several **Thomson Reuters** data products are also available via the **Wharton Research Data Services product** (see WRDS entry later in this chapter for a complete description):

- **Thomson-Reuters Mutual Fund Holdings** database provides security holding information for all registered mutual funds that report their holdings with the SEC, plus an additional 3,000 global funds. Reported securities include all NYSE/AMEX/NASDAQ stocks. This database was formerly known as CDA/Spectrum.
- **Thomson-Reuters Institutional Holdings (13F) Database** provides institutional common stock holdings and transaction data, which are reported on Form 13F filed with the SEC.
- The **Insider Filing Data Feed (IFDF)** is designed to capture all U.S. insider trading activity.
- The **DealScan** database provides extensive and reliable information on the global commercial loan market, currently providing information on over 200,000 loan transactions.
- **Compact D/SEC & Worldscope:** Starting in the late 1980s and into the 2000s, most business libraries subscribed to both **Compact**

Disclosure (Compact D/SEC) and **Worldscope** products on CD-ROM. Compact D/SEC contained SEC filings and financial information for publicly traded U.S. companies and was offered on CD-ROM from 1985 through 2006; Worldscope contained filings and financial information for non-U.S. publicly traded companies and was available on CD-ROM from 1991 through 2006. In 2000, Thomson (now **Thomson Reuters**) acquired these products with its acquisition of Primark. Many business libraries still retain their CD-ROM holdings of these products, primarily for historical research, and data from these products are also available via **Thomson One Banker and LexisNexis**.
- **Academic**. These CD-ROMS are no longer produced.

Capital IQ. Standard & Poor's. http://www.capitaliq.com/. For pricing information, contact the vendor.

Capital IQ was founded in 1999 and currently operates as a division of Standard & Poor's since the 2004 acquisition of the latter by McGraw-Hill Companies. *Capital IQ* is a web-based service that combines information on public and private companies worldwide with a variety of software applications that allow financial professionals to analyze company fundamentals, build financial models, screen for investment ideas, and execute other financial research tasks.

FirstCall. Thomson Reuters. http://thomsonreuters.com/products_services/financial/financial_products/a-z/first_call/. For pricing information, contact the vendor.

First Call, owned by **Thomson Reuters**, is a leading provider of real-time brokerage house reports and earnings estimates. First Call now includes more than 6.5 million research documents from more than 700 brokerage firms. The First Call Historical Database, covering 1990 through 1998, is available through WRDS.

Mergent Online. http://www.mergentonline.com/. Price: Subscriptions start at approximately $5,000/year. Contact vendor for specific pricing information.

Mergent Online (formerly Moody's) provides business and financial information for over 10,000 public U.S. and thousands of international companies. SEC filings (real-time and archived to 1993) are included for the NYSE, AMEX, and NASDAQ exchange companies. Financials for 15 years are "as reported" and can be downloaded to spreadsheet software such as Microsoft Excel, and some financials are available as far back as 1982. The basic subscription includes U.S. and/or International Company Data for both active and inactive companies; Mergent also offers a variety of add-on modules, including institutional holdings data, insider trading data, corporate bond portraits, industry reports, and Dun and Bradstreet's Private Company Business Database. Mergent also offers **Mergent WebReports**, a web product consisting of the PDF searchable versions of the historical Moody's/Mergent print volumes.

Standard & Poor's. http://www.standardandpoors.com/. Contact the vendor for specific pricing information.

In addition to Capital IQ (discussed earlier) and Compustat (discussed later in this chapter), many libraries provide access to information and data from Standard & Poor's via its **Market Insight** and **NetAdvantage** products, and there is overlap between all of these offerings. **Market Insight** provides access to S&P **Stock Reports** for over 5,000 companies; **Industry Surveys**, covering over 110 industries; **EDGAR filings**; and **Excel Analytics**, which draws data from the **Compustat** and **Executive Compensation** databases. Standard & Poor's **NetAdvantage** also provides access to **Stock Reports**, **Industry Surveys**, **Excel Analytics**, the **Corporate Bond Reports**, the **Register of Corporations, Directors & Executives**, the **Security Dealers of North America Directory**, and the **CreditWeek** and **Outlook** publications. NetAdvantage also provides access to current news and market information, and includes a "financial education" section.

Morningstar. http://www.morningstar.com/. Price: Institutional prices start at approximately $16,000/year. Contact vendor for specific pricing information.

Morningstar is best known for its information and performance on mutual funds, providing both performance ratings and holdings analyses. Morningstar provides data on approximately 350,000 mutual funds and stocks, along with real-time global market data on more than 4 million equities, indexes, futures, options, commodities, and precious metals, and on foreign exchange and Treasury markets, primarily through its *Morningstar Direct* product. Morningstar also holds data produced by Ibbotson Associates, primarily covering the areas of asset allocation and capital markets expectations and performance. Specific Ibbotson products include *SBBI* and *Cost of Capital Yearbooks* and data, both providing historical time series data on capital markets and statistics for business valuation. Morningstar started in 1984, and many libraries still hold its CD-ROM product *Principia*. One of Morningstar's most recognizable features is its ninesquare *Morningstar Style Box* as a visual representation of the "investment style" characteristics of a security.

Value Line. http://www.valueline.com/. For pricing information, contact the vendor.

Founded in 1931, Value Line is one of the oldest and most respected investor advisory services. Value Line is best known for its ranking systems.

In addition, it is among the most affordable of the products discussed in this section, and thus it is likely to appeal to libraries with smaller budgets. Its "Timeliness" ranking provides Value Line's prediction for the price performance of a stock over the upcoming 6 to 12 months for actively traded U.S. stocks, ranging from 1 (highest) to 5 (lowest). Value Line also provides both "Safety" (volatility) and "Technical" (short-term statistical) rankings. The company's flagship print product is the *Value Line Investment Survey*, covering about 1,700 U.S. publicly traded stocks. Each weekly update includes three sections: Ratings & Reports (Value Line's well-known one-page overview for each company), Summary & Index, and Selection & Opinion. Its *Small and Mid-Cap Edition* includes an additional 1,800 stocks not included in the *Investment Survey*. Today, Value Line offers a variety of web-based investment advisory products in addition to its stock advisory services. These include the *Value Line Fund Advisor* (mutual funds), the *Value Line Daily Options Survey* (stock and index options), the *Value Line Convertibles Survey* (a convertibles is a hybrid financial instrument that grants its holders the option of exchanging the issue for a predetermined number of common shares at a specific price), and the *Value Line ETF Survey* (exchange-traded funds are funds that are traded on exchanges in the same manner that stocks are traded).

Westlaw Business. http://learn.westlawbusiness.com/index.html. Contact the vendor for pricing information.

Formerly known as GSI (Global Securities Information, Inc.) Online, Westlaw Business (a division of Thomson Reuters) is best known for its **Live-EDGAR** product. LiveEDGAR provides real-time access to SEC/EDGAR filings and other SEC content, along with value-added resources such as *Investext* market research reports. Westlaw Business also offers both a mergers and acquisitions database and a registration and prospectus database. Westlaw Business is also accessible via WRDS.

INDUSTRY/MARKET RESEARCH REPORTS & DATA

In addition to reports and data on companies, business researchers also need access to very current industry and market research reports and data. There are many proprietary databases available to individuals and companies, but this section focuses on those databases that are most widely used in the academic markets. Researchers accessing industry and market research reports are usually very interested in currency of the information (see Chapter 6, "Marketing Research").

Datamonitor 360. http://www.datamonitor360.com. Pricing is based on FTE; contact the vendor for more information.

Datamonitor 360, debuting in November 2010, is a new integrated product consisting of several former individual Datamonitor databases, including *Business Insights* and *MarketLine*. Content includes full-text market research reports, business news and opinions, company profiles and SWOT analyses, and market data and country profiles. Industry reports focus on the consumer goods, health care, financial services, energy, and technology sectors. The integrated platform offers academic institutions the same interface as corporate clients, and users can subscribe to individual components.

eMarketer. http://www.emarketer.com/. Price: Subscriptions begin at approximately $15,000/year. Contact the vendor for specific pricing information.

Established in 1996, *eMarketer* specializes in Internet market research, statistics, and objective analysis on Internet marketing that it compiles from over 4,000 global sources. *Total Access*, *eMarketer*'s primary product, offers its information in a variety of platforms and formats. *eMarketer* also produces over 80 analyst reports per year on a variety of Internet marketing topics including consumers, e-commerce; e-business, marketing and advertising, media and entertainment, demographics and usage, and mobile and wireless devices and usage.

Experian Simmons. Experience Marketing Solutions. http://www.smrb.com/.

Experian Simmons, formerly named *Simmons Market Research Bureau*, is a wholly owned subsidiary company of Experience Marketing Solutions. Simmons, a company founded in 1954 as W. R. Simmons & Associates, is among the most comprehensive and respected consumer marketing data sources available. Experian Simmons conducts ongoing consumer behavior studies that report over 60,000 data variables in over 8,000 product categories and 450 plus brands, as well as major media usage behavior and in-depth consumer behavior demographics. Its most well-known product is the *National Consumer Study*, an annual survey of 25,000 adults in the United States. This survey began in 1960 and was originally known as *The Study of Media and Markets*. Experian Simmons data is available in a variety of segments in addition to the *National Consumer Study*; these include such products as its *Teen Study*; *Kids Study*; *Lesbian, Gay, Bisexual and Transgender Consumer Study*; *New Media Study*; and *National Hispanic Consumer Study*. Most libraries currently use the CD-ROM version of Simmons data called *Choices III*, which provides slightly older data at a more affordable cost. Experian Simmons data are also available via other products including **Simply Map** and **Mintel** (covered in Chapter 6, "Marketing Research").

Faulkner Information Services. http://www.faulkner.com/. Contact the vendor for pricing information.

Faulkner Information Services, a division of Information Today, Inc. (http://www.infotoday.com/), is a leading provider of research in the IT and communications industries. Faulkner's subscription services include *Faulkner Advisory on Computer and Communications Technologies* (FACCTs), a database currently consisting of over 1,200 market research reports related to IT, and *Security Management Practices*, a database of research reports related to IT security.

Forrester Research. http://www.forrester.com/. For pricing information, contact the vendor.

Forrester Research is a publicly traded market research and technology company. Forrester focuses on the impact of technology businesses and consumers. One of its primary areas of strength is its research on Internet commerce, corporate technology, and consumer behavior.

Frost & Sullivan. http://www.frost.com/. Price: Currently, the university program costs $25,000 per year. Contact the vendor for specific pricing information.

Frost & Sullivan provides high-level market research/analyst reports covering about 300 different industries and technologies and some 250,000 global companies. Frost & Sullivan's areas of strength include its in-depth coverage of the technology, chemicals, materials, energy, health care, biotechnology, and communications industries.

Gartner. http://www.gartner.com. Contact the vendor for pricing information.

Gartner, Inc., founded in 1979, is an information technology research and advisory firm providing research reports, news, and support on hundreds of IT research topics. Gartner is unique in that it provides both market research reports on the IT field and also professional support and advice for IT professionals working for subscribing organizations.

Euromonitor Passport GMID Academic. Euromonitor. http://www.euromonitor.com/PassportGMID. Price: Varies by content level and enrollment. Contact the vendor for specific pricing information.

Euromonitor is a premier provider of international market and consumer data and market research reports. Euromonitor has offered a variety of print publications for many years, including *International Marketing Data and Statistics*, *Consumer International*, and many others. Passport GMID (also known as *Global Market Information Database*) is a portal that brings together Euromonitor's vast array of international consumer and market data, including data for many countries on consumer market sizes, market data and forecasts, consumer lifestyles, companies, and brands. Euromonitor reports that *Passport GMID* currently includes over 18,000 market research, industry, and company reports and some 8 million statistics on industries, countries, and consumers.

IBISWorld. http://www.ibisworld.com/. Price: Varies by subscription level and FTE. Contact the vendor for pricing information.

IBISWorld provides highly detailed industry reports covering over 700 different U.S. industries. In addition to their core industry research product, *IBISWorld* also produces over 700 U.S. Industry Risk Rating Reports, brief profiles for more than 8,000 publicly traded U.S. Companies, as well as hundreds of Business Environment Reports (economic and demographic profiles). Most industry reports are approximately 35 pages long, are updated several times per year, and contain nine standard chapters. IBISWorld also offers a less extensive global industry segment and a separate "China Site" covering over 175 industries in China. Given its scope, *IBISWorld* has become one of the most popular sources for industry reports in academic institutions.

MarketResearch.com. http://www.marketresearch.com. For pricing information, contact the vendor. Individual reports can also be purchased; check the website for individual prices.

MarketResearch.com, established in 1998, is a large database of market research reports. Currently, there are over 250,000 reports from over 650 publishers. There are several different products for its customer segments: MarketResearch.com Academic for academic institutions, MarketResearch.com Enterprise for corporate clients, and both alert and custom services where customers can purchase individual reports (pricing per report is available by searching the Web site). Reports can range from 20 to over 400 pages in length, and are regularly updated. MarketResearch.com is considered one of the most authoritative resources for market research reports and is used widely in both academic institutions and the corporate sector.

Mintel. http://www.mintel.com/. For pricing information, contact the vendor.

Mintel International Group, established in 1972, is a London-based producer of high-quality market research reports with an emphasis on consumer products and services, leisure, retail, financial services, sales promotion, and social trends. Mintel provides up-to-date market research reports in a number of modular options, including Mintel Oxygen Academic, its product for academic institutions, which offers over 600 yearly reports focusing primarily on the United States and Europe. Users can also select options that include Mintel Reports within certain market segments such as food and drink, or the beauty industry.

BUSINESS DATA/TIME SERIES

Advanced academic researchers, typically faculty and doctoral students, often require access to historical time series data on companies, industries, markets, or other financial information. The resources discussed in this section tend to be available primarily at larger academic institutions offering advanced business degrees.

Compustat. Standard & Poor's. http://www.compustat.com/myproducts.aspx. Standard & Poor's *Compustat* is one of the largest sets of business data, providing fundamental and market data on over 54,000 securities to users through a variety of databases and analytical software products. The primary databases are Compustat North America, Research Insight, Market Insight, Compustat Global, Compustat Executive Compensation, and Emerging Markets Database. Most major research libraries offer access to Compustat via WRDS (Wharton Research Data Services) or via *Capital IQ* (see separate entries for WRDS and Capital IQ). Institutions can also subscribe to individual segments of Compustat. Major segments are outlined below. Contact the vendor for specific pricing information.

- **Compustat North America** is a database of U.S. and Canadian fundamental and market information on more than 24,000 active and inactive publicly held companies. It provides more than 300 annual and 100 quarterly Income Statement, Balance Sheet, Statement of Cash Flows, and supplemental data items. Compustat North America files are available in both annual and quarterly formats. For most companies, annual and quarterly data are available for a maximum of 20 years and 48 quarters. Compustat North America files also contain information on aggregates, industry segments, banks, market prices, dividends, and earnings. For more detailed information on the Compustat files, consult the Compustat User's Guide.
- **Standard & Poor's Research Insight** provides an easy Windows-based interface to access financial data and company reports from the Compustat database. The database is customizable and accessible through Excel, and users can create financial models, industry analyses, and stock-screening tools.

- **Compustat Global:** The Compustat Global database provides financial and market data, focusing on non-U.S. and non-Canadian companies. Currently, the database provides information on over 28,500 companies, which Standard & Poor's indicates constitutes more than 90 percent of the world's market capitalization.
- **Emerging Markets Data Base:** Standard & Poor's Emerging Markets Data Base (EMDB) provides information and statistics on stock markets in developing countries in Asia, Latin America, Eastern Europe, Africa, and the Middle East. Information includes market performance, indicators, market capitalization, monthly value traded, local stock market price indexes, and prices in local currency and U.S. dollars, back to 1995.
- **Compustat Executive Compensation** provides annual executive compensation data from 1992 forward, on the top five executive officers within a company. The database currently contains information on over 32,000 executives from more than 2,900 companies.

CRSP (The Center for Research in Securities Prices). http://www.crsp.com/. For pricing information, contact the vendor.

CRSP, affiliated with the Booth School of Business at the University of Chicago, is the provider of the most comprehensive historical databases on securities/stock prices. Founded in 1960 through a $300,000 grant from Merrill Lynch, CRSP began work to develop its first database consisting of the stock prices, dividends, and rates of return of all stocks listed and trading on the **NYSE** since 1926. The original database was completed in 1964. Since that time, CRSP has developed several other important financial databases. In 1984, CRSP added data from the **NASDAQ** markets (starting from December 1972); in 2006 it added its **Pre1962** daily stock price data from 1926 through 1962. The **CRSP Survivor-Bias-Free US Mutual Fund Database** was added in the mid-1990s; it provides complete historical information for approximately 39,000 open-ended funds, 13,000 of which are now delisted. Other products are the **CRSP/Compustat Merged Database (CCM)**, comprised of CRSP and Compustat data together with the link and link-history references between these two databases. It includes Standard & Poor's Compustat data, reformatted into CRSP's proprietary database format. Also available is the **CRSP/Ziman Real Estate Data Series** containing historical information on real estate investment trusts (REITs) traded on all three exchanges back to 1980. CRSP is also available via WRDS.

Datastream. Thomson Reuters. http://online.thomsonreuters.com/data stream/. Contact the vendor for pricing information.

Thomson Reuters Datastream is arguably the largest and most comprehensive financial database. Content includes a broad range of financial statistics that is global in coverage. According to the Datastream website, content includes daily prices, trading volumes, and return indexes, updated at the end of every trading day, for over 100,000 equities in nearly 200 countries around the world. Datastream includes over 140 million time series containing over 10,000 data types. Datastream also includes information on options, futures, commodities, derivatives, bonds, mutual funds, market indexes, interest and exchange rates, macroeconomic variables, and corporate financial data. There are a number of different options and features available, and results can be downloaded easily into Microsoft Excel, Word, or PowerPoint. Date ranges vary by type of data, but many are available back to the 1970s.

Global Financial Data. http://www.globalfinancialdata.com. Contact the vendor for pricing information.

Global Financial Data contains historical financial and economic data series data, including inflation data from the thirteenth century to the present, stock market data from the 1600s to the present, and commodities data from the 1500s to the present. This source is unique in that it covers financial and economic data earlier than the twentieth century. Coverage includes more than 150 countries.

I/B/E/S. Thomson Reuters. http://thomsonreuters.com/products_services/financial/financial_products/a-z/ibes/. For pricing information, contact the vendor.

I/B/E/S (Institutional Brokers' Estimate System), now a part of Thomson Reuters, is a database providing analysts' estimates of future earnings for thousands of publicly traded companies worldwide. I/B/E/S contains detailed earnings estimates back to 1982, with summary data back to 1976. U.S. coverage begins in 1976, with international company data starting in 1987. I/B/E/S is also accessible via WRDS.

OptionMetrics. http://www.optionmetrics.com/. Contact the vendor for specific pricing information.

OptionMetrics is a leading provider of historical price and volatility data for the U.S. equity and index options markets. OptionMetrics was formed in 1999 "with the goal of providing accurate and reliable data and services for the econometric analysis of the options markets," and it is the leading database for researchers analyzing options markets and information. OptionMetrics is also available via WRDS.

SDC Platinum. Thomson Reuters.
http://thomsonreuters.com/products_services/financial/financial_products/deal
_making/investment_banking/sdc. For pricing information, contact the vendor.

The SDC (Securities Data Company) Platinum database detailed historical information on new issues/initial public offerings (*Global New Issues*); mergers, acquisitions and joint ventures; and private equity/venture capital (*VentureXpert*). Much of the data goes back to the 1970s. SDC is owned by **Thomson Reuters**.

Trade and Quote (TAQ). New York Stock Exchange. http://www.nyx data.com/Data-Products/Daily-TAQ. Contact the vendor for specific pricing information.

The Daily Trade and Quote (TAQ) database is a collection of intraday trades and quotes for all securities listed on the New York Stock Exchange, American Stock Exchange, NASDAQ National Market System, and SmallCap issues. TAQ provides historical tick-by-tick data of all stocks listed on NYSE back to 1993. TAQ is available for purchase from the New York Stock Exchange, and is also accessible via WRDS. Prices start at $1,000/month of data.

BUSINESS INFORMATION COMPANIES/AGGREGATORS

Many sources of business information are not limited to one kind of data or information, such as only company or industry information. Many providers now offer broader kinds of business databases that cover many areas of business information, encompassing company/industry data, news, investment reports, software or modeling applications, and a variety of other types of information and tools. This section covers some of the most popular databases that fall into this category. (See also Lexis-Nexis, in Chapter 2.)

Factiva. http://factiva.com/. Contact the vendor for pricing information.

Dow Jones Factiva is a leading provider of global business news and information with full-text content from more than 28,000 sources, from 157 countries in 23 languages. Date ranges vary for individual publications. The "News Page" feature allows users to browse the current day's front-page headlines from major U.S. newspapers and magazines, including the *Wall Street Journal*, and is customizable. The "Company/Markets" section allows users to search for company information and current and historical stock quotes.

OneSource. http://www.onesource.com/. For pricing information, contact the vendor.

OneSource provides a range of public and private company and industry information, including company profiles, news, business and trade articles, analyst reports, executive profiles, industry intelligence, and financial data. OneSource, in business for about 20 years, pulls information together from a variety of other sources, including Datamonitor, Thomson Reuters, Investext, and Experian. It currently provides global coverage of over 4 million firms, more than 100 industry sectors, and over 12 million corporate executives.

WRDS (Wharton Research Data Services). http://wrds.wharton .upenn.edu. Price: Currently $37,500 per year. Users must also subscribe to individual data products separately in order to access via WRDS.

Wharton Research Data Services (WRDS) is a web-based business data research service from The Wharton School at the University of Pennsylvania. WRDS was originally developed in 1993 to support faculty research at Wharton; since then, it has evolved into a common tool for business and related research for over 250 top research institutions around the world. WRDS provides web access and a standard interface to a large number of important business research databases and data sets, including Bureau van Dijk, Compustat, CRSP, GSI Online, I/B/E/S, KLD, OptionMetrics, TAQ, and some Thomson data (all of these are discussed elsewhere in this chapter). Institutions pay a standard subscription cost for the WRDS service and must also subscribe directly to the individual data providers for access to specific data products. WRDS allows faculty, doctoral students, and qualified research assistants at subscribing institutions to obtain individual and class accounts that are accessible anywhere in the world via an ID and password that is supplied to the user. WRDS also provides research support to users.

INTERNATIONAL INFORMATION/DATA

In today's global economy, business researchers regularly need data and information related to international companies and industries. Although many of the databases and sources covered in this chapter contain international information (see also Compact D/SEC and Worldscope; Compustat Global; Compustat Emerging Markets Database; IBISWorld; MarketLine; Mergent Online), the resources highlighted in this section specialize in this area.

Bureau van Dijk. http://www.bvdinfo.com/. For pricing information, contact the vendor.

Bureau van Dijk provides international company information through several different products and databases. **ORBIS**, its global database, combines information from around 100 sources and covers nearly 65 million companies.

Another database, **Amadeus**, is a premier source for over 14 million European companies. **Bankscope** provides information on banks and the banking industry; **ISIS** provides insurance company information; **ORIANA** contains comprehensive information on companies across the Asia-Pacific region, and OSIRIS is a database containing financial information on globally listed public companies, including banks and insurance firms from over 190 countries. **Zephyr** contains information on over 800,000 mergers and acquisitions, joint ventures, venture capital/private equity deals, and initial public offerings. Several of the Bureau van Dijk databases are also available via the WRDS platform.

Economist Intelligence Unit (EIU). Economist Group. http://www.eiu .com. Contact the vendor for specific pricing information.
EIU, part of the Economist Group, which also publishes *The Economist* newsmagazine, is one of the oldest and best known providers of country information. The database covers more than 200 markets, including country analysis and forecasts, risk assessment, economic and market data, economic forecasts, daily news analysis, industry trends, and management strategies. EIU provides background information and five-year forecasts on six key industries: automotive, consumer goods, energy, financial services, health care, and technology. Recently, EIU has become well known for its global livability and cost of living surveys and indexes, covering a number of indicators in 140 cities worldwide. EIU has been in business since 1946 and now operates 40 offices worldwide employing more than 150 full-time country specialists.

globalEDGE. Michigan State University. http://globaledge.msu.edu/. Price: Free.
Created by the International Business Center at Michigan State University, globalEDGE is a free web portal providing access to a vast body of international business information. Users can find detailed information on countries and industries; resources on international trade; and many other resources related to international business.

ISI Emerging Markets. Internet Securities, Inc. http://www.securities.com/. Price: Starts at about $500/month.
ISI (Internet Securities, Inc.), established in 1994, provides information on more than 80 emerging markets through its Emerging Markets Information Service. Coverage focuses on Asia, Latin America, Central and Eastern Europe, the Middle East, and Africa, and includes full-text news, financial and economic data, country, company, and market data, and reports.

International Financial Statistics. International Monetary Fund. http:// www.imfstatistics.org/imf/. For pricing information, contact the vendor.

The International Financial Statistics database, produced by the statistics department of the International Monetary Fund, contains time series data back to 1948 (annually) or 1957 (quarterly) on a wide variety of international financial statistics. The database contains approximately 32,000 time series covering more than 200 countries of the world including data on exchange rates, international liquidity, international banking, money and banking, interest rates, prices, production, international transactions, government accounts, and national accounts.

Political Risk Services (PRS). http://www.prsgroup.com/. Contact the vendor for specific pricing information.

PRS produces a number of well-known sources related to international business/political risk and risk forecasting. PRS offers a number of modules, including *Country Reports*, guides to 100 countries, each assessing potential political, financial, and economic risks to business investments and trade. *Country Forecasts*, published semiannually in April and October, provides a four-page summary of forecasts and data for each of the 100 countries monitored by PRS. Most institutions subscribe to PRS Online, which includes both *Country Reports* and *Country Forecasts* as well as *Political Risk Letter*, a monthly newsletter covering key events and a summary of the 100 countries covered.

SELECT SPECIALIZED SUBJECT-SPECIFIC DATABASES

Given the nature of specialized academic research, the types of information needed are almost unlimited. While academic business researchers regularly need data or information from other disciplines, there are also many smaller, very specialized products available to address more focused, subject-specific research needs in business. This section covers just a few of the more well-known products useful to academic researchers.

Audit Analytics. http://www.auditanalytics.com/. Price: commercial pricing is currently $16,000/year; contact the vendor for academic pricing.

Audit Analytics provides detailed research on over 20,000 public companies and more than 1,500 accounting firms. Information includes data sources for tracking and analysis of public company disclosure issues and trends including audits, compliance, governance, corporate actions, and federal litigation. Audit Analytics is also available via the WRDS platform.

BNA (Bureau of National Affairs). http://www.bna.com/. For pricing information, contact the vendor.

BNA specializes in business law and governmental information, news, and data with over 350 separate publications in the areas of corporate law and business; employee benefits; employment and labor law; environment, health, and safety; health care; human resources; intellectual property; litigation; and taxation and accounting. Institutions subscribe to these product segments individually. Each product covers federal and state laws and regulations; legal cases; analysis of laws and cases; news sources; and practice tools in the subject area.

CCH Intelliconnect. Commerce Clearing House. http://intelliconnect .cch.com/. For pricing information, contact the vendor.

CCH's *Intelliconnect* platform allows users to search the entire CCH library of tax and accounting information. Formerly known as the CCH *Tax Research Network*, *Intelliconnect* provides comprehensive coverage of federal, state, and international tax information, as well as a wealth of accounting information. CCH includes full-text legal and news services covering taxation and accounting; also available for licensing within the *Intelliconnect* platform is CCH's **Capital Changes Reporter**, which covers federal taxation consequences of corporate capital changes resulting from stock dividends, stock splits, reorganizations, exchanges, rights, and other changes in the capital structure of a company.

KLD Research & Analytics, Inc. RiskMetrics Group. http://www.kld .com/. Contact the vendor for pricing information. KLD is also available via WRDS.

KLD, recently acquired by RiskMetrics Group, is a leading research company providing information related to socially responsible investing, primarily the impact of environmental, social, and governance factors (ESG). Founded in 1988, KLD offers several different products, including **Global Socrates**, a database of over 2,000 ESG factors for over 4,000 global companies. In 1990 KLD created the Domini 400 SocialSM Index (DS 400 Index), a socially screened, capitalization-weighted index of 400 common stocks that is recognized as the first social investment benchmark.

RIA Checkpoint. Research Institute of America. https://checkpoint.riag .com/. For pricing information, contact the vendor.

RIA (Research Institute of America) *Checkpoint* is a comprehensive federal, state, and international tax database that includes primary source literature, editorial/secondary source materials and analyses, news alerts, a tax thesaurus, several Warren, Gorham & Lamont tax treatises and journals, and some archives dating back to 1860. RIA is owned by **Thomson Reuters**. There are optional additions for **AICPA** (American Institute of Certified Public Accountants), **FASB** (Financial Accounting Standards Board), **GASB** (Governmental Accounting Standards Board), and **IASB** (International Accounting Standards Board) content. AICPA content includes the Audit & Accounting Guides, Professional Standards, Technical Practice Aids, and other alerts while the FASB content includes Original Pronouncements, Current Text, EITF Abstracts, Staff Implementation Guides, Exposure Drafts, and Staff Positions. **GASB** content includes GASB Statements, Interpretations, Technical Bulletins, Exposure Drafts, and Concept Statements. The **IASB** content includes Standards, Interpretations, and Implementation Guide.

RiskMetrics. RiskMetrics Group. http://www.riskmetrics.com/. Contact the vendor for specific pricing information.

RiskMetrics Group, acquired in 2010 by MSCI Barra, consists of three primary business units—risk management, governance services, and financial research and analysis—all of which help investors assess various types of risk through a variety of separate data products. RiskMetrics originally started in 1994 as a part of JP Morgan, but was spun off in 1996 as a separate company, going public in 2008. Its products now include **KLD** (discussed earlier) and **the Investor Responsibility Research Center (IRRC)**. RiskMetrics delivers its data via WRDS in its Governance, Historical Governance, Directors, Historical Directors, Voting Results, and Shareholder Proposal datasets. With the acquisition of RiskMetrics, MSCI Barra continues its growth as a publicly traded risk management company. MSCI Barra (formerly known as Morgan Stanley Capital International) is perhaps best known for its popular MSCI World stock index of 1500 global stocks, which it started in 1969.

CONCLUSION

Selecting and acquiring resources to support academic business researchers is an ongoing challenge. The goal of this chapter is to provide an overview of the most heavily used resources that are typically available in many of the libraries supporting top business schools, particularly those with MBA and doctoral programs. There are many options and platforms available for products supporting various types of academic business research, so librarians are encouraged to consult regularly and often with their faculty and students to ensure that the suite of products selected by a library best supports the range of research needs within a particular institution.

9

Collection Development for Business

Mark E. Andersen

INTRODUCTION

The collections within the business library are a vital source of information to small-business owners, faculty, students, researchers, and the general public. These users come to the business library seeking investment information, in-depth explanations of business processes, or description of a business topic. The business collection is equally important for background information, analysis, research needs, history, biography, "how-to" information, as well as recreational reading. Therefore it is vital for this collection to be up to date, relevant, and utilized.

For all of these reasons, development of the business collection must be a focus of the business librarian. Business collection development requires time, knowledge, concentration, and maintenance. Yet collection development is more of an art than a science. There is no magic formula, and every business collection, every user, and every library is different. Therefore even more time, energy, and knowledge are required to tailor your business collection to your community and its needs. There are some preliminary steps that can be undertaken to ensure that the business library is meeting the needs of your users.

It is a good practice to create a collection development policy for your library that will serve as a guide for the business librarian. The points outlined below can be assembled and used to articulate the needs and policies for your library. This document can guide you through collection development issues as well as being an excellent tool to orient new staff.

MISSION

Understanding the mission of your library, along with an understanding of who your users are, is vital to the success of collection development. These users need to be identified so that their needs can be articulated and met. Their use of your collection will show how much value they find within it. The business collection must also reflect this mission. For printed materials, the mission reflects which resources you purchase, how many copies you purchase, and how long you keep a book or maintain a subscription. If your mission is to be a research library, you will weed very little, keeping materials for historical research value. If your mission is instead to provide practical and "how-to" information, you probably will not keep most books longer than 5 to 10 years. For electronic resources, collections criteria include which resources to purchase, how many users are permitted, and how often you evaluate and renew or cancel these resources. Until recently electronic resources have been mostly limited to databases or electronic reference books. However, e-books are becoming more and more popular and more and more accessible. This demand for e-books will continue to increase and the librarian will be faced with yet another media type to juggle within the business collection.

In an academic library, the collection should reflect the curriculum. Contacts and knowledge of faculty, students, and course listings may be used to determine the types of materials that need to be acquired. Faculty may have suggestions about materials they want for their classes or for their research. In addition to their own research needs, they can also provide guidance on the research needs of their students and the required readings and texts they assign to their students. Good relationships with the faculty are essential for ensuring that your collection is relevant.

Users in public libraries are more difficult to identify or pin down. They can be anyone. Nevertheless, it is important to determine who your users are, and what role the library plays in your community. The public library serves everyone from sophisticated investors and job seekers to small-business owners and casual readers. Therefore, although specific doctoral dissertations may not be needed, some practical "Getting started in . . . " books would be excellent choices. Determining which users you are serving is important. As you are developing and examining your collection, you should also think about who you want your users to be and start acquiring materials that will be of use to them. For example, if you want to attract more entrepreneurs to your library, you may want to start purchasing books about business plans or how to start a business.

BEYOND THE MISSION

In addition to your users, many other factors need to be considered when developing your business collection. Your budget will have a direct influence on which items you can purchase. Some questions to consider: How expensive is an item? Will it be useful to a number of patrons or just one? Does this resource overlap with existing aspects of the collection?

These issues take on a greater significance when you are dealing with materials that are especially expensive, such as large reference sets, a specialized reference item, or electronic resources. Development of your business collection is a constant balancing act. On one hand, the needs and demands of your users are key factors in making your business library useful and meaningful. On the other hand, funding is a finite and shrinking resource. Thus the collections budget will play a critical role in determining which resources are purchased for the business library. If money were no object, every library would have an unlimited supply of resources available in the library and remotely for their patrons. Obviously, this is not the case. It is the job of the business collection development librarian to weigh all of these factors and determine which items to purchase and which ones not to purchase.

Many issues pertain to both printed materials and electronic resources, but there are some topics that are more pertinent to electronic resources, and those need to be explored separately. Theoretically, if there are two books on hedge funds, you could purchase both titles. When you have two electronic resources that cover much of the same material, though, purchasing each one may well not be an option, at least for most business libraries. One electronic resource must be selected over another. An obvious example would be ProQuest's ABI/INFORM and EBSCO's Business Source Premier (covered in Chapter 2). How do you choose? Both provide access to articles in business periodicals (and more), but you will need to decide which resource better serves the needs of your particular community.

The choice of one product/vendor over another product/vendor can be influenced by many factors:

- Cost: We like to believe that price does not drive a collection development decision, but this oftentimes is the sole determining factor in your choice.
- Platform: Can the product easily interface with your library's current ILS platform?
- Choice and selection of materials covered: Your library requires electronic access to a specific periodical. If this title is not available from one of the vendors, you may decide to eliminate that vendor's product from consideration. Another related factor: which product has the stronger holdings in an important subject area for your library?
- Date coverage: Does the product have significant historical coverage? How often is the database updated?
- Full-text, abstracts, indexing: Does the resource provide full text? If not, is indexing and abstracting sufficient reason to purchase?

LICENSING

As more and more printed materials move to an electronic format, the issue of licensing becomes more prominent. These licenses are contracts, and, just as you might suspect, you will need some guidance from your administrative office, IT department, and/or legal department on what kinds of licensing terms and conditions can be permitted or accepted. These issues will vary from library to library as well as university or municipality. Licensing is an area where the business librarian does not act alone. Some major licensing issues include:

- Number of concurrent users: How many patrons can use this product at the same time? This is frequently reflected in the cost. Usually a higher cost will allow for a higher number of simultaneous users.
- Remote users: Are these electronic resources available to your users when they are outside the library? More and more users are accessing our resources from home, or other remote locations.
- Authorized users: Who are your users? Some vendors price their material based on your user population—however that may be defined.

  1. For an academic library, this pricing may be dependent on the size of student enrollment or Full Time Equivalent (FTE). But is it the entire student population, or only the students enrolled in the business program? Can "walk-in" users—users who have no current relationship with the institution as either students or employees—access these products? If the university is state funded, it might be obligated to allow walk-in patrons access to all services and resources.

  2. Public libraries provide access to all users, so it is more difficult for them to limit usage. Again, who are the authorized users: active library cardholders regardless of home address, number of branch locations, or the population numbers for the entire local area? Some vendors of business information see the public library, and even the academic library, as a direct threat to their own business strategy. If users can come to the public library, or log in remotely using a library card ID, and use a resource for free, then the provider may potentially lose a paying customer. Clearly, the terms and conditions that define "authorized" users, and their usage rights both within the library and remotely, are critical considerations.

  3. Some databases are not even available to public libraries. Some vendors see merit in having their products available only in academic libraries. This is seen as a way to familiarize the students

(future businesspeople) with their products and create corporate demand for their product once the students enter the workforce.

- Automatic renewal: Will a renewal notice be sent out each year? Do cancellations or changes need to be made a specified number of days in advance of the contract expiring? Or does the subscriptions renew automatically?
- Content: Does it appear the same in print as it does online? Is the content of the database more textual/narrative or numeric? Does there need to be a balance?
- Future access: Does the library continue to own the previously purchased material, even if the library stops subscribing to new content? If so, how does the library continue or maintain that access? What happens if the vendor goes out of business?
- Hosting fees: Are there additional fees for the vendor to house the information for you?
- Interlibrary loan (ILL) requests: Can ILL requests be filled using these resources? Is interlibrary loan defined in the license or contract as an appropriate or "acceptable" use?
- Usage statistics: Are usage statistics provided? These statistics are an important evaluation tool to see if your patrons are using the product.
- Exporting capabilities: What are the printing, e-mailing, and downloading capabilities of a resource? More and more electronic resources provide citation-generation features. Will your users expect or demand that kind of capability?
- Ease of use: How easy is it for your users to understand the database and use it correctly? What kinds of training materials does the vendor provide? How good is the available online help?

The bottom line is that the business librarian and the purchasing or legal department need to work together so that they can obtain the best licensing agreements for your institution and all of your users. This task is not necessarily as daunting as it may first appear to be. Many publishers and vendors will work with the library if a specific term or condition is not acceptable to the library or its parent institution. It is always worthwhile to ask a vendor to amend problematic licensing terms before eliminating a product from consideration.

And there may be some ways to convert a complicated license into a more readily understandable agreement. Shared Electronic Resource Understanding (SERU)—http://www.niso.org/workrooms/seru—is an agreement whereby database vendors and libraries agree not to have licensing agreements per se but to have a general agreement or guidelines between the specific library and a specific vendor (Hadro 2009). This saves the libraries and database vendors the time and expense of having each other's legal teams write and examine contracts. The actual SERU guidelines are about five pages long and are written in nonlegal language (http://www.niso.org/publications/rp/RP-7-2008.pdf). SERU is still relatively new, having only been established in 2008. Hopefully SERU can ensure that licensing is a win-win for database vendors and librarians alike.

SELECTING AND MANAGING BOOK COLLECTIONS

While collection development of electronic business resources issues usually involves other staff at your library, such as administration and legal personnel, the business book collection can often be handled by one person, the business librarian. In larger business libraries, the business section may be broken down into specific areas, such as accounting, marketing, finance, etc., and responsibilities may be divided among a number of librarians.

However, collection development for business books is not as straightforward as one might imagine. Some business collections encompass related social sciences, including statistics; others may exclude such related areas as economics. It is important to determine which subject areas will be the responsibility of your specific library. Doing so will ensure that each part of the collection is the responsibility of someone. Once you have determined which subject areas will be included in your collection, you need to identify the corresponding call numbers for these subject areas. This may sound basic, but doing so will give your collection some boundaries that will make the rest of your collection development go more smoothly and easily. It is important to know where your business collection begins and ends. While this may not make any difference to your users, it is fundamental to the maintenance of your collection. Know the corresponding call numbers for each subject area for both the Dewey Decimal and Library of Congress (LC) classification systems.

As you will see, many of the collection development tools you may use can be focused on a very specific call number range or an individual call number. And because some of the resources for collection development use Dewey and others use LC, it is useful to have both ranges of call numbers on hand as you start your collection development.

Once you know your users and the subject areas to be covered, you need to determine the budget allocation. How much of your budget will be allocated to each subject area or call number range? How much of your budget is allocated to serials, monographs, online resources, and e-books? These figures can be determined by usage or by the size of a specific department, or the size of the business community. What proportions of the budget do you assign to each call number area? Your decisions may be based on the number of courses taught in each subject area in an academic setting, or on the usage in a public library. Again, this determination will be a reflection of your library's mission. Circulation records may also provide data for usage in a specific area. This allocation may need to be updated and adjusted over time. And special funding allocations may need to be made depending on current events, such as the subprime mortgage crisis, or the introduction of a new course.

The most fun and rewarding aspect of collection development is identifying the books and subject areas you want to acquire. You will not want to add just any book to your collection, so we can turn to some specific resources to provide guidance.

Reviews, Directories, and Other Evaluative Sources

Book reviews are probably one of the most important resources for librarians searching for new titles to acquire. No librarian can read every book in his or her collection, contrary to what some patrons may believe. Since librarians are not necessarily experts in every area of business, book reviews can provide some guidance.

Librarianship has a number of resources that are available in most libraries. The periodicals *Library Journal*, *Booklist*, *Publishers' Weekly*, and *Choice* are probably the most popular in the field. *Choice* targets academic libraries, but it can be useful for large public libraries, too. Some of these professional magazines also have special features, such as *Library Journal's* "Best of {year}: Business Books." Sometimes there is an article or special feature highlighting titles on a specific business topic, which can be very useful. Some of these review sources also have online counterparts, which frequently contain more reviews that the print editions do.

The *American Book Publishing Record* lists books published, and does not provide reviews. However, it can keep the librarian informed of books that have been published in the last month. The entries are listed in Dewey Decimal call number order, so knowledge of the Dewey call numbers for your collection will be useful. If your library uses LC, you should also know the Dewey ranges of your collection.

General and national media are also excellent sources for book reviews. The *New York Times*, *USA Today*, and your local newspapers are excellent resources. These newspapers often have a best-selling books list and sometimes even a bestselling business book list. They also have separate business sections, which may contain book reviews as well. Local and national radio programs are also great resources, but those may be difficult to research if you do not hear them live. However, some of these programs may have online archives, or have transcripts included in general article databases available in libraries. Patrons are likely to ask for a book they have seen reviewed in the local press, online, or on TV/radio. Books of local or regional interest may also appear in local newspapers and media.

The *Wall Street Journal* and the *Financial Times* are two of the most esteemed business newspapers. While they regularly run book reviews, these reviews are not only for business books. However, many of the books reviewed have crossover interest for business patrons. The weekend edition of the *Wall Street Journal* lists the best-selling books: nonfiction, fiction, and business. These lists are a great way to assess your collection and make sure it is up to date.

All of these valuable resources can be shared with other subject collection development librarians at your library, thus spreading the selection work (and potentially the cost) of these materials throughout the library. Make it a practice for all selection librarians to share these resources and inform each other of books in their respective areas.

Many business journals, professional journals, and trade journals carry book reviews that cater to their specific readers. Sometimes the reviews are regular features, while some are published irregularly. These journals are very good at identifying books that may not be considered general interest or mainstream. It would be impossible to subscribe to all of these journals, but it would be worthwhile to see which journals your library subscribes to and determine if they include book reviews.

The periodical databases that index and often provide full texts for magazine and journal articles also provide access to book reviews appearing in these sources. Database providers such from ProQuest and EBSCO (as covered in Chapter 2) provide specific tools to look for book reviews. You can limit your search to your business databases, and look for an advanced search option allowing a limit to a specific document type—in this case a book review. You can then add a specific keyword or limit it to a particular journal title. You may want to perform this search on a regular basis or even set up an automated search, or alert, to notify you when new book reviews are added to a database.

One specialized business is librarianship periodical that can also be useful for collection development are the *Journal of Business & Finance Librarianship* (JBFL). JBFL has a book review section that encompasses large, expensive reference titles, as well as business monographs. There are only a handful of reviews per issue, but the featured titles are prominent and of interest to both public and academic libraries.

Amazon.com is an extremely popular resource for identifying books on any topic, and business is no exception. Although Amazon.com is now an all-around online retailer, it is probably still thought of first and foremost as a bookseller, and as such it has proven to be an excellent collection development tool for libraries. Its ease of use and up-to-date titles makes it an excellent place to begin searching. Keyword searching is perhaps the easiest, although there is some subject heading type searching available based on Amazon.com's unique metadata. You can also search by tags, which are subject headings assigned by other users. Amazon.com allows sorting by publication date, and therefore you can quickly see the latest published materials, as well as forthcoming materials. Other sort functions include relevance, best-selling, price (further sortable in ascending or descending order), and customer review (ranging from one to five stars). One of the advantages of Amazon.com is that is allows you to search a large number of publishers at once.

An additional feature of Amazon.com is the inclusion of professional book reviews, including those from *Booklist*, *Publishers Weekly*, and *Library Journal*. The reviews by individual customers may also be helpful, although one always needs to determine if the reviews are truly objective. Always consider the source of the review.

Although not technically a review source, the list of books acquired at the Baker Library | Bloomberg Center at the Harvard Business School (http://www.library.hbs.edu/bakerbooks/recent/allmonths.html) is another valuable free resource. This is a monthly list of books acquired by the business library of this prestigious university, and many of the titles are relevant for most universities and public libraries. The list is arranged alphabetically by title and includes author, publisher, and publishing date. Click on the title links to go into Harvard's catalog so you can see the catalog record, subject headings, ISBN, or call number.

OCLC Worldcat (http://www.worldcat.org), an online network of library records and holdings from around the world, is also a good tool for collection development. It provides cataloging information, and by using some of the advanced features, you can search for specific call number areas. By utilizing the expert searching feature, you can select "Library of Congress call number" to search for a specific call number. You can get as specific or as general as you need. The * can be used to truncate the call number and search for a wider call number area. For example, by searching "HF5415*" you can locate books within the range HF5415.12 and HF5415.1265. This capability is especially useful if you are searching for books on a narrow topic, and you have a very specific call number. Call number searching can also be done using the Dewey Decimal System. OCLC Worldcat also allows for limiting titles to a specific publication date or date range, subject heading, and keyword.

Although subject bibliographies are becoming less common than they once were, they are still good places to find additional, related titles on a subject. Research organizations and trade and industry associations often publish lists of recommended titles. You should determine which associations pertain to the fields covered by your users, or to which associations your faculty members belong. These associations may also act as publishers. For example, the American Management Association publishes a wide array of books on management, business communication, and leadership.

Bibliographies and notes at the back of well-read books or faculty publications may also yield books to be considered. Consider these bibliographies "social networking" for books. One friend—the trusted book—connects you to a list of other friends, the books listed in the bibliography.

Some business books function as a collection development tool all by themselves. One such title is *The 100 Best Business Books of All Time: What They Say, Why They Matter, and How They Can Help You*, by Jack Covert and Todd Sattersten (Portfolio, 2009). This kind of book can assist in filling gaps in your collection with classics that you may have missed, or may have disappeared from your shelves.

There are also a number of specific business publishers, such as Bloomberg, Portfolio, Entrepreneur Press, Wiley, Nolo (probably best known as a self-help legal publisher), and American Management Association. These publishers have a good reputation for business publications and you will want to watch for their new publications. It is a good idea to create a list of these publishers so you can do this more easily and readily. Publishers' printed catalogs are becoming fewer, and the process of publishers mailing out catalogs is lessening as more and more publishers rely on their websites. These websites provide an easy and inexpensive (and green) way to search these publisher websites and view their book titles. Once you find a publisher you trust and have seen the quality of its books, bookmark the site so you can regularly look for newly published titles. Many publishers will send out announcements or even electronic catalogs to those on their mailing list. So signing up for these lists may be beneficial. A publisher's reputation is a good indicator of quality.

Reading book reviews and assessing publishers' reputations are only two means by which you can build your business collection. Bear in mind, though, that not every book is reviewed, and many books are published by little-known publishers. There are other methods to determine if the book should be acquired by your library, and the industrious business librarian needs to seek out and consider books that may not have been reviewed, applying certain standards when doing so.

Determining if the author has a reputation in the field is another collection development method. Most authors tend to write in the same field because they are experts in that field. If you have determined that the author is known and respected in a specific field, or if the library owns others works by him or her, you can begin to trust the author's reputation. Then you can also search for additional books by the same author.

Many large book distributors, such as Ingram Book Company, Yankee Book Peddler, or Baker & Taylor, have their own databases that list the books they can supply. These databases allow you to search by titles or keywords, and some even allow for some type of call number searching. These are important tools, because they inventory the materials that these distributors can actually supply (and through which electronic orders may be submitted). Discounts may also be available, depending on the specific publishers involved. These companies can provide "shelf-ready" book processing, labels, and cataloging, as well as paperless ordering and billing.

In business (as well as law and medicine), it is important to the credibility of your library to acquire accurate and reputable books. The consequences for users are great if the materials provided by the library are incorrect and/or detrimental to its patrons. Patrons turn to the library as a trusted source of information, so it is our obligation to purchase reliable and accurate books.

Evaluating and Weeding Your Collection

Your book collection is like a garden. In order to grow, both need to be tended to and weeded. And also like a garden, one plant alone does not make your garden beautiful, nor does the lack of one plant make your garden a disaster. It is the overall collection of plants that defines your garden. The same can be said for the business library. Not having one book will not discredit your library (especially thanks to interlibrary loan). And adding just one title will not suddenly make your collection outstanding. It is the overall collection that will determine how your library is viewed and used. The sum is greater than the parts.

Many business books go out of date quickly, and thus need to be regularly monitored. Circulation statistics allow us to see both how often and how recently a book has been used. Many books peak right when they are published, and multiple copies may be needed to keep up with demand. As time goes on, and newer material becomes available, you may want to start weeding the extra copies (especially if circulation data shows little or no activity). Some academic or large public libraries may not want to weed books from the collection, preferring instead to keep a historical record of trends or current theories/thoughts of the time.

It is very important to keep abreast of current events and changes occurring in law and legislation; a collection that includes business law *must* be kept current. For example, in 2005, bankruptcy laws were revised by Congress. These laws changed who could file for different types of bankruptcy and whether repayment was required. This dramatically changed bankruptcy options; therefore any bankruptcy book published before 2005 needs to be discarded and replaced with updated titles (unless it is the mission of the library to retain such material to reflect the historical record).

In other instances, a book already in your collection may come to be revealed to have had some flaws in the original research. Take the example of the once wildly popular "Beardstown Ladies" books (Markin 2002: B7). Reporters and researchers have claimed that their investment returns were not quite what the Beardstown Ladies had claimed in their books. So what do you do? Some libraries might want to weed their books, although some might want to save them for reasons of their fame (or notoriety); another library might want to keep their books for historical reasons. Again, whatever weeding decision might be made, it needs to be made in the context of the mission of the library and its users.

Finally, there is the physical condition of a print book. No one wants to read a dirty or musty book. The same can be said for a book with a broken spine or a torn cover. Regular reviewing of your collection will identify these less than pristine books. If the books are still relevant, you may want to preserve this copy by mending or rebinding. However, it may be cheaper simply to purchase a newer copy of a physically damaged book.

Circulation Records

Thanks to online catalogs, there is a wealth of collection development data waiting to be mined in circulation records. Many circulation systems can produce reports listing popular titles. It is important to see what patrons are reading. You can usually set report parameters for a specific time period. You may also be able to limit a search to a specific call number range so, for instance, you can see the most highly circulating books on bonds (LC classification HG4651). On the opposite end of the spectrum, you can see which titles are not moving. Again, depending on the mission of your library, you may want to keep these titles or maybe you need to promote these books to your users.

Circulation records can also be reviewed to determine what has been lost or kept overdue. When you are looking at your physical library collection you cannot see what has been lost and not returned. The books may be gone for any number of reasons. They could actually be lost; or they could be just "kept" for the patron's own collection. If the book is currently unavailable to users and it is important for your collection, you will try to obtain another copy. Conversely you might want to purchase an updated edition or a more recent book on that subject.

OTHER ISSUES

Patron Requests

You should establish a policy on patron requests. If a faculty member requests a specific title, do you automatically purchase it? What if students request a title? Is cost a deciding factor? Does it need to fit into the mission of your library? Is the request mediated? How do you inform the patron of this decision? Do you purchase textbooks? With the increased cost of textbooks, resourceful students may look to the library. An academic library may have copies of current textbooks on reference or reserve. However, academic libraries generally cannot afford to purchase every text used in a class, much less multiple copies of such texts; a public library certainly cannot purchase every textbook used in every class in every area school.

Self-Published Books

Changes in technology have produced a new phenomenon in the form of self-published books or vanity press books. Previously, it was rather expensive to have your own book published, and only the very rich could afford such a luxury. However, with changes in technology and the ease with which these technologies can be utilized, it is relatively cheap and easy to self-publish. Thus the number of self-published titles has exploded. In the absence of such credentials as reputable authors or publishers, many libraries choose not to purchase self-published books because the credibility cannot be verified. Then again, if author credibility *can* be established, the library may want to consider acquiring a self-published the title.

Donations

Do you add any and every book given to the library? Probably not, but how do you determine which gifts to accept and keep? Again, guidelines for this kind of decision making should be found in your library's collection development policy. If a faculty member wants to donate his or her personal collection, do you accept it even though some of the titles are dated (and many may already be owned)? And what if the book is self-published? Do you reserve the right to discard or sell any books that are not added to the collection? Do you provide appraisals of these donated books and give the donor a receipt that he or she can use for his or her own tax returns? These are all issues that are best to have planned for in advance, and not left to be dealt with in the heat of the moment.

Out-of-Print Titles

It is now easier than ever to search for out-of-print books. In addition to Amazon.com, there are many online out-of-print book dealers who can supply books from around the world. Addall.com, abeBooks.com, and alibris.com are just a few of those that are available. These websites are excellent resources to consult when you need to replace a lost book, or to locate a title published long ago that you did not purchase when it was originally available.

Audiobooks and E-books

Audio books are another nonprint format that is rapidly moving from the realm of fiction into that of nonfiction, including business titles. Many patrons want to listen to a book while driving or relaxing. The ease of use and portability of this medium have also helped it to become more popular than ever.

The steadily growing popularity of electronic books (e-books) in recent years has given rise to a proliferation of platforms, such as (as of this printing) Amazon's Kindle, Sony's E-reader, Barnes & Noble's Nook, and the Apple iPad. In July 2010, Amazon.com reported that sales of its electronic book titles had surpassed its sales of printed books (Miller 2010). This is a huge shift in the book-publishing world. E-books are not only for fiction; many users are demanding that business titles (as well as other nonfiction subjects) be made available for use on their computers or mobile devices. This is a huge opportunity for publishers, but it presents a dilemma for libraries. On the one hand, libraries need to continue to attract and retain the early adopters of technology as allies of the library. On the other hand, very few libraries are increasing their budgets. During the economic downturn in recent years, more and more libraries are facing budget cuts while the demands for library services are increasing. So how do you add a whole new service? Unfortunately, doing so means taking funds that had previously been allocated for print books and periodicals only, and now further dividing these funds to include yet another medium. As a consequence, fewer unique titles are purchased overall, in order that at least some titles will be available in electronic formats.

Further considerations (or complications) continue to rise in collection development for e-books. For example, some titles may be available only in the e-book format, such as *The Great Stagnation: How America Ate All the Low Hanging Fruit of Modern History, Got Sick and Will (Eventually) Get Better* by Tyler Cowen. As of March 2011 this title was available only in electronic format and no print edition has been published. So having titles in electronic form may turn out to be the only way libraries will be able to obtain certain titles. This signals that e-books are less of a supplementary medium and more of a mandatory medium. As this continues to increase, you will need to reexamine the budget allocation for this medium as compared to your print and serial budgets.

And in March 2011, HarperCollins decided it would limit the number of times an e-book could be checked out (Bosman 2010). While libraries pay more for e-books than consumers do, libraries had assumed they would have the e-books forever. However, if e-books are in libraries for only a specific number of circulations, the most popular e-books will "vanish" when that circulation number is reached. Librarians will have to create another model for collection development of e-books.

These are but two examples of some of the challenges facing the collection development librarian regarding e-books. And this is only the beginning in what can be called the e-book revolution.

CONCLUSION

A well-developed business collection supports and enhances the credibility of your library, your staff, your municipality, your university, and your community. If patrons discover relevant, up-to-date, and interesting books in your library, they will become regular users. These regular users will in turn become advocates for the library, and these advocates will see the business library as a valuable, necessary partner in the community. This applies to an academic community as well as a municipality. Developing a business collection cannot be done overnight. But by articulating your library's mission and policies in a collection development policy, your business collection will be built on a strong foundation. Add a well-informed and conscientious librarian and your business collection will produce dividends for years to come.

REFERENCES

Bosman, Julie. 2010. "Publisher Limits Shelf Life for Library E-Books." *New York Times*, March 14. Accessed March 24, 2011. http://www.nytimes.com/2011/03/15/business/media/15libraries.html.

Hadro, Josh. 2009. "More Libraries and Publishers Join SERU Agreement from NISO for E-Resources." *Library Journal*, January 5. Accessed March 24, 2011. http://www.libraryjournal.com/article/CA6625398.html.

Markin, Jerry. 2002. "Disney Unit Settles Suit Over Claims of Beardstown Club." *Wall Street Journal* (Eastern edition), February 27, B7.

Miller, Clair Cain. 2010. "E-Books Top Hardcovers at Amazon." *New York Times*, July 19. Accessed March 24, 2011. http://www.nytimes.com/2010/07/20/technology/20kindle.html.

10

Business Reference:
Advice and Strategy for Serving Today's Business Users

Louise Klusek

TODAY'S LIBRARIES

Librarians are experiencing a "reference renaissance" centered on service and the building of new kinds of relationships with users. This "reference renaissance" will fundamentally change the ways in which reference librarians define their roles.

Ten years ago, many library professionals were predicting the end of reference services (Campbell 2000). It may be that this prediction was premature. Despite data that continue to indicate declining numbers of reference transactions, there is evidence that we are seeing a renewed interest by librarians in reference service. Many librarians, reacting against the simplified environment of the Google world, are meeting their users' needs with Web 2.0 applications, blogs, wikis, tagging, and social networking tools like Facebook and Twitter. Others are taking reference services outside the library's physical confines by means of virtual reference service and embedded-librarian programs. Librarians are dramatically increasing their presence in active teaching, curriculum development, and distance education. Librarians call this renewal of reference services a "reference renaissance" (Zabel 2007, 108). Conferences such as "Reference Renaissance: Current and Future Trends," sponsored in part by the Reference and User Services Association (RUSA), a division of the American Library Association, confirm this renewal.

Renewed focus on reference has arisen simultaneously with a fundamental service-oriented shift in the way libraries operate. This change is noted by Paula Kaufman, Dean of Libraries at the University of Illinois at Urbana-Champaign, who makes a persuasive argument that the twenty-first-century library should be measured by an expanded range and quality of library services (Kaufman 2009). She calls on librarians to collaborate with their faculty or community partners in service to teaching and learning and scholarship. James La Rue, director of Douglas Counties Libraries (Colorado), envisions the future librarian as a community asset, roaming the streets ("Theory Meets Practice" 2010). He proposes a model, the "community reference question," that challenges public librarians to work with users and nonusers alike to help them solve community problems. Reference librarians can naturally be the drivers of a shift to service, but they will have to change the way they define their roles, actively looking for means to engage and build relationships with their community.

THE BUSINESS LIBRARIAN AS CONTENT MANAGER

Business collections have changed, but the business librarian still fills the vital role of managing the collection for the user.

One of the traditional service roles of the reference librarian has been to connect users to the information in library collections. Until relatively recently, library reference collections were finite and in print. The librarian, as intermediary between the print collection and the user, was trained to know the collection, the key reference books, and their contents. The librarian also filled the role of "expert searcher," offering users access to database content through mediated searches. Today, however, we live in an information-rich environment where Google and the Internet bring a variety of basic business sources directly to the user. Researchers and businesspeople are demanding richer resources from libraries and they want these resources in a variety of formats: streaming video, audio, visual, and digital. Business students are asking for real-time data as well as historical-time series and data sets. They want help to map, model, and manipulate the information they find. Academic libraries are building digital collections and open-access research repositories and hiring specialists such as metadata librarians, GIS librarians, and data services librarians to manage information resources. Public libraries are building specialized collections in partnership with groups like the Foundation Center and SCORE (the Service Corps of Retired Executives) that support joint outreach and counseling programs to small-business owners and nonprofits. In this context, the traditional role of the business librarian has become redefined. Today's business librarian must assist users in making connections not only to print collections but to a multilayered electronic information universe. Moreover, the business librarian can no longer act alone but must work as part of an integrated team that helps users understand and interpret information found in their print, digital, and data collections.

One aspect of the changing collection visible to many library users is the shrinking size of the print reference collection. Acknowledging the decline of user reliance upon printed sources (encyclopedias, dictionaries, directories and other hard-copy reference materials), many libraries are dramatically increasing their investment in online reference sources. Digital reference sources help academic libraries reach users needing 24/7 access, as well as those who simply prefer to work outside the library building.

Many corporate libraries are serving fewer "walk-in customers" and are working with users in a virtual environment. They are "right-sizing" their print collections to emphasize core subjects. Librarians are building information portals and virtual reference systems. The NYU Virtual Business Library, for example, offers students a portal to all online resources for business research at New York University. It includes its own specialized search engine and tools that allow students to chat with other VBL users. Increasingly, libraries are actively bringing users to their digital collections by a variety of pathways. User-centered library websites provide tagging to bridge the language gap, as well as "My Library" applications so that users can customize their personal "libraries."

In the multisource electronic information world, the business librarian is faced with mastering an increasingly large and specialized collection of databases and research tools.

Transformations in the information industry demonstrate that we are in a rapidly changing research landscape. Mergers and consolidation of long-established information providers such as Thomson Reuters, the emergence of new niche financial publishers such as Eurekahedge, and the introduction of specialty products in emerging multidisciplinary fields confirm this trend.

At the same time that business researchers expect easy access to local and regional business data, they also depend on librarians to help them find and use databases containing information on emerging markets and international companies and industries. Many of the aggregator databases for business are complex systems. Developed for the trader, financial analyst, or business professional as a desktop work environment, they require considerable investment in librarian training and user support. Bloomberg, Thomson Reuters, and Dow Jones offer users access to an enormous variety of resources in a single platform. Financial data, stock quotes, news, charting, company profiles, public filings, and analysts' reports are only some of the information resources they provide. These databases are sophisticated yet essential tools for navigating the business information landscape.

Business librarians must constantly evaluate their database collection to meet the needs of their users. Many business users want such value-added features as data downloading, modeling analytics, or real-time data. Faculty want historical data sets and specialty databases in emerging research disciplines. Academic business librarians want to offer their students access to products they will use in the corporate workplace. Business librarians in all libraries must make complex purchasing decisions that balance cost, coverage, and value. Can the library depend on the SEC's free EDGAR for access to public company filings, or should it subscribe to EDGAR Online so users have XBRL-enhanced company filings? Should the library purchase an expensive market research database, or buy single reports as needed? While academic business librarians must balance the needs of students and faculty, public librarians must meet community needs, and corporate librarians must decide which databases are necessary for mission-critical decisions. Because of their expertise, corporate librarians often assume the role of content manager for their firms, assessing data needs, analyzing vendor offerings, and negotiating contracts for firm-wide access.

THE BUSINESS LIBRARIAN AS ADVISOR

Library users need an advisor, someone who can be their partner and help them navigate the research universe.

The digital information universe, offering the user an often overwhelming number of specialty resources, makes the role of the librarian as advisor a critical one. Advisory services are growing in all types of libraries, but not all services take place in the physical space of the library building. Many corporate librarians report that they are embedded librarians, working for the long term with business units or client groups (Shumaker and Tyler 2007). Other corporate librarians are collaborating with business teams in short-term project assignments. They are advising groups on research strategies, doing analysis, creating alerting services, and often writing reports and project summaries. Academic librarians, too, are testing the efficacy of being "embedded librarians." They are setting up offices with their departmental faculty, and they are going on the road, offering reference service in college dormitories and student centers. Librarians at Kresge Business Administration Library at the University of Michigan are offering reference service while embedded in action-based learning classes for first-year MBA students (Berdish and Seeman 2010).

Public libraries have long been recognized for offering career advisory services and literacy programs. Today many public libraries are partners with their communities in economic development initiatives (Urban Libraries Council 2007). Some libraries, especially those in rural areas, are part of the "economic gardening" movement (Hamilton-Pennell 2008); others work with local Chambers of Commerce or have established small-business resource centers. Brooklyn Public Library and Berkeley Public Library, for example, offer advisory services in partnership with SCORE. At these sites, librarians work with SCORE counselors reviewing clients' information needs, giving advice on how to gather competitive intelligence, and providing local entrepreneurs with access to the library's business databases and e-resources.

In academic libraries, librarians are engaging their users through research consultation services. Expert help and advice for students and faculty is available by appointment. When students, acting as self-directed learners, request research consultations, they bring the librarian actively into the research process/work flow. The business librarian is recognized by students as a subject expert, offering trusted advice about which sources to use, how to evaluate those sources, and how to incorporate them in their research. Business librarians often use consultation services to offer in-depth reference assistance, working with a single user over several sessions, for example by teaching graduate students how to manage research data or create bibliographies with citation management tools. At the John Cotton Dana Library at Rutgers University, librarians have used the consultation model with the MBA capstone course, Interfunctional Management (Tipton and Au 2009). The librarians function as guides for student teams working on business consulting projects with local businesses.

Librarians also offer advisory services virtually through e-mail, chat, or text/SMS venues. Library websites offer custom-built online knowledge centers with guides, FAQs, and other tools that help users identify and select the best sources. One of the most comprehensive guides for the business researcher was developed at the Rutgers University Libraries by their team of business librarians. The *Research Guide* links to more than 3,000 selected business and management-related Internet resources. Another tool developed specifically for business students is the University of Pennsylvania Lippincott Library's *Business FAQ*, an online knowledge base built on recurring questions answered by Lippincott librarians. *Business FAQ* contains over 500 unique business questions and is now "shared" with 25 other b-school libraries. Users query the FAQ and receive a concise guide to library databases, print sources, and selected websites.

Other libraries have used blogs and wiki platforms to build guides tailored to the research needs of their students. Librarians at the University of Michigan's Stephen M. Ross School of Business have developed the Kresge Business Administration Library Wiki. The Ohio University Libraries Biz Wiki, now the Business Blog, authored by Chad Boeninger, the Business & Economics Subject Specialist, features a continually growing series of research video and screencasts on its pages.

Research guides have been around for years in print form and are now a common tool on websites of public, corporate, and academic libraries. Today

Business Library Research Tools

Babson College. Horn Library. Tutorials
http://libguides.babson.edu/tutorials

Baruch College. Newman Library. SWOT Analysis
http://guides.newman.baruch.cuny.edu/swot

Berkeley Public Library. Small Business Help
http://www.berkeleypubliclibrary.org/community/small_business_help.php

Emory University. Goizueta Business Library. Porter's Five Forces Analysis
http://guides.business.library.emory.edu/porters_five_forces

New York University Libraries. Virtual Business Library
http://library.nyu.edu/vbl/

Ohio University. Ohio University Libraries Business Blog
http://www.library.ohiou.edu/subjects/businessblog/

Rutgers University Libraries. Research Guide—Business
http://libguides.rutgers.edu/business

University of Michigan. Kresge Business Administration Library Wiki
http://webservices.itcs.umich.edu/mediawiki/KresgeLibrary/index.php/Kresge
_Business_Administration_Library_Wiki

University of Pennsylvania. Lippincott Library. Business FAQ
http://faq.library.upenn.edu/recordList?library=lippincott&institution=Penn

they are even more widespread, as Web 2.0 publishing platforms make it possible for librarians to publish guides, add RSS feeds, embed videos, feature books from the catalog, and make lists of links without learning JavaScript or HTML coding. Today's guides are no longer simply lists of sources or sets of links but are active teaching tools in a dynamic electronic work environment. Users can search the catalog or business databases from the pages of a guide. They can work with resources that have been recommended for a specific course or business assignment. They can even talk to the librarian-author and subject expert in chat or by instant messaging. Business librarians have developed guides that are teaching tools; see, for example, Emory University Goizueta Business Library's guide to conducting a Porter's Five Forces Analysis and Baruch College's guide to SWOT Analysis. The Horn Library at Babson College includes two- to three-minute tutorials in their guides that help students learn business research strategies like analyzing market returns, identifying barriers to entry, finding substitutes, and researching the supply chain.

THE BUSINESS LIBRARIAN AS TEACHER

The librarian is a teacher at the reference desk, in the classroom or office, and online.

Where do we situate the reference librarian's role as a teacher? The answer is in all the places where we find our users: in the library, online, and in the classroom or office. Teaching often starts at the reference desk, the first place where librarians have a chance to engage with a potential user. In every reference interview we have the opportunity to pass on knowledge about resources, research strategies, source evaluation, or other information literacy skills. Alternatively, we can meet our users in the virtual reference environment or offer users learning opportunities with a variety of self-help tools.

We are seeing the growth of "Learn-It-Yourself" or "Self-Help" pages such as those at the Thomas J. Long Business Library at UC Berkeley and the Business & Economics Library at Columbia University. These resources respond to students' preference for just-in-time learning tools. In other initiatives designed to provide anytime access, librarians have developed tutorials, podcasts, and instructional videos that are featured on their websites and in iTunes University and YouTube. Podcasts at the Kresge Business Administration Library at the University of Michigan offer instruction on the go. Baruch College has developed business research tutorials specifically for use with large capstone and gateway courses. At Baruch, a tutorial for company research, *The Beginner's Guide to Business Research*, is used in the Introduction to Business course required of all business majors. *Industry Islands*, a game designed to model an industry research project using Porter's Five Forces, was developed for the capstone course in Business Policy.

In the 10 years since the Association of College and Research Libraries issued its standards for information literacy (ACRL 2000), constituencies ranging from accrediting agencies, college and university administrators, to faculty have increasingly recognized the importance of information literacy in education and in the workplace. In 2009, the White House too affirmed that "rather than merely possessing data, we must also learn the skills necessary to acquire, collate, and evaluate information for any situation" (White House 2009). Librarians are taking the lead on campus and are working with faculty writing information literacy standards into college-wide learning goals and serving on committees that assess these learning goals.

Corporate libraries are promoting information literacy by building personal and corporate knowledge bases. Many are actively involved in training programs for incoming associates. They work with information vendors and teach desktop applications as well as how to access shared information resources and use information management tools.

Business Library Teaching Tools and Programs

Baruch College. Industry Islands
http://www.baruch.cuny.edu/tutorials/zicklin/industryislands/

Brooklyn Public Library. Growing Dollars and $ense
http://www.brooklynpubliclibrary.org/growingdollars/

Columbia University. Business & Economics Library. Library Essentials
http://library.columbia.edu/services/workshops/essentials.html

Emory University. Goizueta Business Library. Business Essentials
http://business.library.emory.edu/communities/students/bba-program-0

New York Public Library. Financial Literacy Central @ SIBL
http://www.nypl.org/help/getting-oriented/financial-literacy-central

University of California–Berkeley. Thomas J. Long Business Library. Self-Help
   Tools
http://www.lib.berkeley.edu/BUSI/self_help_tools.html

University of Michigan. Kresge Business Administration Library Podcasts
http://www.bus.umich.edu/kresgelibrary/about/podcasts.htm

College librarians are teaching information literacy in programs that are integrated in the business curriculum. NYU reports that "course embedded librarians" who provide course-integrated instruction are the norm (Whatley 2009, 30). In an example of librarian faculty collaboration, librarians at Pennsylvania State's Schreyer Business Library worked together with the School of Business to create several modules to teach career information literacy in the First Year Seminar (Hickey and White 2009). Librarians teach the units, each with their own problem-based exercises, in several class sessions.

Libraries also target the motivated business student with special information literacy programs. Since 2002, Goizueta Business Library at Emory has sponsored an Advanced Research Certification for students in the undergraduate BBA program. Students learn critical thinking and research skills in a variety of business-related subject areas.

In many of the business schools that have trading rooms, librarians are active in teaching the use of real-time data platforms such as Reuters and Bloomberg. These are financial research tools typically used by investors, analysts, and Wall Street traders. In one notable example, the Finance Department of the University of Illinois at Urbana-Champaign asked their business librarian to develop and teach a financial information applications course using Bloomberg certification (Holler 2009).

Public libraries have traditionally offered workshops for career changers and job seekers and instruction in company and industry research for the small investor. Responding to the recent financial crisis, many are now offering financial literacy classes. Brooklyn Public Library's program, "Growing Dollars and $ense," is a series of workshops, seminars, and one-on-one counseling sessions for teens and adults. At the Science, Industry and Business Library (SIBL) of New York Public Library, a new initiative, Financial Literacy Central, opened in Spring 2010 with 12 mini-courses forming a *Financial Literacy Day*. When SIBL, taking its teaching role seriously, built its NYC Small Business Resource Center (smallbiz.nypl.org), administrators organized the library staff in service teams, rewrote their job descriptions to include formal classroom instruction, and offered training programs to teach them how to design syllabi and deliver instruction (SLA, Business & Finance Division).

THE BUSINESS LIBRARIAN AS EDUCATIONAL PLANNER

For librarians to be truly involved in knowledge creation, they must be organically involved in curriculum design.

Information literacy will become more fully integrated in the teaching mission of the university when librarians champion their role as educators. In a major study at the University of Washington that looked at "How Students Seek Information in a Digital Age," authors Alison J. Head and Michael B. Eisenberg found that students typically relied on a small set of common sources and underutilized librarians. They recommended that librarians partner with the faculty to identify research-based assignments and teach critical thinking skills (Head and Eisenberg 2009). Concurrent with these recommendations, research libraries are looking for new ways to realign the roles of their subject specialists to emphasize curriculum design and course creation (Dupuis 2009). In one recent strategic initiative, the Baker Library at the Harvard University Business School developed a new model for the business subject specialist: the librarian as curriculum services specialist (Wallace, Cullen, and Esty 2007). The librarians in Baker's Curriculum Services unit work with the faculty to integrate information resources in the curriculum. They work with faculty on the design of new courses, they design information resources or services for the curriculum, and they create web resources, workshops, resource guides, and self-service reference tools. Librarians gather data sets, course readings, and other course support materials. They sometimes build knowledge centers for specific courses.

The key component of this curriculum development model is collaboration with faculty at the start of the course-design process. Resources are not merely identified, they are created and they are designed in ways that inform student learning. This model moves the librarian's instruction role from one that is focused on teaching research skills to one whereby the librarian, in partnership with the faculty, becomes the creator of learning opportunities for students.

The business librarian's role as educator is centered on taking a more strategic role in curriculum development. Librarians who understand information literacy as it is applied to the business discipline can partner with faculty to design assignments that help students understand the research process. They can help faculty incorporate the use of library collections into their course syllabi, and they can design online modules for course management systems. They can work with faculty on curriculum committees and participate in learning assurance teams.

CONCLUSION

Reference service is not going to go away. However, the reference model is changing, and the role of the business librarian is changing with it. Today the subject librarian, the business specialist, has a bigger role than ever connecting students and clients to information. Librarians are moving closer to the center of the research process as both advisors and teachers. Personal contact between librarians and users is increasing. Some of this contact is off-line and virtual, as seen in the growth of virtual reference service, and in outreach efforts with blogs, wikis, FAQs, and social networking. Librarians are also offering in-depth and face-to-face assistance in many new venues. They meet with users in research consultations, work with faculty and business units, teach information literacy, and develop curricula. The new model showcases librarians as valued partners in research and knowledge creation.

REFERENCES

ACRL. 2009. "Information Literacy Competency Standards for Higher Education." http://www.ala.org/ala/mgrps/divs/acrl/standards/informationliteracycompetency .cfm.

Berdish, Laura, and Corey Seeman. 2010. "A Reference-Intensive Embedded Librarian Program: Kresge Business Administration Library's Program to Support Action-Based Learning at the Ross School of Business." *Public Services Quarterly* 6:208–24.

Campbell, Jerry D. 2000. "Clinging to Traditional Reference Services." *Reference & User Services Quarterly* 39:223–27.

Dupuis, Elizabeth A. 2009. "Amplifying the Educational Role of Librarians." *Research Library Issues* 265:9–14.

Hamilton-Pennell, Christine. 2008. "Public Libraries and Community Economic Development: Partnering for Success." *Rural Research Report* 18:1–8.

Head, Alison J., and Michael B. Eisenberg. 2009. "Finding Context: What Today's College Students Say about Conducting Research in the Digital Age." http://projectinfolit.org/pdfs/PIL_ProgressReport_2_2009.pdf.

Hickey, Daniel, and Gary White. 2009. "Career Information Literacy for Freshmen Business Students." Poster presented at the annual conference of the Special Libraries Association, Washington, DC. June 16, 2009.

Holler, Carissa. 2009. "From Reaching Out to Working Within: Evolving toward Embeddedness at the University of Illinois." Poster presented at the annual conference of the Special Libraries Association, Washington, DC, June 16, 2009.

Kaufman, Paula T. 2009. "Carpe Diem: Transforming Services in Academic Libraries." Presentation made in Xi'An, China; New Delhi, India; and Taipei, Taiwan, June 2009.

Shumaker, David, and Laura Ann Tyler. 2007. "Embedded Library Services: An Initial Inquiry into Practices for Their Development." Paper presented at the annual conference of the Special Libraries Association, Denver, CO, June 6, 2007.

SLA. Business & Finance Division. Centers of Excellence Award Recipients. Last modified June 28, 2010. http://units.sla.org/division/dbf/awards/coe/pastwinners.html.

"Theory Meets Practice: Educators and Directors Talk." 2010. In *Reference Renaissance: Current and Future Trends*, edited by Marie L. Radford and R. David Lankes, 17–36. New York: Neal-Schuman.

Tipton, Roberta, and Ka-Neng Au. 2009. "Information Literacy and the Real World of Business: Interfunctional Management at Rutgers." Poster presented at the annual conference of the Special Libraries Association, Washington, DC, June 16, 2009.

Urban Libraries Council. 2007. "Making Cities Stronger: Public Library Contributions to Local Economic Development." Evanston, IL: Urban Libraries Council.

Wallace, Debra, Ann Cullen, and Barbara Esty. 2007. "Shifting Gears: The Role of Reference and Research in Curriculum Design." Paper presented at Columbia University Libraries Reference Symposium, New York, March 9, 2007.

Whatley, Kara M. 2009. "New Roles for Liaison Librarians: A Liaison's Perspective." *Research Library Issues* 265:29–32.

White House. 2009. "National Information Literacy Awareness Month." Accessed March 28, 2011. http://www.whitehouse.gov/the_press_office/Presidential-Proclamation-National-Information-Literacy-Awareness-Month/.

Zabel, Diane. 2007. "A Reference Renaissance." *Reference & User Services Quarterly* 47:108–10.

11

2010 and Beyond

Howard F. McGinn

Every weekday morning Whelan Mahoney boards the New Jersey Transit commuter train for the 30-minute ride into New York City. Mahoney's work-day had started much earlier. He had already caught the latest news on WINS, an all-news-format radio station in New York. He scanned the *New York Times*, especially the business section, while eating breakfast. Now, on the train, he is reading through several trade newsletters. Mahoney is the publisher of *Inc.com*, the website for *Inc.* magazine. The website "delivers advice, tools, and services to help business owners and CEOs start, run, and grow their busi-nesses more successfully" (Mansueto Ventures LLC 2008). The full *Inc.* brand publishes a robust array of information media that encompasses more tradi-tional delivery modes such as the magazine, an online site, newsletters, and videos. However, *Inc.* has also ventured into Twitter, Facebook, Buzz, LinkedIn, and other social networking arenas. Mansueto Ventures LLC, the parent company of Inc.com, *Inc.* magazine, *Fast Company*, and *Fast Company.com*, leveraged its important brand names, its editorial and market-ing staff, and its library of editorial content to expand its delivery modes in order to grow its customer base. Such brand migration—from simple but glossy magazines to a complex information distribution system specializing in delivery to new businesses and entrepreneur—mirrors the transformation that must also take place in the future in business libraries, especially academic and public libraries.

In the previous edition of this book, Jane Moore McGinn summarized the significant changes taking place in business librarianship. She identified the following dynamics:

- Reengineering of business libraries
- Changes in the information seeking behaviors of users
- Changes in the format of business information
- Changes in collection development and collection access (J. M. McGinn 2002, 110)

In this chapter I will examine how these dynamics continue to make an impact on the practice of business librarianship. I will discuss trends I have identified that offer glimpses into the future of business libraries, especially those in academic and public libraries. My perspectives may be idiosyncratic, but as a former general manager of a New York Times Company subsidiary and product line sales manager at the J. B. Lippincott publishing company, an academic library dean, an urban and rural public library director, and a state librarian, I have spent decades attempting to serve the business community or, in the case of the New York Times Company and J. B. Lippincott, as a consumer of the business information I needed to manage. I ask your forbearance with my use of anecdotes from my work in these varied settings. Perhaps the best place to start is with my list of predictions for the future of business library services. These predictions are safe. Most have been under way for many years as noted by McGinn in 2002.

GENERAL PREDICTIONS

1. Libraries as physical spaces in most corporations will disappear.
2. Corporate libraries involved in complex product research that leads to the creation of significant intellectual property will persist—but in digital form.
3. Digital archivists will become crucial team members in corporate operations.
4. Academic business library services will continue to increase their value to the college or university through collaborative efforts with faculty and off-campus business and corporations.
5. Public libraries will continue to see significant increases in the demand for business services.
6. Public libraries will expand distribution methods for business information, especially through the use of Internet social networks, bookmobiles, and stand-alone "retail" outlets.
7. Quality business services will be characterized by the ability of a librarian or nonlibrarian to deliver information efficiently and accurately.
8. Librarians will need to have actual business or nonprofit management experience and/or earn graduate degrees in business and management.

I will use a simple framework to discuss these and other items. The framework is Corporate Business Information Services, Academic Business Information Services, and Public Library Business Information Services.

CORPORATE BUSINESS INFORMATION SERVICES

The revolution started here. Companies had been accumulating data in digital form for decades. Starting with the capture of sales, inventory, costs, and other data essential to estimating profit and loss, companies developed sophisticated software applications that enabled them to use the captured data for operations, strategic planning, product development, and the like. It was only natural, then, for employees to rapidly accept and use electronic information accessible over the Internet and from commercial business information providers. As sources of electronic business information increased and employees became skilled in accessing and using information, the need for a corporate library as a place with a business collection declined. Employees not only could access substantial amounts of information, they could download it into spreadsheets and other utilitarian software for crunching, massaging, and other human body descriptors we tend to use to describe what we do to data. In effect the employee was able to focus on the exact data or data range that she or he needed to do the job. Moreover companies, especially small businesses, are already using social networks not only to gain information for planning, market analysis, and recruiting but to launch new products themselves to a customer base developed on Facebook, Twitter, and other networks. Here is an example.

Founded in 1971 by Michael Powell, a graduate student at the University of Chicago, Powell's Books in Portland, Oregon, has assumed an almost cult-like status for readers, librarians, and anyone who just wants to wander around an old building examining millions of new and old books stored on homemade wooden shelves. When my wife and I lived in Portland we would make monthly pilgrimages to the store, and we usually had to hire a cab to take our stash of books home. As dean of university libraries at Seton Hall University, I would use the Powell's website to purchase rare theological and liturgical books for the university's theology library. Yet this old-style used-book store thrives because of its ability to blend the past and the future. In 2008, Powell's began to place mini-ads on its website asking customers to "find us on Facebook" and "follow us on Twitter."

Over the course of a year, the company went from roughly 3,000 fans on Facebook to 38,500 and from a few hundred followers on Twitter to more than 12,000. Although the campaign has not directly produced a large revenue increase, Megan Zabel, Powell's manager of social media efforts, "says the fans' and followers' online purchases have more than offset the cost of the campaign. In addition, having a large fan base creates the impression of a vibrant community that she thinks will help Powell's in the long run.

"The more fans we have, the more people are proselytizing our brand," she says. "Word of mouth is one of the most powerful selling tools" (Mansueto Ventures, LLC 2010).

The story about Powell's is fascinating for two reasons in particular. The first is the use of social media to market products and to expand a company's customer base. The second is Ms. Zabel's job title: *Manager of Social Media*. Direct marketing via social media lends itself to product development and to other marketing functions that tend to be research-heavy. Moreover, the use of social media drastically reduces marketing expenditures. The focus of marketing research is moving from a corporate institutional library to employees using not only social media but other Internet-based and commercial resources. This trend will only accelerate.

Corporate Research Library

When Whelan Mahoney arrives at the *Inc.com* offices he continues to access information that he needs to direct the operations of his website. There is no corporate library or librarian on site to help him find the information. The "corporate library" is simply a collection of trade journals and other items of general interest. The "collection" is maintained by two staff members. I asked Mr. Mahoney how he acquires the information he needs without a library. His response: by using commercial databases targeted to his needs that he searches himself, such as the *Nielsen @ Plan* that provides net ratings and analysis. Other daily sources of information include electronic surveys from trade conferences, e-mail summaries from *Inc.* salespeople, electronic newsletters, news of account movements, and other forms of industry information. And of course CNN is a constant presence on television monitors in the *Inc.* offices.

Mr. Mahoney's process of acquiring information is the norm in today's corporate world, yet the traditional corporate research library is not entirely dead. And back from the dead are the corporate archives. How important is a corporate research library? In today's business environment, and more so in the business environment of the future, the research required for product development and government compliance is significant. In the pharmaceutical industry alone, for example, research and development costs of the members of the Pharmaceutical Research and Manufacturers of America (PhRMA) totaled $45.8 billion in 2009. The pharmaceutical industry as a whole invested $65.3 billion in 2009. R&D expenditures in 2009 for the pharmaceutical industry increased $17.7 billion since 2004 (Pharmaceutical Research and Manufacturers of America 2010). In like manner, the American Association for the Advancement of Science, using data reported to the National Science Foundation, estimated that all U.S. industries in 2007 would invest $247 billion in R&D. This is an increase in expenditures of $17 billion in just two years (American Association for the Advancement of Science 2009). This research, obviously, must be facilitated by corporate research libraries. And a product of the research is a significantly valued asset called "intellectual property."

Intellectual Property

Corporate research libraries of the future will see their role in the preservation of intellectual property grow.

> Intellectual property (IP) refers to creations of the mind: inventions, literary and artistic works, and symbols, names, images, and designs used in commerce. IP is divided into two categories: Industrial property, which includes inventions (patents), trademarks, industrial designs, and geographic indications of source; and Copyright, which includes literary and artistic works such as novels, poems and plays, films, musical works, artistic works such as drawings, paintings, photographs and sculptures, and architectural designs. Rights related to copyright include those of performing artists in their performances, producers of phonograms in their recordings, and those of broadcasters in their radio and television programs. (World Intellectual Property Organization n.d.)

The types of intellectual property noted above require the application of traditional librarian skills, especially information management, control, and access. As all types of intellectual property wind their way through the Internet maze, safeguarding their asset value will become an increasingly critical component of the work portfolio of the librarian in a corporate research library. Management, control, and access issues will continue to increase, but continued creation and/or expansion of digital archives will, in turn, make this work more manageable.

Corporate Archives

Digitization has breathed new life into American and worldwide archival collections. Out of necessity, archival collections had to be used on site because of the rare nature of the materials or the fragile condition of manuscripts, books, photographs, and other archival materials. Many archival items were also inaccessible because they contained proprietary information, were sealed by the donor of the materials, or fell under other personal, governmental, or institutional restrictions. Because digitization is now somewhat affordable—the main cost is labor—items can be scanned for use via the

Internet. Many restricted items, of course, will continue to be restricted once digitized, but these items now become more accessible to those afforded access privileges, especially because they are often able to be full-text searched. In like manner, jobs for "digital librarians" are increasing rapidly, and a new type of corporate librarian/archivist is becoming commonplace in business information services.

Victoria McCargar, a preservation consultant in Los Angeles and a lecturer at UCLA and San Jose State University, "estimates that 20,000 people work in the field today—plus others in related areas—and she expects that to triple over the next decade, assuming that economic conditions stabilize before long" (Aenlle 2009). Where digitization was once considered part of the IT empires in corporations or on college campuses, the creation of digital libraries and archives is increasingly being done *within* libraries by librarians and archivists. As McCargar notes, "People with I.T. backgrounds tend to be wrong for the job. They tend to focus on storage solutions: 'We'll just throw another 10 terabytes on that server.'" A result, she said, can be "waxy buildup"—a lot of useless files that make it hard to find the good stuff (Aenlle 2009). Most librarians and archivists are averse to "waxy buildup." Librarians and archivists are skilled at creating valuable files that enhance access to the "good stuff."

It is probable that corporate digital archives will grow at a rapid pace in the future. That growth will be driven by the need to enhance investment in corporate intellectual property assets, the need to support legal issues, the need to comply with government regulations, and the old-fashioned need to preserve a company's history. Notice the recent resurrection of advertising themes that were prominent in the 1950s and 1960s. Corporate marketing departments have discovered that there is money to be made from the corporation's history.

Corporate Business Information Services—Predictions

In summary, I suggest that the following dynamics, as discussed above, will drive the future development of corporate business information services:

1. General corporate libraries and information centers will disappear because of changes in information-seeking behavior and practices by employees. We have entered the "do-it-yourself" generation.
2. Libraries and information centers in corporations that engage in significant research will grow.
3. Digital archives for the protection and preservation of corporations' intellectual property assets will grow rapidly.
4. Digital archivists will become crucial team members in corporate operations, especially in legal and marketing efforts.

ACADEMIC BUSINESS INFORMATION SERVICES

Because many aspects of academic business libraries have been expertly discussed in earlier chapters of this book, I will limit my discussion to the interlocking roles of librarians, business school faculty, and students. I do so because I believe that the most significant changes in the academic business library will occur in how the librarian goes about her or his work. Other changes in the academic business library and its relationship with business education have already occurred, or are deep into the evolutionary process. I began to see these changes in overall business services in 2000 when I was dean of libraries at Clarion University of Pennsylvania. I noticed the faculty in the university's AACSB-accredited business school rarely used the library. They relied substantially on electronic journals. Reference volume was decreasing. More acquisitions funds were used to purchase databases rather than monographs. Clarion's experience was not unique at that time. In 2001, Abels and Magi identified these trends occurring in business school libraries:

- The trend to develop Web sites that offer access to a variety of services and resources is now well established.
- Also well established is the offering by libraries of a variety of commercial online databases, normally made accessible through their Web sites.
- A clear trend is the growing reliance by libraries on e-mail reference service.
- There seems to be a preference for user education sessions that focus on topics over resource-specific sessions.
- It appears that interactive tutorials may grow in number but will remain as supplements to and not as replacements for classroom instruction.
- Reference desk hours are expected to remain stable in the short term, but will likely begin to decrease five years from now.
- There is at least a tendency for libraries to spend more of their materials budget on serials than on monographs. (Abels and Magi 2001)

These trends have generally held true since 2001. The Internet provides an enormous array of business services and resources. Commercial databases have proliferated on academic library websites. Library reference, while using e-mail plentifully, has jumped to delivery of services using social networks. Sophisticated online tutorials are commonplace. A disproportionate amount of an academic library's budget is spent on electronic sources of business information, including journals. I argue that it is now common for libraries to be open 24/7 and to offer reference services into the early morning (budgets permitting). Abels and Magi examined business school libraries only, but the transformation of many academic libraries to social learning centers will continue to diffuse business services to other libraries on campus because of dependence on easily accessible electronic information.

Absent from their study, however, is the change in the nature of the work of the librarian produced by these changes. Academic business librarians increasingly are entering a workday marked by collaboration rather than traditional reference, collection development, and so forth. This trend will accelerate. In the near future more academic librarians will be collaborators with the business school faculty in teaching as well as research. They will collaborate, as well, with alumni in the business world, especially those who are entrepreneurs or employed in small businesses. A model for this kind of collaboration by librarians has existed for decades in medical librarianship. Brown notes that "clinical reference librarians stepped out of the library and joined the patient care team in the early 1970s beginning in Kansas City, Missouri and then Hartford, Connecticut" (Brown 2004, 45). At first these medical librarians offered an expanded reference service providing literature to aid in patient care planning. In 2000, however, Brown writes that the scope of work of the librarians had expanded considerably with the introduction of the concept of the "informationist." The position of the informationist began with "clinical medical librarianship and [expanded] to this information specialist in context, being based and salaried in a clinical setting, having information-seeking skills, knowledge of informatics and the clinical subject area. Both the clinical medical librarian and the clinical informationist contribute to better patient care, medical education and clinical research" (Brown 2004, 45). This idea of the librarian as part of the patient care, medical education, and clinical research team can easily be applied to the role of the academic business librarian, especially incorporating the use of social networks.

Social Networks

Websites discussing the applications of social networking by small businesses are plentiful. Much of the discussion, of course, centers on the use of Twitter, Facebook, LinkedIn, and even Flickr. There are still more specialized business sites that offer social networking opportunities. Examples of these networks are *biznik.com*, *cofoundr.com*, *e.factor.com*, and *ziggs.com*. The use of these networks offers a great opportunity for academic business librarians to add increased value to their daily work with faculty and students. In a manner similar to the "informationist" work of medical librarians, business librarians can take the lead in creating "teaching" business networks.

One way to do this would to be to work with the institution's business school or business department's internship program. Each network would have at least four participants: student, businessperson, faculty member, and the librarian. The work of the student would be monitored by the faculty member and businessperson. The librarian would work with the student, in particular, by providing searching instruction and sources of business information relevant to the intern's project. This model would be especially valuable in the public library setting, as I will discuss shortly.

Signs of Change

I suggest that the role of the business librarian has the potential to change even more in its importance to the institution. The innovative work of Richard Stern with Consumers Union offers a glimpse of such change. Stern is the business librarian at Seton Hall University. His work is casting the role of librarian into a new form that transports the provision of business information service from the library to the classroom and corporate setting. In 2006 Stern began to take business students on a tour of Consumers Union in Yonkers, New York. "Consumers Union (CU) is an expert, independent, nonprofit organization whose mission is to work for a fair, just, and safe marketplace for all consumers and to empower consumers to protect themselves" (Consumers Union 2010). Consumers Union is the publisher of the highly successful magazine *Consumer Reports*, the website *ConsumerReports.org*, and other consumer-related newsletters and websites. Consumers Union conducts extensive research on products and services ranging from the Apple iPhone to Toyota. In its publications and websites, it offers rankings of product reliability and performance based on the publisher's research.

Stern's tours proved to be so popular that the dean of Seton Hall's Stillman School of Business asked him to develop a course for undergraduate business majors. Access to the course is now provided to business and economics majors. The course, Consumer Product Testing, carries one or two credits, depending on the scope of the student's involvement, and is available to juniors and seniors. The course objectives describe the intersection of business education and the role of the librarian.

The objectives are straightforward:

> To develop a greater understanding of our consumer-oriented society through a basic familiarity with:
>
> • Consumer product testing environment and processes;
> • Sources and use of consumer product information including testing, rating, opinion;

- Operation of Consumers Union, the largest non-profit consumer product testing organization in the world. (Stern 2009)

The objective stated in the second bullet point above is key. It shows the centrality of the role of the librarian in the course because information *is* the core of the course. In reality the librarian, Stern, is the faculty member for the entire course, not just for the information segment. His role is also reflected in his dual appointment to the School of Business's Marketing and Economics faculty. (Librarians at Seton Hall have faculty status.) The librarian thus becomes an information provider *and* content provider embedded in the pedagogical process.

Students typically have one classroom session before traveling to Consumers Union. The trip is mandatory and is scheduled for the day in October when Consumers Union conducts its annual meeting. After attending the meeting, students meet with Consumers Union research staff to learn about consumer research methodology, the evaluation of research, and other aspects of the process. Stern conducts three classes following the trip. The director of marketing for Consumers Union is the guest speaker at the last class. Each student is required to complete an analysis of a specific product by addressing the following questions:

Part 1:
Pick a product that you have purchased within the past two years or intend to purchase. Specify the product. Describe the product selection process taken or intended to be taken. Include in your description, sources of information you used including acquaintances; commercials on TV, web, or radio; sales personnel; expert reviews or owner comments; any other sources. Indicate which sources were important in your decision-making. Be ready to speak in class on this process if requested.

Part 2:
Select a product type reviewed in Consumer Reports and about which you have personal knowledge. The product may be the same one that you picked for the first assignment. What are the product characteristics evaluated in the report? What are the characteristics that are counted in the ranking? Compare the rating of a particular product and model with your own opinion of the product, expert opinion, and/or general user opinion that you find at another website. Do you find anything in the CR report to be of special value? (Stern 2009)

The project offers an excellent example of the value the librarian brings to the course because of the project's emphasis on the acquisition and analysis of information. The project is also a basic primer that teaches a student how to develop a business plan. Stern's course has become so popular that the university's Marketing Club now piggybacks on the visit to Consumers Union. Consumers Union, in turn, has expanded access to its testing program for Stern by permitting him to take students to CU's automotive testing track in Connecticut.

Academic Business Information Services—Predictions

In summary, I suggest that the following dynamics, as discussed above, will drive the future development of academic business information services:

1. Academic business collections will disappear except for print materials that have not been digitized.
2. The traditional business reference function (e.g., reference desk hours) will disappear as librarians become integrated into collaborative activities.
3. Collaborative ventures between teaching faculty, librarians, students, and businesspeople will increase using social media networks.
4. The business librarians will become course providers themselves because of the high degree of dependence by businesses on information.

PUBLIC LIBRARY BUSINESS INFORMATION SERVICES

In late 1985, at the State Library of North Carolina, I began construction of the North Carolina Information Network. The Internet as we came to know it did not exist. In order to link all 100 counties of a very large state, I strung together a series of telephone networks using the telecommunications system of the University of North Carolina system as the base. Each of the 100 public libraries, all of the state's academic institutions, and many special libraries agreed to participate. Western Union was used to provide e-mail and electronic bulletin board service. OCLC (Online Computer Library Center) borrowing service was extended to all public libraries by running two T1 lines from OCLC's Dublin, Ohio, headquarters to the campuses of the University of North Carolina at Chapel Hill and North Carolina State University. Even then Governor James G. Martin joined the network. He held a PhD in chemistry from Princeton University and was a former professor at Davidson College—he wanted access to be able to keep up to date in his field. Most public libraries and academic libraries were given fax machines. One university special library refused the fax machine because it did not see any value in the gadget. Another held a special library faculty meeting to discuss acceptance of the machine. It all seems so primitive now. Although OCLC access was the main attraction, the network also offered important state-generated information about jobs, state construction contracts, and opportunities to bid on all goods and services purchased by the state. I believed the network would contribute to the economic development of the rural areas of the state by providing information about business opportunities to rural citizens that had not been available before. However, I was wrong. Even though the state library was able to provide business information from the mountains to the coast, few librarians knew how to market this new service and many businesspeople were skeptical about its value.

Today, of course, the opposite is true. The provision of business services by public libraries is arguably the fastest-growing sector of the business librarian "industry." The reasons for growth are clear. The Internet is now a common part of daily life. Entrepreneurs in ever-increasing numbers are discovering the value of public librarians in acquiring business start-up information. Public librarians are becoming more aggressive in marketing their services and resources to the business community. The realities of library budgets and their dependence on the political process are forcing public librarians to become aggressive in building constituencies that will, in turn, provide political support. In this section I will discuss examples of current public library business practice that I believe will have to increase if public libraries themselves are to thrive.

Public Libraries and Small-Business Development

A local news story in the *New York Times* began with this sentence: "A product hitting shelves this week at New York area motorcycle dealerships has a surprising history: It was created at the New York Public Library's Science, Industry and Business Library" (Kramer 2006). The investor, Sean Sabol, told of his experience with the library. " 'You have no idea what they have here. I'm not the college-educated guy. I'm the street-educated guy. This has been my college.' Mr. Sabol, 49, is one of more than 63,000 entrepreneurs, investors and small-business owners who have been trained at the business library to search its thousands of print and electronic resources for real-life business applications. The library is one of four specialized research centers operated by the New York Public Library" (Kramer 2006). Programs similar to the New York Public Library's have been developed across the United States and Canada. The Toronto Public Library's SmallBizExpress offers a wide array of services to the business community including special business services to Canada's aboriginal citizens. The Johnson County Public Library in Overland Park, Kansas, offers small-business start-up information, tax advice, and many other business information services to the business community. In Seattle, a government publication entitled "10 Essential Steps in Starting a Business in Seattle" tells readers that they should go to the Seattle Public Library at the beginning of their planning for a small-business start-up. It might seem that only the major urban public libraries are able to offer extensive small-business services. This assumption would be only partly true. In reality small and rural public libraries have access to the same electronic business information as do the larger libraries. These business databases are usually offered through a state-supported network, often by the state library. Lack of personnel, unfortunately, hinders the ability of small and rural public libraries to offer business services.

As public libraries develop existing services to small businesses, they will find ways to collaborate with small businesses. As I mentioned above in my discussion about academic librarians' involvement in social networks, so too must public librarians collaborate with important people in their town's business community. The librarian should link, through social networks, an entrepreneur or small-business person with people who can help the entrepreneur or small-business person develop his or her plans. Examples of these collaborative contacts would be experts at the local Chamber of Commerce, the Small Business Administration, SCORE (Service Corps of Retired Executives), the local agricultural extension service, and experts at the local community college. The key, however, is the librarian as collaborator, as the central contact point and intermediary in aiding the small-business person or entrepreneur. Because information is crucial to the small-business development operation and to the planning for the small-business start-up, information accessed or coordinated by the librarian will be essential.

Branch Libraries and Bookmobiles

Many public libraries have "hidden assets" that they can use to deliver business services more directly to the consumer in the neighborhood. These assets are the branches and bookmobiles. Branch and bookmobile librarians have tremendous contact with their communities. A good branch or bookmobile librarian will know the people in the neighborhood, their problems, and their needs. A good branch or bookmobile librarian will have performed a community analysis that enables her or him to craft information programs tailored to the neighborhood. Because of this intimate knowledge of the community, the librarian can make business information much more personal. A good branch or bookmobile librarian can form collaborative ventures to serve the business needs of the neighborhood. When I was City Librarian in New Haven, Connecticut, I worked with the branch director and chairman of the library board of trustees to establish a business information center in the Stetson Branch in New Haven's Dixwell neighborhood. The business information center was a collaborative venture with Yale University's Office of New Haven and State Affairs and the New Haven Public Schools. Yale students and the branch librarians contributed an enormous number of hours helping people in the neighborhood develop resumes, search for jobs, develop business plans for small-business start-ups, and create websites. The school system, in turn, helped train the Yale students to teach basic-business practices. By creating this mini business center in the city's Dixwell neighborhood, more people were served and more value was brought to the community. It is not improbable that urban libraries in the future will build on existing business services by establishing small "storefront offices" to provide business information services to neighborhoods. The storefronts would be similar to a Sir Speedy copy center or UPS store. This model is also applicable in rural areas. For example, Lyon County, Kansas, has three rural libraries served for administrative purposes by the Emporia Public Library in the county seat of Emporia. Each of the rural libraries is located in a small town dependent on agribusiness. Because of access to electronic information, business services for these libraries could be developed by the much larger Emporia Public Library. In effect, public libraries would franchise business information services. One final note—bookmobiles are very valuable service delivery units in rural and many urban areas. It is easy to equip them to access the Internet. They offer the possibility of door-to-door business service.

Several years ago I was asked to write a column for the magazine *The Bottom Line*. The magazine publishes articles about financial and other business information for librarians. One of my columns was entitled "State Libraries: Ten Actions to Promote Business and Economic Development" (McGinn 1992/1993). I offer these ideas once again here (with a little editing, upgrading, and truncating) as suggestions for public libraries to take in the future to develop business services. I believe the recommendations I made in 1992 remain valid today.

Public Libraries: Seven Actions to Promote Business and Economic Development in the Future

- **Action 1:** Continue to invest in technology and its applications. Explore the use of any new communications devices to expand the library's contact with its customers and to collaborate.
- **Action 2:** Change the perception of the public library, especially through the formation of collaborative relationships with business leaders.

- **Action 3:** Have businesspeople appointed to the library board of trustees.
- **Action 4:** Work with federal, state, and local government authorities to encourage and promote entrepreneurial development in your community.
- **Action 5:** Tap into federal, state, and local sources of funding to help local entrepreneurs develop product. Develop new information products yourself.
- **Action 6:** Protect the public library's turf. Because of the probable availability of funding for small businesses, it is probable that other government agencies will suddenly develop services to the small-business community. Make sure funding officials understand that the library is always there through good and bad economic times.
- **Action 7:** Make sure you have access to business information provided by state information networks. Do not forget about the wealth of federal government information available.

Public librarians in the future must run their libraries as small businesses. They must supplement traditional roles by entering into collaborative business relationships with customers and local important business helpers.

Public Library Business Services—Predictions

1. Public library business information services will expand significantly.
2. Public libraries will find innovative ways of delivering services in increasingly effective ways.
3. Collaborative ventures between the public librarian, neighborhoods, and businesspeople will increase using social media networks.
4. Expansion of quality business services directly to the neighborhoods will be a positive force in the never-ending public library funding battle.

CONCLUSION

There was a famous scene that took place at the Battle of Yorktown in the American Revolution. Tradition has it that when British General Cornwallis surrendered to General George Washington, a British military band played a song called "The World Turned Upside Down." Though not nearly as critical as in the American Revolution, the sentiment expressed by that song title is a good way to describe the future of business information services. The work of the business librarian, as we know it, will not exist in the relatively near future. Much of the traditional work has already disappeared. There is a substantial amount of free business information available on the Internet. Access to business information is already a privilege of those who can afford to pay for the services. Whelan Mahoney has significant personal access to the information he needs to do his job because *Inc.com* makes this information available to him. An essential role of the business librarian in the future, whether in an academic or public library, will be to assure that the customers of the library will have good access to business information *and* know what to do with the information found.

Business librarians must understand the corporate and technology dynamics that threaten their jobs. They must be willing to change. Edgar describes what must be done: "[It] is clear that circumstance, technology, economics and resistance to change have been major factors in the demise [of corporate information centers]. Going forward there will be challenges and excitement for those Information Managers who have a thirst for adventure" (Edgar, 2009, 201). Just as Mansueto Ventures leveraged the success of their brand names *Inc.* and *Fast Company* into the development of a strong portfolio of websites, video, conferences, and other media, so too can libraries, especially academic and public business libraries, expand their "brand names" into services beyond the walls of the library building using service delivery methods such as social networks and storefront information centers. Librarians will need to retool themselves as well. Librarians will have a role only if they remake themselves into businesspersons through business experience and/or education. It will be imperative that business librarians in any setting acquire an MBA, MPA, or related degree. It will be imperative that we attract students into the profession of librarianship who have business or nonprofit business experience. If we do not begin to make these changes now, the future of business librarianship will be dim. More is at stake than just the future of business librarianship. The future of our students is at stake. The preservation of important corporate history is at stake. But most important, the economic well-being of our neighborhoods and small towns needs modern business services. Librarians must change in order to help these towns change, thrive, and survive. The opportunities for expanded and exciting new opportunities for librarians are excellent in all types of libraries if we choose to grab them.

REFERENCES

Abels, E. G., & Magi, T. J. 2001. "Current Practices and Trends in 20 Top Business School Libraries." *Journal of Business & Finance Librarianship* 6(3):3–19.

Aenlle, C. D. 2009. "Digital Archivists, Now in Demand." *New York Times*, February 8.

American Association for the Advancement of Science. 2009. *R&D Budget and Policy Program*. Accessed July 9, 2010. http://www.aaas.org/spp/rd/totalr07t.pdf.

Brown, H.-A. 2004. "Clinical Medical Librarian to Clinical Informationist." *Reference Services Review* 32(1):45–49.

Consumers Union. 2010. *ConsumersUnion.org*. Accessed July 25, 2010. http://www.consumersunion.org/about/.

Edgar, S. 2009. "Is the Bell Tolling for the Death of the Corporate Information Unit?" *Business Information Review* 26(3):201–4.

Kramer, L. 2006. "All You Need Is an Idea, and Good Connections." *New York Times*, April 16.

Mansueto Ventures LLC. 2008. *About Inc.com*. December 21. Accessed June 23, 2010. http://www.inc.com/about/index.html.

Mansueto Ventures, LLC. 2010. "How to Getcustomers on Facebook and Twitter." March 1. Accessed July 16, 2010. http://www.inc.com/magazine/20100301/how-to-get-customers-on-facebook-and-twitter.html.

McGinn, H. F. 1992/1993. "State Libraries: Ten Actions to Promote Business and Economic Development." *The Bottom Line*, 34–39.

McGinn, J. M. 2002. "Business Libraries: Changing Collections, Services, and Roles." In *The Basic Business Library: Core Resources*, 4th ed., edited by R. S. Karp, 109–26. Westport, CT: Greenwood Press.

Pharmaceutical Research and Manufacturers of America. 2010. *Industry Profile 2010*. Washinigton, DC: Pharmaceutical Research and Manufacturers of America.

Stern, R. E. (2009, August 15). Stillman School of Business. Syllabus. South Orange, NJ: Seton Hall University.

World Intellectual Property Organization. n.d. *What Is Intellectual Property?* Accessed July 18, 2010. http://www.wipo.int/about-ip/en/.

Index

About the Editors and Contributors

ERIC FORTE holds degrees in Economics and Library and Information Science. Eric has many years' experience as a business and economics librarian at Boise State University, the University of California at Santa Barbara, and Western State College of Colorado, serving undergraduate, graduate, faculty, and members of the business community in finding and using business data and information, from economics and finance to marketing and accounting. Eric has numerous publications and presentations on finding and using business information, statistics, and government resources. Highlights include *Fundamentals of Government Information* (Neal Schuman, 2011, coauthored with Cassandra Hartnett and Andrea Sevetson), and chapters in *The Basic Business Library: Core Resources* (Oryx Press, 4th edition) and *Reference and Information Services* (Libraries Unlimited, 3rd and 4th edition). During writing of most of this book, Eric was Associate Dean for library services at Boise State University. He is currently a Member Services Consultant with OCLC.

MICHAEL OPPENHEIM has been Collections & Reference Services Librarian in the Rosenfeld Management Library, UCLA Anderson Graduate School of Management since 1997. Michael is active in the American Library Association (ALA) and has held various offices in its Business Reference and Services Section (BRASS), the Government Documents Roundtable (GODORT), as well as in the California Library Association, the Business & Finance Division of the Special Libraries Association, and California Academic and Research Libraries (CARL). With Wendy Diamond (California State University–Chico), he is coauthor of *Marketing Information: A Strategic Guide for Business and Finance Libraries* (Haworth Press, 2004). Also: chapters on government information for business in *Government Online* (Neal-Schuman, 2001), and, with Eric Forte, in *The Basic Business Library: Core Resources* (4th ed., Oryx Press, 2002). He edited the "Local Publications and Resources" column for the annual Notable Documents issue of *The Journal of Government Information*, 1998–2004, and he has also written for H. W. Wilson's Current Biography and, for nearly 18 years, Sage Publications' social sciences abstracting services.

In addition to being Head of Reference at St. John's University, Prof. **LUCY HECKMAN** is also Business Bibliographer and author of the books: *Franchising in Business: A Guide to Information Sources* (1989); *The New York Stock Exchange: A Guide to Information Sources* (1992); *NASDAQ: A Guide to Information Sources* (2001); and *Damascus* (Blood Horse Thoroughbred Legends Series, 2004). Her latest book, *How to Find Business Information*, is scheduled for publication in 2011. Prof. Heckman also reviews books in Business and Economics for Library Journal and ARBA.

RUTHIE BROCK is a business librarian for accounting, finance, and marketing for the College of Business at University of Texas–Arlington. The fifth edition of *The Basic Business Library* will be the third time Ruthie has contributed to the publication. For the two prior editions, Ruthie co-authored the "Core List."

CAROL BYRNE is a business librarian for economics, information systems/operations management, and management at University of Texas–Arlington. This will be Carol's second contribution to the publication. Carol co-authored the "Core List" in the fourth edition.

MADELEINE COHEN, Assistant Director, New York Public Library, Science, Industry and Business Library, has an MLS from Queens College, City University of New York, and an MA from City University of New York Graduate Center. Madeleine has worked for the New York Public Library for more than 20 years in a variety of positions, including head of technical processing, head of information services, and assistant director, with a focus on electronic resources, in the Science, Industry and Business Library (SIBL).

WENDY DIAMOND is Business and Economics Librarian and Head of Reference at California State University–Chico. She has presented and written on marketing information and has been active in ALA's Business Reference and Services Section (BRASS) and in California Academic and Research Libraries (CARL).

CHRIS LeBEAU currently holds a joint appointment between the University of Missouri's School of Information Science & Learning Technologies, where she serves as an Assistant Teaching Professor, and the University of Missouri–Kansas City, where she is the Research and Instruction Librarian for Business and Public Administration for the Henry Bloch School of Management.

GARY W. WHITE is Head of the Schreyer Business Library and Acting Head, Department of Reference, Collections and Research at Penn State University. He holds an MLS and MBA and is ABD in the Department of Higher Education at Penn State. Gary is active in ALA, serving as RUSA (Reference and User Services Association) President in 2011–12 and was formerly chair of the Business Reference and Services Section of RUSA. He also served as editor of the *Journal of Business & Finance Librarianship* from 2005 to 2010 and was awarded the Gale Cengage Award for Excellence in Business Librarianship in 2008.

MARK E. ANDERSEN is the Division Chief for the Business Science Technology Division at the Chicago Public Library (CPL). He has a BS in Commerce, with a major in marketing, from DePaul University and an MS in Library and Information Science from the University of Illinois at Urbana Champaign. He has been an active member of the American Library Association's Business Reference and Services Section (BRASS), chairing many committees and being elected Member-at-Large 2003–6 and Chair from 2010 to 2011.

LOUISE KLUSEK is an Associate Professor in Baruch College's William & Anita Newman Library. She has 17 years of business research experience in corporate libraries at Salomon Brothers and Citigroup where she was Assistant Vice President and Manager of Research Services. She earned her MLS from the University of Pittsburgh and MBA from Temple University. At Baruch she teaches LIB 3040, "Information and Society."

HOWARD F. McGINN, PhD. is Dean Emeritus of University Libraries at Seton Hall University. His career includes management positions in the corporate sector, academic libraries, and public libraries. Positions held include general manager of the Microfilming Corporation of America, a subsidiary of the New York Times Company; sales manager with the J. B. Lippincott Publishing Company; State Librarian of North Carolina; City Librarian of New Haven, Connecticut; and Dean of University Libraries at Clarion University and Seton Hall University. A graduate of Villanova University, he holds an MSLS from Drexel University, an MBA from Campbell University, an MA (Theology) from Seton Hall University, and a PhD (Information Management) from Emporia State University.